3·99

Qt Programming for Linux® and Windows® 2000

ISBN 0-13-027001-6

9 780130 270016

90000

Hewlett-Packard® Professional Books

OPERATING SYSTEMS

Fernandez	Configuring CDE: The Common Desktop Environment
Lund	Integrating UNIX® and PC Network Operating Systems
Madell	Disk and File Management Tasks on HP-UX
Poniatowski	HP-UX 11.x System Administration Handbook and Toolkit
Poniatowski	HP-UX 11.x System Administration "How To" Book
Poniatowski	HP-UX System Administration Handbook and Toolkit
Poniatowski	Learning the HP-UX Operating System
Poniatowski	UNIX® User's Handbook
Rehman	HP Certified, HP-UX System Administration
Sauers, Weygant	HP-UX Tuning and Performance
Stone, Symons	UNIX® Fault Management
Weygant	Clusters for High Availability: A Primer of HP-UX Solutions

ONLINE/INTERNET

Amor	The E-business (R)evolution: Living and Working in an Interconnected World
Greenberg, Lakeland	A Methodology for Developing and Deploying Internet and Intranet Solutions
Greenberg, Lakeland	Building Professional Web Sites with the Right Tools
Ketkar	Working with Netscape Server on HP-UX
Klein	Building Enhanced HTML Help with DHTML and CSS

NETWORKING/COMMUNICATIONS

Blommers	OpenView Network Node Manager: Designing and Implementing an Enterprise Solution
Blommers	Practical Planning for Network Growth
Bruce, Dempsey	Security in Distributed Computing: Did You Lock the Door?
Lucke	Designing and Implementing Computer Workgroups

ENTERPRISE

Blommers	Architecting Enterprise Solutions with UNIX® Networking
Cook	Building Enterprise Information Architectures
Pipkin	Halting the Hacker: A Practical Guide to Computer Security
Pipkin	Information Security: Protecting the Global Enterprise
Sperley	The Enterprise Data Warehouse, Volume 1: Planning, Building, and Implementation
Thornburgh	Fibre Channel for Mass Storage
Thornburgh, Schoenborn	Storage Area Networks: Designing and Implementing a Mass Storage System

PROGRAMMING

Blinn	Portable Shell Programming
Caruso	Power Programming in HP OpenView
Chaudri, Loomis	Object Databases in Practice
Chew	The Java™/C++ Cross-Reference Handbook
Grady	Practical Software Metrics for Project Management and Process Improvement
Grady	Successful Software Process Improvement
Lewis	The Art & Science of Smalltalk
Lichtenbelt, Crane, Naqvi	Introduction to Volume Rendering
Mellquist	SNMP++
Mikkelsen, Pherigo	Practical Software Configuration Management
Norton, DiPasquale	Thread Time: The Multithreaded Programming Guide
Tapadiya	COM+ Programming: A Practical Guide Using Visual C++ and ATL
Wadleigh, Crawford	Software Optimization for High Performance Computing
Ward	Qt Programming for Linux® and Windows® 2000

IMAGE PROCESSING

Crane	A Simplified Approach to Image Processing
Day	The Color Scanning Handbook
Gann	Desktop Scanners: Image Quality

OTHER TITLES OF INTEREST

Kane	PA-RISC 2.0 Architecture
Markstein	IA-64 and Elementary Functions

Qt Programming for Linux and Windows 2000

PATRICK WARD

Hewlett-Packard Company

www.hp.com/go/retailbooks

Prentice Hall PTR
Upper Saddle River, New Jersey 07458
www.phptr.com

Library of Congress Cataloging-in-Publication Data

Ward. Patrick, 1955-
    Qt programming for Linux and Windows 2000 / by Patrick Ward
        p. cm. -- (Hewlett-Packard professional books)
    ISBN 0-13-027001-6
    1. Graphical user interfaces (Computer systems) 2. Application software--Development. 3. Linux. 4. Microsoft Windows (Computer file) I. Title II. Series.

QA76.9.U83 W37 2000
005.4'28--dc21

                                                                    00-055758

Production Supervisor: Wil Mara
Acquisitions Editor: Jill Pisoni
Editorial Assistant: Justin Somma
Marketing Manager: Dan DePasquale
Manufacturing Manager: Alexis Heydt
Buyer: Maura Zaldivar
Page Layout: Pine Tree Composition
Cover Designer: Talar Agasyan
Proofreader: Anne Trowbridge

Manager, Hewlett-Packard Retail Book Publishing: Patricia Pekary
Editor, Hewlett-Packard Professional Books: Susan Wright

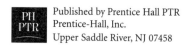

Published by Prentice Hall PTR
Prentice-Hall, Inc.
Upper Saddle River, NJ 07458

The publisher offers discounts on this book when ordered in bulk quantities. For more information contact: Corporate Sales Department, Prentice Hall PTR, One Lake Street, Upper Saddle River, NJ 07458. Phone: 800-382-3419; FAX: 201-236-7141; E-mail: corpsales@prenhall.com

Printed in the United States of America

10 9 8 7 6 5 4 3 2 1

ISBN 0-13-027001-6

Prentice-Hall International (UK) Limited, *London*
Prentice-Hall of Australia Pty. Limited, *Sydney*
Prentice-Hall Canada Inc., *Toronto*
Prentice-Hall Hispanoamericana, S.A., *Mexico*
Prentice-Hall of India Private Limited, *New Delhi*
Prentice-Hall of Japan, Inc., *Tokyo*
Pearson Education Asia Pte. Ltd.,
Editora Prentice-Hall do Brasil, Ltda., *Rio de Janeiro*

This book is dedicated to Leslie, Queen of Denial, whose encouragement, support, and patience made this book possible.

Contents

PART II   QT WIDGETS AND CONVENIENCE CLASSES   61

3   USER INTERACTION OBJECTS   63

4   PROGRAM OUTPUT OBJECTS   109

5   QT CONVENIENCE OBJECTS   125

6   THE QT NAMESPACE AND QT EXTENSIONS   157

PART III   DEVELOPING PROFESSIONAL QT APPLICATIONS   163

7   QT DEVELOPMENT CONSIDERATIONS   165

Foreword

In the summer of 1991, I sat together with Haavard Nord on a park bench in Trondheim, Norway. We were both working on the same medical database project at the Regional Hospital in Trondheim. We were discussing how to proceed with the user interface when Haavard said, "We need an object-oriented display system."

A year later I had made a C++ GUI toolkit because of that statement. After another year the company I had made it for (and was then working for) decided to scrap it for Motif. I thought they were crazy. Haavard called me up one night and said, "Let's build a new and better toolkit from scratch. Quit your job and start a company together with me."

Haavard first did his thesis on making the first Qt kernel. Then, for a year, we hacked day and night in a small office and lived off our wives. We had the luxury of working undisturbed. Qt gradually took form, we polished the details, designed and re-designed until things just felt right (a design rule Trolltech still follows). We then got a small consultancy contract where we used our still quite primitive version 0.60 of Qt, hired Arnt Gulbrandsen for a ridiculously low salary, and the snowball started rolling.

I had never imagined that one day I would write a foreword for a book about Qt from Prentice Hall. Many of our dreams have come true, and this is another one of them.

I have had the pleasure of meeting Patrick Ward, the author of this book. In addition to being a mighty fine Qt hacker, he is also a very nice guy with a good sense of humor. I think that's a perfect combination for writing a book like this one. Now sit back and enjoy the wonders of Qt, as narrated by Patrick Ward. The word is yours, Pat.

Eirik Eng,
President, Trolltech AS

Preface

This book is a guide to writing applications for Linux, Microsoft NT 4.0, Windows 2000, Windows 95, and Windows 98, using the Qt software toolkit from Trolltech AS. As any respectable programming guide should, it provides a working knowledge of the Qt software distribution and the objects, widgets, and conveniences that the Qt toolkit provides. In addition, it explores some aspects of Qt programming for enterprise application development that are not obvious from the toolkit vendor's documentation.

AUDIENCE

This book is for C++ programmers and students that want to write effective application software using the Qt toolkit. The focus is primarily on platform-independent software, but some platform-specific topics are unavoidably covered.

ASSUMPTIONS

This book is not a reference manual for the Qt objects and widgets—Trolltech has done an excellent job of providing reference documentation in HTML and Adobe Postscript formats. Their documentation is included with both the Qt-Free edition and the

Qt-Professional edition licenses, and is available from the Troll web site. http://www/trolltech.com\

This book is written for both the experienced C++ programmer and the knowledgeable beginner. It is assumed the reader is familiar with standard C++ data types and how new data types are created. The reader should be familiar with the basic concepts of object-oriented (OO) design and implementation, particularly the concept of object inheritance. I have avoided using multiple inheritance in my examples for purposes of clarity, but the reader is encouraged to experiment.

While the title of this book implies a focus on Linux and Windows 2000, the actual scope is much larger. Most of the examples, as well as the code provided on the CD, will compile and function correctly on virtually any platform that Qt will.

If you are an experienced Microsoft developer, some of the coding style presented here may cause mild confusion. Please remember that with a few exceptions, the code presented in this book is intended for cross-platform use. As a result, you will seldom see references to DWORD, LPVOID, and LPSTR data types because they are undefined on platforms outside the Microsoft arena, and since most of the standard *Unix* data types are compatible with Windows development, they are used instead. The "correctness" of either is purely subjective.

Microsoft platform-specific examples require a Qt-Professional license. Licensing can be obtained directly from Trolltech, and is discussed in some detail in Chapter 1. While Qt software development can be done using the Borland compiler and tools, it is far more common for developers to use Microsoft Visual C++. As a result, it is assumed that the Windows developer has access to Microsoft Visual Studio 6.0 and VC98 (Visual C++).

It is possible, in theory, to compile and use Qt-Free edition applications on a Windows platform, using the Cygnus Win32 implementation, the ming32 compiler distribution, the X11R6.3 development kit for Win32, and an appropriate X server. Since this is an incredibly esoteric environment, it isn't addressed by any of the examples in this book. However, any of the Linux examples should work, assuming you succeed in compiling the Qt-Free edition with the Cygnus compiler distribution—something I haven't tried yet.

Linux development can be accomplished using the Qt-Free edition. You will need a C++ compiler. This book assumes a generic gcc/g++ distribution (gcc-2.95 was used for the examples) from the Free Software Foundation (FSF), in the assumption that it is a reasonably low common denominator.

Many other platforms are supported out-of-the-box by Troll. I have had virtually no trouble using Qt on HP/UX or AIX.

HOW THIS BOOK IS ORGANIZED

This book is organized into three parts. Part One is an introduction to the Qt toolkit. It provides some initial programming examples, and discusses some of the unique features that set Qt development apart from other toolkits. Part Two is a detailed discussion of toolkit components. Part Three discusses project-level considerations and debugging techniques.

Appendix A maps the contents of the accompanying CD-ROM. Appendix B (and the index) help to map the contents of this book.

TYPOGRAPHICAL CONVENTIONS

Text in *italics* is used to emphasize a point, introduce new terms, or, as is the case in chapters 5 and 6, as a heading for basic examples.

Examples of command-line text appear in a different typeface and will usually appear on a line by themselves as in this example of a Linux command-line:

```
find . -name "*.cpp" -exec findtr {} >> ./tr_text \;
```

Examples and source fragments also appear in a distinct typeface, as in this example:

```
#include <stdio.h>
int
main( int argc, char **argv )
{
        printf( "Howdy, Terre!\n" );
        return( 0 );
}
```

THE ACCOMPANYING CD-ROM

The CD-ROM that comes with this book is in ISO9660 format with Joliet extensions (long filenames). The root directory of the CD-ROM contains a number of subdirectories with names that are (hopefully) descriptive of their contents. The only file in the root directory is a file named "contents.txt" that surprisingly, contains a text map of what the CD-ROM contains, along with some brief descriptions of those contents.

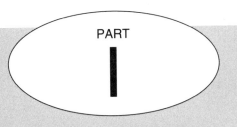

PART

I

Getting Started

Introduction to Qt

Qt (commonly pronounced *cute*) is a C++ class library and GUI toolkit that provides the basic set of services needed for most common application development on Linux (or nearly any UNIX) platforms and Microsoft Windows 2000 (and all its ancestors, back to Windows 95). Qt is the product of Trolltech AS (hereafter referred to as Troll, Trolltech, or more informally as "the Trolls"). Trolltech AS is a Norwegian company based in Oslo, Norway, founded in 1994 by Eirik Eng and Haavard Nord.

This chapter will introduce you to the toolkit and some of the common programming issues that Qt helps to eliminate.

The application development services provided by the Qt toolkit include:

- A full complement of GUI widgets (often referred to as "controls" in the Windows community)
- A comprehensive set of file and filesystem manipulation tools
- Classes for manipulating images, arrays, and internationalized text
- Collection classes and template classes

This is to name but a few. All these classes are either functionally complete and platform-independent or are provided to ease transition between the target platforms the toolkit supports.

3

Qt has rapidly grown in popularity since the K Desktop Environment (KDE) team chose Qt as its base toolkit in 1996 (though the Qt story dates back to 1991). KDE was (in the author's opinion) the first graphical desktop environment for Linux of a truly Enterprise-Quality nature. Other UNIX users had CDE, OpenWindows, VUE, and others, while the Linux users had only fancy window managers. Qt provided the look-and-feel and basic GUI framework, while KDE provided an integrated desktop environment. Application software could be rapidly developed, deployed, and integrated into the end-user's desktop.

Until Qt came along, writing software for both UNIX and Windows platforms usually required two development efforts and, usually, two development teams. Let's take a minute to explore some of the reasoning for this:

UNIX programmers often view the PC (and Windows) as a toy, unworthy of serious programmer attention. These programmers sometimes view the popularity of the Windows software phenomena as a symptom of intellectual or technical decay within the user base. Many UNIX programmers refuse to acknowledge Windows software as anything more than "software for the point-n-drool masses," and flatly refuse to take any part in development of Windows software. With an attitude such as this (and it's not at all uncommon), and with the coding style of traditional Windows software that is so different from UNIX coding styles, plus the nearly complete nonportability of the code between UNIX and Windows platforms, you have a stalemate.

Windows programmers, on the other hand, usually consider UNIX programming as unnecessarily cryptic, complex, and confusing in terms of coding style. The availability of tools to ease the coding effort is poor (at best) and many Windows programmers detest command-line programming—especially the use of the standard editor, vi. Again, we have a stalemate.

UNIX programmers often refuse to write Windows code and Windows programmers often can't, or won't, write UNIX code. The solution of most organizations is usually to hire two programming teams and provide them with their preferred development environment—even when both teams are writing code in the same language. This approach more than doubles the costs of a typical development effort. It increases the risk of project failure by increasing the probability of encountering issues that cannot be resolved to the mutual satisfaction of both teams (lots of deadlines are missed because of this, and many projects are scrapped in their infancy as a result). In fact, the double-team solution increases the workload of every member of the project team—from the person who empties the wastebaskets to the person who processes medical claims.

Qt addresses nearly all the issues of inconsistent UNIX GUI toolkits and cross-platform development without sacrificing anything. Does this sound ideal? It isn't, but it comes much closer than any toolkit that preceded it, and newer releases are closer still. After all, "ideal" is a purely subjective term.

Qt has its share of shortcomings, and this book will make note of some of them, but the developers at Troll are always making improvements and adding functionality—to the extent that each new release still surpasses my expectation.

WHAT THE TOOLKIT DOES

In order to provide GUI development capabilities on Linux and Windows platforms, Qt emulates the high-level interface components of popular toolkits using the underlying, low-level API calls of the target platform. The toolkit performs this task with nearly seamless precision, making it very difficult to identify which platform is in use, if your only cue is the appearance of an application's pushbuttons, listboxes, dialogs, and text.

For UNIX and Linux systems, this means that Qt uses the base X11 API calls available from libX11 (and to a limited degree, libXext), and performs all the appropriate steps involved in producing some visually pleasing and familiar controls. Those familiar with Xlib programming know this is a tedious and daunting task, and the results are almost never aesthetically pleasing. Those familiar with Motif or Xt programming will undoubtedly appreciate the higher performance of Qt and the greatly simplified development model. Motif programmers will, however, mourn the loss of the thousands of resource settings that they have become accustomed to, as well as the loss of their beloved UIL code.

On Microsoft Windows systems, Qt uses the SDK calls to create components that closely resemble some of the familiar MFC components and controls that are available on Windows NT 4.0 and Windows 98 systems. The visual changes and components that have been introduced with Windows 2000 are not present in the current release of Qt, but I seriously doubt that the Trolls will tolerate a gap in functionality or appearance for very long.

Qt provides classes to perform many of the common platform-dependent operations that are normally a source of headaches for the programmer, such as file and directory manipulation and handling of internationalized text.

Veteran Microsoft Windows programmers will experience a short period of confusion as they begin exploring typical Qt development practices. The absence of the familiar but confusing initialization and event-handling code has caused more than one instance of culture shock. However, the simpler, and more intuitive, programming style that the toolkit encourages makes the adaptation easy and rewarding. Although you are free to use type definitions that are unique to Windows such as DWORD and LPSTR, you should avoid them when possible to prevent future portability issues. You should also be aware that Qt methods won't accept many of these data types as arguments for that very reason.

WHAT THE TOOLKIT INCLUDES

Qt provides a great deal of functionality and is an ever-changing work in progress. As a summary of features only, Qt provides the following groups of application development resources:

- Graphical user interface components that closely resemble those available from the Microsoft Foundation Class and platform SDK libraries, and from OSF Motif and the Common Desktop Environment (CDE, which is based on Motif)

- A natural and intuitive object interaction model, based on "signals" and "slots" that works effectively the same way a patch panel does
- Platform-independent services for file and directory manipulation
- Asynchronous I/O abstraction
- A powerful, efficient, and fast string storage and manipulation class that supports single-byte or Unicode text
- Simple Rich Text Format manipulation
- Image manipulation classes for image I/O and format conversions
- Very fast drawing capability
- Dictionary collections
- Date and time abstraction
- Cache manipulation
- Elegant event encapsulation
- Binary data serialization/deserialization
- All toolkit source code
- Many example applications that demonstrate portions of the toolkit
- Plus a *lot* more

A set of add-ons, called Qt Extensions, is provided for creating Netscape plug-ins, OpenGL graphic applications, extended image format manipulation, and support for legacy Xt/Motif application development. Available from the Troll Web site is a Qt add-on that offers a growing family of network programming classes and network protocol encapsulations.

Qt includes a comprehensive overview, tutorials, programming guides, and reference documentation in HTML format. While most will probably prefer the HTML documentation, those who have need of hard-copy reference material can obtain an Adobe PostScript version from the Troll Web site (although as of this writing, the Trolls have not updated the Web link to point to the newer release's documentation). You can access the different versions using their FTP server. Be warned that the PostScript documentation is extremely large, comprising more than 1,000 pages.

USING THE QT ONLINE REFERENCE DOCUMENTATION

Documentation is the usual drawback to the best applications, utilities, and APIs. Either it is poorly organized, inaccurate, or perhaps nonexistent. Even when the product is documented well, you still have the problem of finding the book when you need a piece of information. If your desk is anything like mine, you spend a lot of time searching all horizontal surfaces within arm's reach of your chair, looking for a manual that's the size of a postage stamp. Once you've located the book, untangled your headphone cable from its tacky spiral binding, and applied the proper unguent to the abrasions the headphones made on your forehead when you picked up the book too fast, you're still faced with the task of finding the needed information. Instead of a hard-copy book, Troll chose to use HTML documentation for the Qt toolkit. It is very well organized, and uses a consistent and predictable approach—much like the Qt toolkit itself.

Because the documentation is supplied in HTML form, you will need a Web browser to read it. Just about anything will work: Netscape Communicator/Navigator, Microsoft Internet Explorer, Opera, even Lynx. Try several and use the one you like best.

I strongly recommend that you read the reference documentation for each new object or widget as it is presented in following pages. This will help you to become accustomed to finding needed information in the reference material—a skill that is easily adapted and essential to successful development with Qt.

Assuming you have installed the Qt distribution and you have an environment variable, either $QTDIR or %QTDIR%, that points to the top of the Qt directory structure, you can easily view the documentation by opening the Qt main page, $QTDIR/doc/index.html, by whatever means your preferred browser provides. You will want to create a bookmark in your Web browser to this page to ease future reference.

General

This section is Troll's marketing page. It provides a brief description of the vendor and the product. The "Common Problems" section can save you more than one e-mail seeking for support.

- **About Qt**: A brief description of the toolkit with links to Troll's Web site and licensing information.
- **Common Problems**: The list of most commonly reported problems (usually mistakes on our part) with information on how to resolve them.
- **How to Buy Qt**: Contains links on licensing information.

Getting Started

Unlike Motif, the Qt toolkit provides excellent training materials to help you jumpstart your new skill set. This section provides a complete tutorial and links to the example applications.

- **Tutorial**: The tutorial exercises provided with the toolkit walk the user through the process of creating a rather enjoyable game.
- **Walkthrough**: An explanation of how a typical application is created, the steps involved, and a description of what each step's purpose is.
- **Examples**: HTML links to HTML versions of all the example program's source code listings.

What's New

Trolltech is always working to improve and enhance the toolkit. You can expect to see a new release every six months or so. The "What's New" section makes it possible for you to quickly catch up with a new release.

- **Key Features in Qt 2**: Summarizes the significant changes in the current release.
- **Detailed Changes Notes**: Provides detailed information about the changes in the current release and the previous release.
- **Porting From Qt-1.X to Qt-2.0**: Discusses the incompatibilities between the current release of Qt and the previous major release versions. Troll includes the steps required to make your legacy applications work with the new release.

API Reference

You will want to bookmark this section in your Web browser. This section provides the details about the Qt toolkit widgets and other classes.

- **Alphabetical Class List**: The per-class reference documentation for the toolkit application programming interface. This will likely be the most heavily used portion of the documentation. You will find links to the detail information for all the Qt widgets and classes in this section.
- **Structure Overview**: This section is not named correctly. It is supposed to be titled "API Structure Overview." It provides a reorganized reference source—one organized by functionality groups. It serves as a good complement to the alphabetical class list mentioned above.
- **Annotated Class List**: An alphabetical listing of the Qt classes with a brief description of their purpose.
- **Inheritance Hierarchy**: Provides an outline perspective of each class' inheritance tree, with links to each class' reference documentation.
- **All Functions (long)**: As the title implies, this is a complete listing of every method exposed by the Qt classes with HTML links to the reference documentation. It is very long, as the title also implies.
- **Header File Index**: HTML links to the HTML versions of the header files. Note that this is a poor source for documentation, because the headers describe the internal implementation of widgets and classes, and it is always subject to change in subsequent releases.

Overviews

In some respects, Qt programming is a little different than programming for other toolkits such as MFC or Motif. This section describes these differences in enough detail to allow you to become productive in a short time frame.

- **Introduction to the Qt Object Model**: Provides a brief discussion of some of the unique aspects of Qt programming.
- **Using the Meta-Object Compiler (moc)**: This is more a user's guide than an overview. It discusses the Qt Meta-Object Compiler (moc or moc.exe) usage, capabilities, and limitations.
- **Geometry Management**: A discussion of the Qt *layout* mechanism with many examples.

- **Drag 'n Drop (DnD)**: A discussion of how Qt implements drag and drop functionality with some examples.

- **Internationalization (i18n)**: This section discusses the facilities provided by the toolkit to help the programmer create applications that are multilingual, and use varying character sets and input methods.

- **Debugging Techniques**: Provides some useful techniques for debugging Qt applications, beyond those provided by a specific platform's development environment.

- **Network Programming**: This section covers the network programming objects that are not a part of the Qt toolkit itself, but distributed as a separate extension toolkit. It provides an overview of the Qt network programming model and the abstractions that make it possible. Nearly all of these objects are new with the release of Qt 2. The documentation is included with Qt because the objects will become an integral part of the toolkit in a future release.

- **Widget Screenshots**: This is a list of nearly all the different visual components (widgets) of the Qt toolkit. Each is usually displayed in the various GUI styles that Qt provides.

Trolltech

This section provides information about the vendor. It discusses Qt support and the qt-interest mailing list.

- **About Trolltech**: Provides contact information (phone numbers, fax numbers, addresses, e-mail addresses, and HTML links to their Web site).

- **How to Report a Bug**: Provides basic instructions on how to report possible defects to Troll.

- **Mailing List Information**: Provides a description of the available Qt e-mail lists that you can subscribe to. The page even provides a "Subscribe" button to make it easier.

Products for Qt

This used to be a fairly large section. With the 2.1 release, the Trolls opted to move a lot of functionality to external toolkits. The OpenGL interface remains, I suspect, simply because it is a widget.

- **Qt OpenGL 3D Graphics**: A discussion and reference to the Qt extension that allows you to perform OpenGL rendering in a Qt application.

Appendix

This section covers some miscellaneous topics that didn't fit in other categories, although the licensing discussions probably belong under the "About Qt" section.

- **Standard Accelerators**: This is the complete list of standard keyboard accelerators provided by Qt. Where Qt's accelerators differ from the Open Group standard, explanations are provided.

- **Qt Free Edition License**: This is the official end-user license that governs use of the Qt Free Edition.
- **Other Licenses used in Qt**: This section describes and documents the licensing information for the products provided with Qt that are not part of the Qt toolkit and not governed by the Q Public License.
- **Credits**: A list of people who deserve honorable mention for one reason or another.

QT PORTABILITY

If you need to concern yourself with issues of portability between UNIX and Windows platforms—and only the myopic developers will exclude themselves from that classification—you will delight in the features Qt provides to implement cross-platform solutions. Using the Qt toolkit, it is very easy to create complex and elegant applications that need only be recompiled on the target platform. There are several other toolkits that offer that degree of portability, but the price is usually in the performance. Qt applications will typically outperform applications written for these other toolkits on any given platform, without sacrificing any of its substantial aesthetic benefits.

To this purpose, the toolkit will *help* break down the barriers that exist between Windows and UNIX platforms, but there are, and will always be, certain platform-dependent hurdles that no toolkit will leap without a few nudges from a platform-savvy programmer. Issues regarding OS-dependent low-level I/O, proprietary protocols, and the like, are not directly handled by the Qt toolkit but there are several basic frameworks to help support your task, should you need to address those issues.

Interfacing Qt with other platform services can be accomplished with relative ease. This is more obvious in a Linux or UNIX environment than it is in a Windows environment, but this book will cover enough of this topic in later chapters that the reader should feel comfortable when facing any routine task in either environment. All the examples provided in this book should compile and run equally well on any of the platforms supported by Qt, except when explicitly described as being platform-dependent (as some of the Windows 2000-only examples are—they will still compile, just don't expect them to *do* much).

MICROSOFT WINDOWS LOGO PROGRAM

It seems that many Windows programmers have the notion that an application that doesn't use MFC can't be certified for the Windows Logo program. This is not the case. Any Qt application can comply with either the Windows Logo Program specification or the Application Specification for Windows 2000. Compliance with all the recommendations contained in these specifications is not a requirement for certification, and will prove somewhat difficult using Qt, but it is not impossible.

For document-based applications, the specification insists that you use a MAPI-compliant procedure to implement a "Send To" menu item on the File menu of your application. Since the MAPI "standard" changes (presumably whenever Microsoft encounters a new bug in their Exchange product) your software may become noncompliant in the time it takes to have it certified by the independent testing agents. At any rate, Qt interfaces to whatever MAPI you have at the moment, with no problems.

With the exception of the MDI (Multiple Document Interface) example provided with the Qt distribution, all the examples comply with Microsoft's Windows Logo Program, although I doubt that Troll has taken the time to actually have them certified by a third party as Microsoft dictates.

The MDI example itself can be easily modified for compliance by adding the required "Send To..." menu item to the provided "File" menu and calling the Windows default e-mail client (Outlook, cc:Mail, OpenMail WinGUI, etc.) to perform the actual send operation.

BUILDING AND INSTALLING QT

Since Qt is distributed as source code, you will need to build the toolkit library and install the toolkit in a convenient location. A file named INSTALL can be found at the toplevel directory and provides detailed instructions on building and installing Qt. The process is extremely simple, but you are encouraged to read the INSTALL file and the release notes that accompany every Qt release.

The Qt configure script supports the following platforms, although it is relatively easy to port Qt to other platforms as well:

- IBM AIX with GNU g++ or xlC compilers
- BSD with GNU g++ compiler
- Data General DGUX with GNU g++ compiler
- Free BSD with GNU g++ compiler
- Hewlett-Packard Co. HP/UX with aCC, CC, or GNU g++ compilers
- Silicon Graphics Inc., Irix
- Linux with GNU g++
- NetBSD with GNU g++
- OpenBSD with GNU g++
- OSF-1 with CC and GNU g++
- QNX with GNU g++
- SCO UNIX/UNIXWare with GNU g++
- Sun Microsystems Solaris with GNU gcc, g++ and CC
- SunOS with GNU g++
- Digital Equipment Ultrix with GNU

In addition to the above, the Qt Professional license includes support for Microsoft Windows family, with Visual C++ 4.2, 5.0, or 6.0, or Borland C++.

If you acquire the Cygnus Solutions *CygWin32* distribution and the XFree86 developer's kit for *CygWin32*, you should have little trouble creating native NT X11 applications with the Qt Free Edition, compiling as you would for a Linux and g++ environment. I have not actually tried it, nor do I know of anyone who has. It would seem to have very limited potential for real-world projects, but I mention it for the purpose of speculation.

QT LICENSING

Unfortunately, Qt licensing is not currently available from software resellers. The only way to obtain a Qt license is directly from *Trolltech,* via the Web, fax, postal mail, etc. The software can be obtained from the Troll Web site, and the Qt Free Edition is frequently bundled with other software distributions for Linux. The Qt Free Edition is also available on the CD that comes with this book. The reader is encouraged to check the Troll Web site, as the newer versions and enhancements are always nice to have.

Troll provides time-limited evaluation copies of Qt, and two forms of toolkit licensing, Qt Professional Edition, and The Qt Free Edition. The QPL, or Q Public License, governs the Qt Free Edition. QPL qualifies as an OpenSource license and provides a generous degree of freedom to the OpenSource developer. The QPL is also very easy to understand—a refreshing alternative to most end-user licensing. QPL also grants the right to use the QPL itself for your own software as long as the terms of the QPL are preserved.

The QPL Version 1.0, which governs your use of the Qt Free Edition, permits you to develop applications with Qt and to distribute those applications with the following (and other) related constraints:

- You can charge a fee for your software.
- The source code for your application must be made available to anyone who wants it, without charge, except to recover distribution costs.
- You must permit users of your application to redistribute your application and its source code without any charges, to whomever they choose.
- If your application is not generally available and a representative of Troll asks for a copy, you must provide it, free of charge.
- You are not entitled to product support—Qt Free Edition is available "as-is."
- You won't be able to develop Native Microsoft Windows applications.

The QPL also governs redistribution of the Qt Free Edition and derived works, such as patches, bug-fixes, and enhancements. It also grants the right to distribute binary compilations of Qt and/or modifications, such as shared or static libraries. Just make sure you don't modify any of Troll's copyright notice information.

The Qt Professional License removes the constraints for software that you develop, and adds an excellent e-mail-based technical support system. Professional licensing is available in three types: UNIX-only, Microsoft Windows-only, and the "Duo-Pack," which is a Professional License for both UNIX and Windows. The latter two provide native Microsoft Windows development capability. Of course, with all types of professional licensing you lose the right to redistribute the Professional Qt source and development code, but the runtime shared library can be redistributed without royalties. The technical support alone makes the Professional License worthwhile.

Much of the material in this book assumes a Professional "Windows" or "Duo-Pack" License as it covers aspects of Microsoft Windows development.

The CD that comes with this book includes a copy of the Qt Free Edition source code and a separate Linux binary installation, already compiled, ready to install and use. Note that only a static compilation is provided, but feel free to reconfigure for shared library support.

Whether you are a serious and experienced developer or a knowledgeable novice, you should realize the importance of understanding your software distribution rights and responsibilities. Please read the license that accompanies this distribution before you do anything else.

SUMMARY

The Qt toolkit provides the tools, documentation, and functionality to create first-rate applications that will compile and run on most of the popular computer platforms, and for many developers, the toolkit is completely free. This will continue to be a winning combination for everyone involved, although I suspect the advantage lies more strongly with the software development community than with the vendor.

CHAPTER

2

Creating Your First Qt Applications

Given the premise that the simplest solutions are inherently the most elegant, this chapter will demonstrate just how elegant Qt applications can be. For those accustomed to writing GUI applications for Microsoft Windows, you may think there's been a mistake—or that I forgot to include the Windows example. That is not the case. The following examples will work on any platform that supports Qt development. In fact, the screen shots are performed on a Windows 98 system.

Each example will be followed by some typical methods for getting it running. Examples presented in subsequent chapters will assume successful compilation, unless extra or obscure techniques are required. For now, I'll avoid Makefiles and VC++ projects and use the command line.

Keep in mind that you aren't expected to understand what's happening in the source code for these examples. Their intent is more to dazzle you with the elegance of the Qt toolkit than as a training exercise. Some, however, will find these examples are adequate to begin writing serious software without further explanation. I would discourage that tendency—at least until you have finished this chapter.

If you are relatively new to C++ or GUI programming, it is *highly* recommended that you actually enter these examples and compile them, as this tends to reinforce the concepts that are covered. You will need an editor, a C++ compiler that is compatible with the compiler used to create the Qt library, and you will need a link editor. For Windows developers, you will need to invoke a command prompt and execute the VC++-provided script *VCVARS32.BAT* to set the appropriate environment. You can use the

Windows Notepad to enter the source code, or create a new, empty "Win32" application project with VC++.

For this book, I use the following tools (other than Qt, of course):

```
Linux: (kernel release 2.3.18)
vim—editor
gcc-2.95
XFree86 4.0beta from nVidia

Microsoft Windows 2000 Server, Windows 98:
Cygnus Solutions cygwin32 release of 'vi'
Microsoft Visual C++ 6.0 (SP3)
```

HELLO WORLD EXAMPLE

No book on programming is complete without a hello world example. As strong as the urge is to break with tradition, I'll resist . . . for a moment at least:

```
Hello.cpp
#include <qapplication.h>
#include <qlabel.h>

int
main( int argc, char **argv )
{
    QApplication *app = new QApplication( argc, argv );
    QLabel *1 = new QLabel( "Hello World", 0, 0 );
    app->setMainWidget( 1 );
    1->show();
    app->exec();
    delete app;
    return( 0 );
}
```

On Linux systems, this can be compiled and linked via the following command line (it is assumed you followed the instructions given in the INSTALL file that comes with the distribution, and that your environment variable QTDIR is set to the root directory of the compiled distribution and that you are performing a *shared* compile):

```
g++ -I$QTDIR/include hello.cpp -o hello -L$QTDIR/lib -lqt
```

Microsoft Windows developers can use a similar approach, although it is slightly more complicated than a Linux compile:

```
cl -nologo -I%QTDIR%\include -c hello.cpp
link -nologo hello.obj %QTDIR%\lib\qt.lib user32.lib gdi32.lib \
comdlg32.lib ole32.lib uuid.lib imm32.lib wsock32.lib
```

The example will produce output similar to that shown in Fig. 2.1:

Figure 2.1   Output of hello.cpp

For nearly every Qt object, there is a suitably named header file that will provide all the definitions needed to use that object. In the example above, we make use of two objects, QApplication and QLabel, which are supported by the respective header files, qapplication.h and qlabel.h. Most of Qt's classes are supported by header files that are named in a similar and sensible manner.

The QApplication class is required for any Qt application that makes use of events or visuals, but not for Qt applications that only use QString, the container classes, and so on. There can and *must* be only one instance of this class in visual or event-driven applications. The QApplication class is covered in some detail further on in this chapter, but for now just assume that QApplication takes care of all the underlying, platform-specific startup and initialization details.

The example creates an instance of QApplication on the heap and passes the command-line arguments. It then creates a QLabel instance on the heap and sets the label text to the argument string. We then tell the QApplication object that the QLabel is the *widget* that QApplication will manage. Next, we tell the QLabel to display itself. Finally, we pass control to the QApplication event-loop.

If your development background is primarily with Microsoft Windows, you're probably wondering "What's a widget?" The word *widget* is slang for Window Gadget, and dates to the X Window System's X Toolkit (Xt) and Athena Widget (Xaw) libraries. I've heard some claim that it comes from Motif, based on Xt and Xlib, but Motif came along after the Athena Widgets were already popular. All three of these toolkits are pseudo-object-oriented C language code that many GUI programmers began their GUI development careers with. You will frequently hear Qt people bantering hither and yon about this widget or that widget. In Qt circles, they are likely referring to visual components of Qt or a derived work. If you substitute the term "control" for "widget," their conversations will make more sense.

If you're an experienced Windows or Motif programmer, you're probably surprised at the simplicity of the example—but I assure you, it's only the first of many advantages that Qt offers. Now, let's try an example that has potential for real-world application.

The following example could be used as a basic contact-list database interface. For now, we won't worry about saving the data it produces, as this is only an exercise in creating the user-interface, nor will we concern ourselves with providing for a formal, multi-line address.

CONTACT LIST INTERFACE EXAMPLE

Hello world examples are a good way to demonstrate an easy first application, but they don't really do anything useful. A toolkit that makes useless applications easy to create is about as useful as those same applications. Fortunately, Qt can produce very useful applications with very little coding on your part. The following example demonstrates a simple contact-list application that accepts names, a number, and an address.

```
Contact List UI

#include <qapplication.h>
#include <qlabel.h>
#include <qlineedit.h>
#include <qpushbutton.h>
#include <qlayout.h>
#include <qstring.h>

//
// ContactUI—a contact list data-entry widget
class ContactUI : public QWidget
{
    // Signal/Slot support
    Q_OBJECT
public:
    // CTOR -
    ContactUI( QWidget *parent=0, const char *name=0 );

    // methods to retrieve current field values
    // expect a compiler warning here—this is an
    // example!
    const QString &name()    { return(theName->text());   }
    const QString &number()  { return(theNumber->text()); }
    const QString &address() { return(theAddr->text());   }

public slots:
    // methods to set current field values
    void   setName( const QString & );
    void   setNumber( const QString & );
    void   setAddress( const QString & );

// Here's that 'slot' thing again
protected slots:
    // Internal method to end the dialog
    void   ok();

private:
    // So we can reference each field
    QLineEdit *theName;
    QLineEdit *theNumber;
    QLineEdit *theAddr;
};

// Constructor—inherits QWidget functionality
ContactUI::ContactUI( QWidget *parent, const char *name )
: QWidget( parent, name )
{
    // QLayouts manage placement and resizing
    QVBoxLayout *top = new QVBoxLayout( this, 5 );
```

```
    // The name widget group
    QLabel *l = new QLabel( "Contact Name:", this );
    // Add the label to the layout
     top->addWidget( l );
     // A textfield to add/edit the name
    theName = new QLineEdit( this );
    top->addWidget( theName );
    // Add a little extra spacing
    top->addSpacing( 5 );

    // The number widget group
    l = new QLabel( "Phone Number:", this );
    top->addWidget( l );
    theNumber = new QLineEdit( this );
    top->addWidget( theNumber );
    top->addSpacing( 5 );

    // The address widget group
    l = new QLabel( "Address:", this );
    top->addWidget( l );
    theAddr = new QLineEdit( this );
    top->addWidget( theAddr );
    top->addSpacing( 10 );

    // An OK button
    QPushButton *pb = new QPushButton( "OK", this );
    top->addWidget( pb );

    // Connect the pushbutton's clicked signal to
    // our own ok slot
    connect( pb, SIGNAL(clicked()), SLOT(ok()) );
}

// The OK pushbutton will send a signal to this slot.
// each time the user clicks the button. We can then
// close the widget or exit, or do something else.
void
ContactUI::ok()
{
    // Call the QApplication's quit slot via the Qt
    // global QApplication reference.
    qApp->quit();
}

// Set the name field
void
ContactUI::setName( const QString &s )
{
    theName->setText( s );
}

// Set the number field
```

```
void
ContactUI::setNumber( const QString &s )
{
    theNumber->setText( s );
}

// Set the address field
void
ContactUI::setAddress( const QString &s )
{
    theAddr->setText( s );
}

// So we can see what it does
int
main( int argc, char **argv )
{
    QApplication app( argc, argv ); // Stack OK for main()
    ContactUI *cui = new ContactUI();
    app.setMainWidget( cui );
    cui->show();
    return( app.exec() );
}

#include <cui.moc>
```

The output of the example looks like Figure 2.2.

Figure 2.2   Output of Cui.cpp

On Linux systems, compile via:

```
moc Cui.cpp -o cui.moc
g++ -I. Cui.cpp -o cui -L$QTDIR) -lqt
```

On Windows systems, via:

```
moc Cui.cpp -o cui.moc
cl -nologo -I%QTDIR%\include -I. -c Cui.cpp
link -nologo Cui.obj %QTDIR%\lib\qt.lib user32.lib gdi32.lib \
comdlg32.lib ole32.lib uuid.lib imm32.lib wsock32.lib
```

This example introduces four new objects and four new (but related) concepts. First to appear is the QString object. QString is the Troll encapsulation of the string concept. It provides, among many things, "safe" string storage, UNICODE or ASCII string interpretation, searching, tokenizing, etc. Next to make the scene is the QLineEdit object. This is the standard "textfield" object for Qt and permits the user to enter and edit a single line of text. QPushButtons are what you most likely suspect they are—pushbuttons with a text or picture label. QLayouts help manage the overall layout of an interface.

The four new concepts introduced in the example are the "Q_OBJECT" line at the top of the class definition, the "slot" keywords in middle of the class definition, the connect() call at the end of the constructor, and the last line, which includes a mysterious, nonexistent file, cui.moc. These four are all related to Qt's signal/slot mechanism.

Qt provides a relatively unique mechanism for connecting one object's behavior to another. The Trolls call this the signal/slot mechanism, and it is used extensively throughout Qt and derived works. This mechanism is discussed in detail in the following chapter, so for now just pretend that it's not important but is somehow related to the four strange references in the example. There are two simple rules that cover virtually any Qt coding situation:

- If your class will emit or accept signals (via slots), the class definition must contain the term "Q_OBJECT" at the top.
- Any source file containing the term Q_OBJECT will need to be "meta-compiled" with the meta compiler, "moc," which is provided as part of the Qt toolkit. This meta-code must then be compiled by the platform compiler and linked with the final binary.

To support the use of the Qt signal/slot mechanism, there is an extra step involved in compiling this example. You must preprocess the source file using a Qt-supplied tool to produce the additional code that will support the signals and slots. The new step is the same for Linux or Windows and looks like:

```
moc Cui.cpp -o cui.moc
```

The moc program is created during the Qt build and should be located in $QTDIR/bin/moc under Linux, or %QTDIR%\bin\moc.exe on Windows systems. It is a good idea, for either platform, to add this directory to the PATH environment variable.

For those who are using a VC++ project to enter the examples, I've found it most convenient to add a "Custom-Build Step" to the source file. Specifying something like:

```
moc $(InputDir)\file.cpp -o $(InputDir)\file.moc
```

where "file" is replaced by the source file name. Once you've meta-compiled the source, you're ready to compile the source with the platform compiler. You can platform-compile the output of "moc" or, as I have done in the example, you can simply include it with the source. I have used the #include method for brevity.

You probably noticed that I used a different number of arguments in the QLabel constructor for this example. The Qt classes usually provide several overrides for the constructors and any of the C++ operators that make sense. You can also set or test most value settings of Qt classes after instantiation. Statements such as:

```
...
QLabel *myLabel = new QLabel( this );
myLabel->setText( "Hello World" );
QString ltext( myLabel->text() );
cout << (const char *)ltext << "\n";
...
```

will work like Troll Magic. Motif programmers will probably ask themselves, "Where's the tradeoff?" There is a tradeoff for Motif developers—you sacrifice difficult coding and have to settle for superior performance. Sigh.

STACK VS. HEAP

It is extremely important that you either always instantiate classes on the heap (via the "new" keyword) *or* have intimate knowledge of how your compiler will treat objects created on the stack or within a particular scope. Astute coders will have noticed that I use both methods for the QApplication class in the two examples. This is intentional. Both are legal and will work just fine—unless someone creates a new compiler or runtime that makes a persistent main() function unreliable.

I've heard arguments that stack instantiation is always a bad idea. As with anything else, if you don't know what you're doing—or in this case, what your compiler is doing—nearly everything is a bad idea. Stack instantiation can cause some serious problems that are difficult to debug, and it can also yield significant supportability and performance improvements. If you are in doubt, use the heap. A really nasty stack allocation bug is an excellent learning opportunity—that most people won't have time or patience for.

QT TOOLKIT BASICS

If you learn just the following basic principles, you'll be more than half way toward being a proficient Qt developer. As a reader and frequent contributor to the Qt-interest mailing list, I frequently see questions posted that would have been unnecessary if the person was familiar with the Qt basics. When someone answers these questions, you can almost picture a forehead being slapped somewhere in self-frustration.

Here are the basic concepts that you should acquaint yourself with before going any further:

* QApplication—the Qt application startup class handles most of the platform-specific initialization procedures.
* Qt uses a signal/slot model of message passing instead of the callback approach used by the X Toolkit (the basis for Motif) or the Microsoft Foundation Class Library.
* QObject—inherited by any Qt class that sends signals or provides slots, the QObject is the basis for nearly every Qt class. This is very short and easy to digest but extremely important because it is the base class of most Qt classes.
* QWidget—inherited by all the Qt widgets, QWidget provides most of the consistent features and functionality of the Qt widgets.

QAPPLICATION CLASS

For any given Qt application you create that uses any visual components, or processes input or events of *any* kind, you must create one (and *only* one) instance of the QApplication class, and you must create this one instance before you create other interface components. The toolkit will warn you if you attempt to create more than one instance of QApplication. It is QApplication that performs all the tedious initialization of the underlying, platform-dependent graphics and event notification functionality. Global desktop preferences such as default font, font properties, window colors, and mouse behavior are all copied to the Qt application's space, so your Qt application will appear as your user expects, despite the varying desktop themes. QApplication provides the event dispatch loop that allows your application to receive events from the underlying window manager.

If Qt was *not* compiled with the QT_NODEBUG flag defined, the following debugging options are available:

* **-nograb**: Qt must never grab the mouse or keyboard focus.
* **-dograb**: This is the counterpart to the –nograb option, and permits your Qt application to grab mouse or keyboard focus. This is sometimes necessary when executing your Qt application within a debugger. This option is only meaningful on X11 platforms.
* **-sync**: Normally, an X11 application will queue requests to the X server—they are buffered and serviced in FIFO order. This flag disables that normal buffering for the target application. This can be very useful for initial debugging, but you are warned that your application's performance will be extremely poor. This option is only meaningful on X11 platforms.

All Qt applications understand the following arguments:

- **-style=**<*style*> Where *style* is "motif," "windows," or "platinum."
- **-session=**<*session_id*> Where *session_id* is the *session manager* specific identifier for the session you want to restore. This is only useful on platforms that provide a full session management system, such as KDE, CDE, VUE and others. Microsoft Windows doesn't provide any true session management. Windows does, however, provide logout and shutdown notifications that can be used to save changes or to prompt the user, possibly canceling the logout or shutdown.

Qt Applications running in an X11 environment can use the following command-line arguments to alter the runtime behavior:

- **-display** <*Display*> Where *Display* is the display name and screen where the application's interface should manifest itself. This is specified in the usual *hostname:screen_number* syntax, and the environment variable $DISPLAY is the default.
- **-geometry** <*geometry_spec*> Where *geometry_spec* is a standard X11 geometry specification. Examples:
  ```
  myapp -geometry +600+200 # Start myapp at X=600, Y=200
  myapp -geometry 400x200 # 400 pels wide, 200 pels high
  ```
- **-fn/-font** <*font*> Set *font* as the default application font.
- **-bg/-background** <*color*> Use *color* as the default widget background color.
- **-fg/-foreground** <*color*> Use *color* as the default foreground color.
- **-btn/-button** <*color*> Use *color* as the default pushbutton background color.
- **-name** <*name*> Sets the application name to *name*. Note that this sets the name of the application as far as the X server is concerned, and won't necessarily affect the name displayed in the window manager title bar.
- **-title** <*name*> Sets the applications caption in the window manager's title bar to the specified *name*. Most applications will set this explicitly with a call to QWidget::setCaption().
- **-visual** <*visual*> Where *visual* is the type of visual you want the application to use. Currently, only the "TrueColor" visual type is defined and provides a truecolor visual on 8-bit displays—if the X server will support it.
- **-ncols** <*num_colors*> This option limits the number of colors your Qt application will allocate for its color cube on an 8-bit display to the number specified by *num_colors* if the QApplication::ManyColor color allocation specification is being used.
- **-cmap** This option will cause the application to install a private color map.

QApplication exposes a considerable number of methods. Table 2.1 lists these methods with a brief overview of their purpose:

Table 2.1   Public Slots, Public Functions, and Static Public Members

Public Functions	Purpose
QApplication(int &argc, char **argv)	Constructor
QApplication(int &argc, char **argv, bool GUIenabled)	Constructor
virtual ~QApplication ()	Destructor
int argc()	Returns number of command line arguments
char** argv()	Returns the array of command line arguments
QWidget* mainWidget()	Returns a pointer to the QApplication's main widget
virtual void setMainWidget(QWidget *)	Sets the QApplication's main widget
virtual void polish(QWidget *)	Invokes the QStyle::polish() function for the argument widget
QWidget* focusWidget()	Returns a pointer to the widget that currently has focus
QWidget* activeWindow()	Returns a pointer to the toplevel window that currently has focus
int exec()	The built-in event loop
void processEvents()	Processes all outstanding events, returns when they are complete
void processEvents(int maxtime)	Processes outstanding events for, at most, the argument number of milliseconds
void processOneEvent()	Processes one outstanding event
int enter_loop()	Recurses one additional level into the event loop. Returns zero on success, non-zero on failure
void exit_loop()	Forces a return from a recursed entry into the event loop
int loopLevel() const	Returns the number of recursions into the event loop
virtual bool notify(QObject *, QEvent *)	Sends an event to the argument QObject. Returns the value returned by the receiver's event handler
void setDefaultCodec(QTextCodec *)	Sets a different text encoding for the application. The default is Latin1.
QTextCodec * defaultCodec()	Returns a pointer to the default text encoding.
void installTranslator(QTranslator *)	Installs a new translator for the application
void removeTranslator(QTranslator *)	Removes the current translator from the application

(continued)

Table 2.1   (Continued)

Public Functions	Purpose
QString translate(const char *scope, const char *key)	Translates a string and returns the result.
bool isSessionRestored()	Returns true if this is a restored session
QString sessionId()	Returns the session ID (if available)
virtual void commitData(QSessionManager &sm)	This method is invoked when the session manager wants the application to commit all its outstanding data
virtual void saveState(QSessionManager &sm)	Causes the session manager to save the current state of the application
void wakeUpGuiThread ()	On Microsoft Windows systems, this method causes the GUI thread to execute

Public Slots	Purpose
void quit()	Causes the event loop to return a zero. This will typically cause the application to exit
void closeAllWindows()	This method causes all of the top-level windows to close

Static Public Members	Purpose
QStyle & style()	Returns the current style
void setStyle(QStyle *)	Sets a new style for the application
int colorSpec()	Returns the color allocation style for the application
void setColorSpec(int)	Sets a new color allocation style for the application
QCursor * overrideCursor()	Returns the current override cursor
void setOverrideCursor(const QCursor &, bool replace=FALSE)	Sets a new override cursor for the application
void restoreOverrideCursor()	Restores the previous override cursor (setOverrideCursor() pushes the current cursor onto an internal stack)
bool hasGlobalMouseTracking()	Returns true if this application has enabled global mouse tracking
void setGlobalMouseTracking(bool enable)	Enables or disables global mouse tracking

(continued)

Table 2.1   (Continued)

Static Public Members	Purpose
QPalette palette(const QWidget *w = 0)	Returns the default application color palette
void setPalette(const QPalette &, bool informWidgets=FALSE, const char * className = 0)	Sets the default application color palette
QFont font(const QWidget *w = 0)	Returns the default application font
void setFont(const QFont &, bool informWidgets= FALSE, const char *className = 0)	Sets the default application font
QFontMetrics fontMetrics()	Returns the current font metrics of the current application font
QWidgetList * allWidgets()	Returns the list of all widgets
QWidgetList * topLevelWidgets()	Returns the list of all top-level widgets
QWidget * desktop()	Returns a pointer to the desktop as a widget
QWidget * activePopupWidget()	Returns a pointer to the currently active popup widget (if one exists)
QWidget * activeModalWidget()	Returns a pointer to the currently active modal widget (if one exists)
QClipboard * clipboard()	Returns a pointer to the Qt clipboard interface
QWidget * widgetAt(int x, int y, bool child=FALSE)	Returns a pointer to the widget at the given coordinates
QWidget * widgetAt(const QPoint &, bool child=FALSE)	Returns a pointer to the widget at the given coordinates, represented by the QPoint argument
void exit(int retcode=0)	Causes the QApplication event loop to return the argument return code
bool sendEvent(QObject *rcvr, QEvent *event)	Sends the argument event to the argument object
void postEvent(QObject *rcvr, QEvent *event)	Places the argument event on the internal event queue and returns immediately
void sendPostedEvents(QObject *rcvr, int event_type)	Immediately dispatches all events of the argument type and that are targeted at the argument receiver
void sendPostedEvents()	Immediately dispatches all posted events
void removePostedEvents(QObject *receiver)	Immediately dispatches all events posted for the argument receiver
bool startingUp()	Returns true if the application object has not been created yet

(continued)

Table 2.1   (Continued)

Static Public Members	Purpose
bool closingDown()	Returns true if the application objects are being destroyed
void flushX()	Flushes the X11 event queue (only valid for X11)
void syncX()	Causes the Qt notion of the application display to synchronize with the X server (only valid for X11)
void beep()	Sounds the platform bell
void setDesktopSettingsAware(bool)	When the false argument is used, Qt's default behavior of using system default fonts, colors, etc., is disabled
bool desktopSettingsAware()	Returns false if the standard behavior of inheriting desktop font and color settings has been disabled
void setCursorFlashTime(int)	Sets the number of milliseconds for the total time period of a text cursor blink
int cursorFlashTime()	Returns the total time period for a text cursor blink
void setDoubleClickInterval(int)	Sets the mouse's double-click interval in milliseconds
int doubleClickInterval()	Returns the current mouse double-click interval in milliseconds
void setWheelScrollLines(int)	Sets the number of lines to scroll when the mouse wheel is rotated
int wheelScrollLines()	Returns the current number of lines to scroll when the mouse wheel is rotated
void setStartDragTime(int)	Specifies the time delay, in milliseconds, between the time the mouse button is pressed and the time a drag event begins
int startDragTime()	Returns the current delay, in milliseconds, between the time the mouse button is pressed and a drag event begins
void setStartDragDistance(int)	Specifies the distance the mouse must move following a mouse click before it is interpreted as a drag event
int startDragDistance()	Returns the distance the mouse must move following a mouse click before it is interpreted as a drag event

QApplication's Purposes

The QApplication class functions as the main interface between your application and the underlying window system and serves as a base object for all of the visual components of that application. The following features will give you an overview of functionality the QApplication class provides:

- QApplication encapsulates the *look and feel* of the application by means of a concept referred to as *Style*. The global style can be changed at runtime using the QApplication::setStyle() method. You can exercise per-widget style control as well, but it tends to make the interface confusing. Styles themselves are encapsulated via QStyle.

- QApplication specifies how the application will allocate and use colors via the *QApplication::setColorSpec() method*. You *must* set the color specification before you instantiate the QApplication object itself, or the specification will have no effect. (The Qt color allocation model is discussed below.)

- QApplication sets the default text codec (see QApplication::setDefaultCodec()), which defines how strings will be localized or translated via the QApplication::translate() method.

- QApplication encapsulates some extremely platform-dependent concepts, such as the "desktop" and the "clipboard," so that your application will work as you expect on whatever platform you deploy it. The Trolls define this as "Troll magic"—but it's just a lot of hard work on their part.

- QApplication provides adequate window interrogation and management functionality through the methods QApplication::widgetAt(), QApplication::topLevelWidgets(), and QApplication::closeAllWindows().

- QApplication provides the event dispatch mechanisms that every application needs; i.e., it receives events from the underlying window system and sends them to the appropriate widgets. You can use QApplication::postEvent() and QApplication::sendEvent() to send your own messages to your application's widgets. What could be more fun than that?

- QApplication manages how mouse events are handled and provides adequate control for customizing this handling via QApplication::setOverrideCursor() and QApplication::setGlobalMouseTracking(). You will hardly ever use these functions, however; you can usually accomplish the desired effect at the QWidget level.

- In X11 environments, QApplication provides methods to control the X11 protocol stream via QApplication::flushX() and QApplication::syncX().

- QApplication provides the needed framework to implement full session management control—even on a Microsoft Windows platform. This functionality is provided via the QSessionManager class and the QApplication::isSessionRestored(), QApplication::sessionId(), QApplication::commitData(), and QApplication::saveState() methods.

Color Management

Qt provides several methods of managing color allocation for your application. If you are primarily used to X11 programming, you have no doubt read the MIT documentation on the subject and have scars from scratching your head to prove it. The X11 color models for the various visual types can be confusing. Qt makes color allocation simple and predictable for most (not all) applications, and the QApplication class plays a significant role in that simplicity.

Qt provides more options on X11 platforms than on Microsoft Windows platforms, but the usage is consistent and simple. Qt manages color allocation in one of several ways, depending on the use of QApplication::setColorSpec() and QColor::enterAllocContext().

QApplication::setColorSpec() accepts an enumerated value that is one of the following:

- **QApplication::NormalColor**—This is the default. It causes your application to use the default system colors, which will work well for any application that uses very little color. This can lead to noticeable color dithering on Windows platforms.
- **QApplication::CustomColor**—This setting is useful for applications that have a small number of specific colors that must be allocated. This setting has no effect on X11 platforms as compared with the default setting. On Windows systems, this setting causes a new color palette to be created and colors are allocated from it as needed.
- **QApplication::ManyColors**—This setting is appropriate when your application will need many (even thousands of) colors.

You can gain an additional degree of color allocation control at application runtime via the QColor::enterColorContext() method, which permits the application to allocate many colors on a temporary basis. But if your application's help file refers to the name Pantone anywhere, you will need to add your own refinements to QColor to get the exact color you're after.

QWIDGET CLASS

QWidget is the abstraction of a user interface object and is the atom of Qt interface design. QWidget provides a great deal of functionality and performs many useful tasks. It receives events from the underlying window system and provides the methods you will most likely need to put those events to work. It maintains properties such as the font and a color palette, although it doesn't directly use them. All of the visual objects in the Qt toolkit are a *subclass* of QWidget, so all of the visual objects inherit QWidget methods and functionality. Table 2.2 represents the methods exposed by the QWidget class:

Table 2.2   QWidget Class Methods

Public Members	Purpose
QWidget(QWidget *parent=0, const char *name=0, WFlags f=0)	Constructor. The default behavior, with a widget argument equal to zero, constructs a top-level widget
QWidget ()	Destructor
WId winId()	Returns a platform-independent window ID
QStyle & style()	Returns the current Qt style of this widget
void setStyle(QStyle *)	Sets a new style for this widget
bool isTopLevel()	Returns true if this is a top-level widget
bool isModal()	Returns true if this widget is modal (true implies top-level)
bool isPopup()	Returns true if this widget has the WType_PopUp flag set
bool isDesktop()	Returns true if this widget refers to the desktop
bool isEnabled()	Returns true if this widget is enabled
bool isEnabledTo(QWidget *)	Returns true if this widget would be enabled or disabled along with the argument widget
QRect frameGeometry()	Returns the geometry of this widget relative to its parent (including the window frame)
const QRect & geometry()	Returns the geometry of this widget relative to its parent
int x()	Returns the x coordinate of this widget, relative to its parent
int y()	Returns the y coordinate of this widget, relative to its parent
QPoint pos()	Returns the QPoint coordinate of this widget, relative to its parent
QSize frameSize()	Returns the size of the window system frame (only valid for top-level widgets)
QSize size()	Returns the size of the widget
int width()	Returns the width (in pixels or pels) of the widget
int height()	Returns the height (in pixels or pels) of the widget

(continued)

Table 2.2   (Continued)

Public Members	Purpose
QRect rect()	Returns the internal geometry of the widget, without a window frame
QRect childrenRect()	Returns the geometry of the bounding rectangle of this widget's children
QRegion childrenRegion()	Returns the combined region of this widget's children
QSize minimumSize()	Returns the current minimum size for this widget
QSize maximumSize()	Returns the current maximum size for this widget
int minimumWidth()	Returns the current minimum width for this widget
int minimumHeight()	Returns the current minimum height for this widget
int maximumWidth()	Returns the current maximum width of this widget
int maximumHeight()	Returns the current maximum height of this widget
void setMinimumSize(const QSize &)	Sets the minimum size of this widget
virtual void setMinimumSize(int minw, int minh)	Sets the minimum width and height of this widget
void setMaximumSize(const QSize &)	Sets the maximum size of this widget
virtual void setMaximumSize(int maxw, int maxh)	Sets the maximum width and height of this widget
void setMinimumWidth(int)	Sets the minimum width of this widget
void setMinimumHeight(int)	Sets the minimum height of this widget
void setMaximumWidth(int)	Sets the maximum width of this widget
void setMaximumHeight(int)	Sets the maximum height of this widget
QSize sizeIncrement()	Returns the current size increment value (ignored on Microsoft Windows, probably ignored by the window manager)
void setSizeIncrement(const QSize &)	Sets the resize increment value. Windows will resize in steps of this amount (ignored on Microsoft Windows, probably ignored by the window manager)

(continued)

Table 2.2   (Continued)

Public Members	Purpose
virtual void setSizeIncrement(int w, int h)	Sets the resize increment width and height. Windows will resize in steps of this amount (ignored on Microsoft Windows, probably ignored by the window manager)
QSize baseSize()	Returns the current base widget size (only useful for size increments)
void setBaseSize(const QSize &)	Sets the widget's base size (only useful for size increments)
void setBaseSize(int w, int h)	Sets the widget's base width and height (only useful for size increments)
void setFixedSize(const QSize &)	Sets a fixed size for the widget
void setFixedSize(int w, int h)	Sets a fixed width and height for the widget
void setFixedWidth(int)	Sets a fixed width for the widget
void setFixedHeight(int)	Sets a fixed height for the widget
QPoint mapToGlobal(const QPoint &)	Translates the argument widget-relative coordinate to a global (window system) coordinate
QPoint mapFromGlobal(const QPoint &)	Translates the argument global (window system) coordinate to a widget-relative coordinate
QPoint mapToParent(const QPoint &)	Translates the argument widget-relative coordinate to a coordinate in the parent widget
QPoint mapFromParent(const QPoint &)	Translates the argument parent widget coordinate to a coordinate relative to this widget
QWidget * topLevelWidget()	Returns a pointer to the top-level widget that is an ancestor of this widget
BackgroundMode backgroundMode()	Returns the current background mode. The default is PaletteBackground
virtual void setBackgroundMode(BackgroundMode)	Sets the current background mode
const QColor & backgroundColor()	Returns the current background color of this widget
const QColor & foregroundColor()	Returns the current foreground color of this widget

(continued)

Table 2.2   (Continued)

Public Members	Purpose
virtual void setBackgroundColor(const QColor &)	Sets the widget's background color. This is probably not what you want! *Use setPalette()!*
const QPixmap * backgroundPixmap()	Returns a pointer to the background pixmap
virtual void setBackgroundPixmap(const QPixmap &)	Wrong. It sets the background pixmap
const QColorGroup & colorGroup()	Returns the current color group
const QPalette & palette()	Returns the current palette for the widget. If no custom palette has been set for this widget, this method returns the widget class palette, the parent's palette, or the application palette
virtual void setPalette(const QPalette &)	Sets a new palette for this widget
void unsetPalette()	Removes a custom palette, restoring the default
QFont font()	Returns the current widget font
virtual void setFont(const QFont &)	Sets a custom font for this widget
void unsetFont()	Removes the custom font, restoring the default
QFontMetrics fontMetrics()	Returns the current font metrics for this widget
QFontInfo fontInfo()	Returns the current font information
const QCursor & cursor()	Returns the current cursor used when the mouse is over this widget
virtual void setCursor(const QCursor &)	Sets the cursor shape that will appear when the mouse pointer is over this widget
virtual void unsetCursor()	Removes custom cursor settings, restoring the default
QString caption()	Returns the current widget caption (window frame title bar on top-level widgets)
const QPixmap * icon()	Returns a pointer to the pixmap that is currently set as this widget's icon
QString iconText()	Returns the icon text (if it has been set, otherwise it returns NULL)

(continued)

Table 2.2   (Continued)

Public Members	Purpose
`bool hasMouseTracking()`	Returns true if mouse tracking is enabled for the widget
`virtual void setMask( const QBitmap & )`	Sets a widget mask from the argument bitmap that controls how the widget is clipped (this is how you create round buttons)
`virtual void setMask( const QRegion & )`	Sets a widget mask from the argument region information that controls how the widget is clipped
`void clearMask()`	Disables widget masking from a previous setMask()
`bool isActiveWindow()`	Returns true if this widget is in the active window
`virtual void setActiveWindow()`	Sets this window to be active
`bool isFocusEnabled()`	Returns true if this widget can receive keyboard focus
`FocusPolicy focusPolicy()`	Returns the current focus policy of the widget
`virtual void setFocusPolicy( FocusPolicy )`	Sets or changes the current focus policy of the widget
`bool hasFocus()`	Returns true if this widget has keyboard focus
`virtual void setFocusProxy( QWidget * )`	Sets the argument widget to proxy keyboard focus for this widget
`QWidget * focusProxy()`	Returns the widget that proxies the keyboard focus for this widget (Null if none)
`void grabMouse()`	Grabs the mouse input. No other widget will receive mouse input until releaseMouse() is called
`void grabMouse( const QCursor & )`	Grabs the mouse input and changes the mouse appearance to that of the argument. No other widget will receive mouse input until releaseMouse() is called
`void releaseMouse()`	Releases the mouse after a widget has called grabMouse()
`void grabKeyboard()`	Grabs the keyboard input. No other widget will receive keyboard input until releaseKeyboard() is called
`void releaseKeyboard()`	Releases the keyboard after a widget has called grabKeyboard()
`bool isUpdatesEnabled()`	Returns true if updates to this widget are enabled

(continued)

Table 2.2   (Continued)

Public Members	Purpose
virtual bool close(bool)	Closes the widget. If the argument is true, the widget will be deleted along with its children
bool isVisible()	Returns true if the widget is (or could be) visible. A widget obscured by another widget could be visible in this sense
bool isVisibleTo(QWidget *)	Returns true if this widget would become visible if the argument ancestor widget is made visible
QRect visibleRect()	Returns the currently visible rectangle of the widget
bool isMinimized()	Returns true if this widget is minimized
virtual QSize sizeHint()	Usually overridden in a subclass, this method returns a suitable size for this widget
virtual QSize minimumSizeHint()	Usually overridden in a subclass, this method returns the smallest useable size for this widget
virtual QSizePolicy sizePolicy()	Returns the current size policy of this widget. Widgets such as QPushButton and QLineEdit "like" to grow/shrink horizontally but not vertically. This is an effect of QSizePolicy values
virtual int heightForWidth(int)	Returns a preferred height, given an argument width. The default returns zero (doesn't care).This does not take layouts into account.
virtual void adjustSize()	Adjusts the size of this widget to fit the content widgets. Uses sizeHint() if it's valid, otherwise it attempts to fit the bounding rectangles of child widgets
QLayout * layout()	Returns a pointer to the QLayout that manages this widget's children or NULL if no layout is in use
void updateGeometry()	Notifies a layout that this widget's geometry has changed.

virtual void
reparent(QWidget *parent,
  WFlags, const QPoint &,
  bool show=FALSE)
	Reparents the argument widget to this widget, positioning it at the argument point and applying the argument window flags to it. If show == true, the widget will be shown immediately

(continued)

Table 2.2   (Continued)

Public Members	Purpose
void reparent(QWidget *parent, const QPoint &, bool show=FALSE)	Reparents the argument widget to this widget, positioning it at the argument point. If show == true, the widget will be shown immediately
void erase()	Erases the entire widget to the background color
void erase(int x, int y, int w, int h)	Erases the rectangle described by the arguments to the background color
void erase(const QRect &)	Erases the rectangle described by the argument to the background color
void erase(const QRegion &)	Erases the rectangle described by the argument to the background color
void scroll(int x, int y)	Scrolls the widget x pixels to the right and y pixels down. If x and y are negative, the scrolling is reversed
void scroll(int x, int y, const QRect &)	Scrolls the argument rectangle of the widget x pixels to the right and y pixels down. If x and y are negative, the scrolling is reversed
void drawText(int x, int y, const QString &)	Draws the argument string on the widget at the point referenced by the x and y coordinates
void drawText(const QPoint &, const QString &)	Draws the argument string on the widget at the argument point
QWidget * focusWidget()	Returns a pointer to the widget in the current window that has focus
QRect microFocusHint()	Returns the current focus position and size for platform-dependent input methods
bool acceptDrops()	Returns true if this widget accepts drop events
virtual void setAcceptDrops(bool)	Sets this widget to accept drop events if the argument is true
virtual void setAutoMask(bool)	Enables/disables automatic calls to the widget's updateMask() method whenever a resizeEvent or a change in focus occurs
bool autoMask()	Returns true if automatic calls to updateMask() are enabled for resize events and focus changes

(continued)

Table 2.2   (Continued)

Public Members	Purpose
void setBackgroundOrigin(BackgroundOrigin)	Sets the widget's background to be drawn relative to the argument origin type, either WidgetOrigin (the default) or ParentOrigin (typically used to blend the background of adjacent widgets to make them appear as one)
BackgroundOrigin backgroundOrigin()	Returns the current background origin type of this widget (either WidgetOrigin or ParentOrigin)
virtual bool customWhatsThis()	Returns true if this widget handles What's This popup help manually. The default value is false
QWidget * parentWidget()	Returns a pointer to the parent widget. Returns NULL if this is a top-level widget
bool testWFlags(WFlags)	Returns true if the argument window flag is set

Public Slots	Purpose
virtual void setEnabled(bool)	Enables/disables this widget. This affects both behavior and appearance
virtual void setCaption(const QString &)	Sets the widget's caption text. For top-level widgets, this will set the title bar string in the window frame
virtual void setIcon(const QPixmap &)	Sets the icon pixmap for this widget. For top-level widgets, this will set the icon displayed on the title bar on the window frame
virtual void setIconText(const QString &)	Sets the icon text
virtual void setMouseTracking(bool)	Enables/disables mouse tracking. When disabled (default) mouse move events are only received when a mouse button is pressed. When tracking is enabled, the widget receives move events whether a button is pressed or not
virtual void setFocus()	Sets this widget (or its focus proxy) to receive keyboard focus
void clearFocus()	Removes focus from this widget (or its proxy)
virtual void setUpdatesEnabled(bool)	Enables/disables the widget to receive updates. Calls to repaint() have no effect if updates are disabled

(continued)

Table 2.2   (Continued)

Public Slots	Purpose
void update()	If updates are enabled, any invalid regions of the widget are erased and repainted
void update(int x, int y, int w, int h)	If updates are enabled, this will update the specified region
void update(const QRect &)	If updates are enabled, this will update the specified region
void repaint()	If updates are enabled and the widget is visible, this method will erase and repaint the entire widget
void repaint(bool erase)	If updates are enabled and the widget is visible, this method will repaint the entire widget. If the argument is true, the widget is erased first
void repaint(int x, int y, int w, int h, bool erase=TRUE)	If updates are enabled and the widget is visible, this method will repaint the specified rectangle of the widget. If the erase argument is true (default), the widget is erased first
void repaint(const QRect &, bool erase=TRUE)	If updates are enabled and the widget is visible, this method will repaint the specified rectangle of the widget. If the erase argument is true (default), the widget is erased first
void repaint(const QRegion &, bool erase=TRUE)	If updates are enabled and the widget is visible, this method will repaint the specified rectangle of the widget. If the erase argument is true (default), the widget is erased first
virtual void show()	Causes the widget and its children to become visible. You almost never need to call this method
virtual void hide()	Makes this widget and its children invisible
virtual void showMinimized()	Causes the widget to appear minimized (as an icon). This is only useful for top-level widgets
virtual void showMaximized()	Causes the widget to appear maximized. This is only useful for top-level widgets
void showFullScreen()	Causes the widget to appear in full-screen mode. This is only useful for top-level widgets
virtual void showNormal()	Causes the widget to appear normally

(continued)

Table 2.2   (Continued)

Public Slots	Purpose
virtual void polish()	This slot is called after the widget has been created but before it is displayed. This is useful for performing additional initialization
void constPolish()	Ensures that a widget is fully initialized by calling polish(). Don't call this method from the constructor!
bool close()	Sends a QCloseEvent to the widget. If the event is accepted (default behavior), the widget will be hidden. Returns true if the close event was accepted
void raise()	Raises this widget to the top of the parent's stack if sibling widgets are obscuring it
void lower()	Lowers this widget in the parent's stack, possibly causing it to become obscured by sibling widgets
virtual void move(int x, int y)	Moves the widget to the new coordinates, relative to the parent (and any window frame)
void move(const QPoint &)	Moves the widget to the new coordinates, relative to the parent (and any window frame)
virtual void resize(int w, int h)	Resizes the widget to the specified size (assuming the size is between the minimum and maximum sizes). If the widget is visible, it will receive a resize event immediately. Otherwise, it will receive a resize event before it becomes visible
void resize(const QSize &)	Resizes the widget to the specified size (assuming the size is between the minimum and maximum sizes). If the widget is visible, it will receive a resize event immediately. Otherwise, it will receive a resize event before it becomes visible
virtual void setGeometry (int x, int y, int w, int h)	Sets the widget's geometry to the argument values (assuming the size is between the minimum and maximum sizes)
virtual void setGeometry (const QRect &)	Sets the widget's geometry to the argument values (assuming the size is between the minimum and maximum sizes)

(continued)

Table 2.2   (Continued)

Static Public Members	Purpose
void setTabOrder(QWidget *first, QWidget *second)	Sets the widget tab order. This is done in pairs, i.e., first to second, second to third, etc.
QWidget * mouseGrabber()	Returns a pointer to the widget that is currently grabbing the mouse, NULL otherwise
QWidget * keyboardGrabber()	Returns a pointer to the widget that is currently grabbing the keyboard, NULL otherwise
QWidget * find(WId)	Returns a pointer to the widget whose window has the argument window ID

Protected Members	Purpose
virtual bool event(QEvent *)	The main event handler. An event is compared to all registered event types and dispatched to a specialized event handler
virtual void mousePressEvent(QMouseEvent *)	Called when a mouse button is pressed
virtual void mouseReleaseEvent(QMouseEvent *)	Called when a mouse button is released
virtual void mouseDoubleClickEvent(QMouseEvent *)	Called when a mouse button is double-clicked
virtual void mouseMoveEvent(QMouseEvent *)	Called whenever the mouse moves if tracking is enabled. Otherwise, it is called whenever the mouse moves while a mouse button is pressed
virtual void wheelEvent(QWheelEvent *)	Called when the mouse wheel is rotated
virtual void keyPressEvent(QKeyEvent *)	Called when a keyboard key is pressed
virtual void keyReleaseEvent(QKeyEvent *)	Called when a keyboard key is released
virtual void focusInEvent(QFocusEvent *)	Called when the widget receives keyboard focus
virtual void focusOutEvent(QFocusEvent *)	Called when the widget loses keyboard focus
virtual void enterEvent(QEvent *)	Called when the mouse pointer enters the widget's region
virtual void leaveEvent(QEvent *)	Called when the mouse pointer leaves the widget's region
virtual void paintEvent(QPaintEvent *)	If updates are enabled, the function is called when a portion of the widget needs to be repainted

(continued)

Table 2.2   (Continued)

Protected Members	Purpose
virtual void moveEvent(QMoveEvent *)	Called when the widget is moved
virtual void resizeEvent(QResizeEvent *)	Called when the widget is resized
virtual void closeEvent(QCloseEvent *)	Called by a prior call to the close() method. The default behavior is to accept() the event which will hide the widget
virtual void dragEnterEvent(QDragEnterEvent *)	Called when a drag operation is in progress and the mouse enters the widget's region
virtual void dragMoveEvent(QDragMoveEvent *)	Called when a drag operation is in progress and the mouse moves within the widget's region
virtual void dragLeaveEvent(QDragLeaveEvent *)	Called when a drag operation is in progress and the mouse leaves the widget's region
virtual void dropEvent(QDropEvent *)	Called when a drag operation is in progress and the mouse button is released within this widget's region
virtual void showEvent(QShowEvent *)	Called before the widget is shown
virtual void hideEvent(QHideEvent *)	Called after the widget is hidden
virtual void customEvent(QCustomEvent *)	Called explicitly from QApplication's sendEvent() or postEvent() methods to implement a custom event type
virtual void updateMask()	Called automatically if autoMask() is true. This updates the widget mask to account for resize and focus changes
virtual void styleChange(QStyle &)	Called when the widget's style has been changed
virtual void enabledChange(bool)	Called whenever the widget's enabled state changes
virtual void backgroundColorChange(const QColor &)	Called when the widget's background color is changed by a call to setBackgroundColor()
virtual void backgroundPixmapChange(const QPixmap&)	Called when the background pixmap is changed
virtual void paletteChange(const QPalette &)	Called when the widget's palette is changed
virtual void fontChange(const QFont &)	Called when the widget's font is changed

(continued)

Table 2.2   (Continued)

Protected Members	Purpose
virtual void create(WId = 0, bool initializeWindow = TRUE, bool destroyOldWindow = TRUE)	Creates a new widget window if the window ID argument is zero, otherwise the widget is moved to the window with that ID. The initializeWindow argument specifies whether the new window's geometry will be initialized or not. If the destroyOldWindow argument is true, the previous window will be destroyed
virtual void destroy(bool destroyWindow = TRUE, bool destroySubWindows = TRUE)	Destroys the widget window if destroyWindow is true. If destroySubWindows is true, destroy() is called recursively for child widgets
WFlags getWFlags()	Retrieves the current widget flags
virtual void setWFlags(WFlags)	Sets the specified widget flag
void clearWFlags(WFlags)	Resets (clears) the specified widget flag
virtual bool focusNextPrevChild(bool next)	Finds a new widget to accept keyboard focus in the current tab order. Returns true if successful, false otherwise
QFocusData * focusData()	Returns a pointer to the focus data for the top-level widget ancestor of this widget
virtual void setKeyCompression(bool)	Enables/disables key event compression. When enabled, more than one key event can be processed in a single event, useful for multi-character unicode input. The default is disabled
virtual void setMicroFocusHint(int x, int y, int w, int h, bool text=TRUE)	Sets the focus position and size for platform-dependent input methods

Parent/Child Relationship

QWidget maintains a list of its *child* widgets (accessible via the QWidget::children() method). A child of a given widget is any widget whose *parent* widget (passed as the first argument to the constructor) is the given widget. The default QWidget destructor will delete all of its children before it deletes itself. All you need do to delete a chain of widgets is delete the parent.

The parent/child relationship rule is simple: A QWidget that has no parent is a *top-level* widget (usually with a window manager border, title bar, etc.), and all QWidgets that have this top-level widget as a parent are children of that widget.

QApplication maintains a list of the top-level widgets in your application, and these top-level widgets maintain the list(s) of their children. If you delete a widget, its destructor will first delete all its children. (The symbiosis is nearly perfect. You will spot the occasional memory leak but they are always very small and nonpropagating.)

The geometry of a Qt widget is constrained by the geometry of its parent. Creating a 300 by 200 pixel list view as a child of a 50 by 50 frame widget will not appear as you intended.

The following example will help to illustrate the parent/child relationship.

```
NewW.h

#ifndef _NEWWIDGET_H
#define _NEWWIDGET_H

#include <qlabel.h>
#include <qlayout.h>
#include <qstring.h>

// A subclass of QWidget
class NewWidget : public QWidget
{
    // To make our two slots work:
    Q_OBJECT
public:
    // The constructor accepts a widget parent but the default
    // behavior is a toplevel widget.
    NewWidget( QWidget *parent=0, const char *name=0 );

public slots:
    void setLabel( const QString &s ) { left->setText( s ); }
    void setValue( const QString &s ) { val->setText( s ); }

private:
    QLabel *left, *val;
};
#endif // _NEWWIDGET_H


NewW.cpp


NewWidget::NewWidget( QWidget *p, const char *n )
: QWidget( p, n ) // Pass the arguments to the base class
{
    // Add a layout
    QHBoxLayout *top = new QHBoxLayout( this, 5 );
    // "left" is the label in the pair
    left = new QLabel( this );
```

```
    left->setAlignment( AlignVCenter|AlignRight );
    top->addwidget( left );
    // val displays the value in the pair
    val = new QLabel( this );
    top->addWidget( val );
}
#include "NewW.moc"
```

OK, we have a new widget. It exposes all the same methods, signals, and slots of a QWidget, adding two new slots in the process. Internally, it maintains a layout and two label widgets, but you needn't concern yourself with how the management is accomplished—for the purpose of this discussion, it just *is*.

Now, we'll make use of our new widget. We'll create two instances of NewWidget and delete one when the user clicks a button, then we'll discuss what you can expect to happen:

main.cpp

```
#include "NewW.h"
#include <qapplication.h>
#include <qpushbutton.h>

class screen : public QWidget
{
    Q_OBJECT
public:
    screen();

protected slots:
    void delbot() { delete bottom, bottom = 0; }

private:
    NewWidget *above, *bottom;
};

screen::screen()
: QWidget( 0, 0 )
{
    // Vertical layout—two NewWidgets and a button
    QVBoxLayout *top = new QVBoxLayout( this );
    above = new NewWidget( this );
    above->setLabel( "Upper Value:" );
    above->setValue( "Above it all" );
    top->addWidget( above );
    bottom = new NewWidget( this );
    bottom->setLabel( "Lower Value:" );
    bottom->setValue( "Bottomed-out" );
    top->addWidget( bottom );
    QPushButton *pb = new QPushButton( "Delete Bottom", this );
    connect(pb, SIGNAL(clicked()), SLOT(delbot()) );
}
```

```
int
main( int argc, char **argv )
{
    QApplication app( argc, argv );
    screen *s = new screen();
    app.setMainWidget( s );
    s->show();
    return( app.exec() );
}


// We have slots in the above class, so we have to meta compile
// this code and link to it (or just include the moc output)
#include "main.moc"
```

The above code defines a subclass of QWidget, screen, that manages two New-Widget widgets and a pushbutton in a vertical layout. In screen's constructor, the clicked() signal that is emitted by the pushbutton is connected to the delbot() slot of the screen widget. The delbot() slot simply checks to see if the bottom NewWidget (a pointer) is equal to zero and if not, deletes the object it points to.

Since each instance of a widget that is created will allocate resources, what happens to all the resources allocated by the instance of NewWidget, pointed to by the bottom pointer, when you click the button? You guessed it—all of the children of that particular NewWidget will be deleted first. That means *all* the children. This behavior is present in QWidget, QObject, and their subclasses, and it is very important that you take this into account. If you delete the *main widget*, the widget passed as the argument to QApplication::setMainWidget(), your application will exit.

Widget Flags

A top-level widget is any widget that has no parent. Sometimes, you will want to create top-level widgets with different *widget-flag* values from the default. The following example illustrates a simple dialog-style top-level widget. Notice the addition of a widget-flag argument.

```
dialog.h

#include <qlabel.h>
#include <qlayout.h>
#include <qpushbutton.h>

class dialog : public QWidget
{
    Q_OBJECT
public:
    dialog( const QString &, const QPixmap & );
```

```
public slots:
    void setText( const QString &s ) { msg->setText( s ); }

protected slots:
    virtual void byebye();

private:
    QLabel *msg;
};


dialog.cpp

#include "dialog.h"

dialog::dialog( const QString &mesg, const QPixmap &pix )
: QWidget( 0, 0, WStyle_Dialog|WType_Modal )
{
    // Something for the title bar
    setCaption( tr("Alert!") );
    // Use the same pixmap for a window icon
    setIcon( pix );
    // Vertical layout (overall)
    QVBoxLayout *top = new QVBoxLayout( this );
    // Horizontal layout for an icon and a message
    QHBoxLayout *hb = new QHBoxLayout();
    // The icon and the message get all the vertical stretch
    top->addLayout( hb, 5 );
    QLabel *l = new QLabel( this );
    l->setPixmap( pix );
    hb->addWidget( l );
    msg = new QLabel( mesg, this );
    hb->addWidget( msg, 2 );
    // An OK button
    QPushButton *pb = new QPushButton( tr("OK"), this );
    connect( pb, SIGNAL(clicked()), SLOT(byebye()) );
    top->addWidget( pb );
}

void
dialog::byebye()
{
    delete this;
}
#include <dialog.moc>
```

It's a lot easier to do this with the QMessageBox class, of course, but this illustrates a top-level widget a little better.

The widget-flag value will normally only be specified for top-level widgets. Here are the current widget-flag values and their meanings (it's subject to change from one release to another, so it's a good idea to check the qnamespace.h file and read the documentation for the Qt class). They are arranged into three groups: those that affect type, style, and modifiers.

Widget Type Flags

The type flag influences how the window is treated by the application and the underlying window system.

- **WType_TopLevel**—sets this widget to be a top-level widget, implying that it will have window manager decorations, a border, etc.
- **WType_Modal**—indicates that this is an application-modal top-level widget. No other top-level widget in the application can receive input until this widget is closed. This widget type also implies a style of *WStyle_Dialog*.
- **WType_Popup**—sets this widget to be an application-modal top-level widget with a style appropriate for popup menus.
- **WType_Desktop**—indicates that this widget is the window system desktop. See the *WPaintDesktop* modifier flag below.

Widget Style Flags

The style flag determines what window decorations the window manager will add to the widget, i.e., borders, resize gadgets, etc.

- **WStyle_Customize**—provides no window decorations, icon (system menu), title bar (caption), buttons (minimize, maximize, and close), or resize gadgets. It implies that you will set all of the style hints using WStyle_XXX widget flags. This is useful by itself for splash screens.
- **WStyle_NormalBorder**—provides the standard window decorations, icon, title bar, buttons, and resize gadgets. You can't combine this flag with *WStyle_DialogBorder* or *WStyle_NoBorder*.
- **WStyle_DialogBorder**—provides a tile bar, icon, and a close button. This flag can't be combined with WStyle_NormalBorder or WStyle_NoBorder.
- **WStyle_NoBorder**—provides a normal window without the decorations. This flag can't be combined with WStyle_NormalBorder or WStyle_DialogBorder.
- **WStyle_Title**—provides a title bar.
- **WStyle_SysMenu**—provides a system menu icon.
- **WStyle_Minimize**—provides a minimize button.
- **WStyle_Maximize**—provides a maximize button.
- **WStyle_MinMax**—provides both a minimize and a maximize button.
- **WStyle_Tool**—provides a title bar and a close button.
- **WStyle_StaysOnTop**—causes the window to remain on top of other windows.
- **WStyle_Dialog**—provides an appearance appropriate for dialog boxes. It has a title bar, an icon, and a close button. This flag will prevent the creation of an additional icon on the system taskbar, and the dialog will (usually—it depends on the underlying window system) minimize along with the parent.
- **WStyle_ContextHelp**—adds a context-sensitive help button.

Widget Modifier Flags
The modifier flags alter the behavior of the other flag values.

- **WDestructiveClose**—causes the widget to be destroyed when the widget accepts a *closeEvent()* or when it attempts to ignore a closeEvent() and fails.
- **WPaintDesktop**—causes the widget to receive paint events for the desktop.
- **WPaintUnclipped**—causes all *painters* to paint in an unclipped manner. All children of this widget, and all widgets in front of it (above this widget in Z-order) will not clip the areas the painter can paint on.
- **WPaintClever**—indicates that Qt should not try to optimize repainting for the widget and that the underlying window system will pass repaint events directly to the widget. This may generate more events, but usually reduces the size of the areas that will be repainted (e.g., by expose events).
- **WResizeNoErase**—indicates that the widget should not erase its contents when resized. This can reduce possible flicker during a resize caused by using WPaintClever.
- **WRepaintNoErase**—indicates that the widget takes responsibility for painting (and repainting) all its pixels. Scrolling, expose events, updating, and focus changes will not erase the contents. This can reduce possible flicker that can result from using the WPaintClever modifier.
- **WMouseNoMask**—causes a masked widget (one with an irregular shape) to receive mouse events for the entire widget window (which is always rectangular or square).
- **WNorthWestGravity**—indicates that the widget's contents are statically aligned to the top-left corner. A resize event will only create repaint events for newly exposed contents of the widget.

All the above flags can be combined to achieve a desired special effect, although the default flags for the higher-level (subclassed) Qt widgets are usually adequate.

QOBJECT CLASS

Nearly every Qt class inherits the QObject class behavior. It is the base class for the Qt object model and provides the functionality that makes the signal/slot mechanism (discussed next) work. QObject contains an optional object name value and can report its class name (if the class definition contains the Qt-specific keyword Q_OBJECT in its class definition). It can receive events via the QObject::event() method, filter events for other QObjects, and can intercept events for its children. QObject manages a parent/child object-tree in a manner that is similar to QWidget. If you delete a QObject, all of its children will be destroyed first.

The occasion may arise where you need QObject functionality in a subclass of a widget that doesn't inherit QObject. A good example is QListViewItem. You can use the

C++ multiple-inheritance feature to derive a new class from both QObject and QList-ViewItem, but you must always derive from QObject first. The following code fragment illustrates what this looks like:

```
#include <qobject.h>
#include <qlistview.h>

class myItem : public QObject, QListViewItem
{
Q OBJECT
public:
myItem( QWidget *p=0, const char *n=0 );
…
};
```

If you were to derive from QObject after QListViewItem, you would waste a lot of time trying to figure out why your slots and signals weren't working as expected.

While you will rarely see an example in this book that makes use of the *name* parameter to QObject, QWidget, and their subclasses, it is usually a very good idea to do so (I leave them out because they make the examples larger and because I wanted to keep the examples simple). The Qt error-handling mechanism will report the name of an object that experiences or causes a problem. (While there is no formal Qt-specific exception handling mechanism, the built-in error handling mechanism is usually adequate.)

Table 2.3 lists the methods exposed by the QObject class:

Table 2.3   QObject Class Methods

Public Members	Purpose
QObject(QObject * parent=0, const char * name=0)	Constructor
virtual QObject()	Destructor
virtual bool event(QEvent *)	Receives events for an object and should return true if the event is recognized and processed
virtual bool eventFilter(QObject *, QEvent *)	Filters events if this object has been installed as an event filter for other objects
virtual QMetaObject * metaObject()	Returns a pointer to the meta object of this object
virtual const char * className()	Returns the class name of this object or an invalid name if the Q_OBJECT keyword is missing
bool isA(const char *)	Returns true if this object matches the argument class type, otherwise it returns false

(continued)

Table 2.3   (Continued)

Public Members	Purpose
bool inherits(const char *)	Returns true if this object instance inherits the argument class type
const char * name()	Returns the instance name of this object
const char * name(const char *)	Returns the instance name of this object if one exists, otherwise the argument is assigned as the new instance name
virtual void setName(const char *)	Sets the instance name of this object
bool isWidgetType()	Returns true if this object instance is a widget
bool highPriority()	Returns true if this object is a high priority object
bool signalsBlocked()	Returns true if signals are blocked by this object
void blockSignals(bool b)	Enables/disables blocking of signals by this object
int startTimer(int)	Starts a timer with a period equal to the argument number of milliseconds. It returns a timer ID
void killTimer(int)	Stops the timer with the argument ID
void killTimers()	Stops all timers associated with this object
QObject * child(const char *name, const char *type = 0)	Returns a pointer to the object with the specified name and type, NULL otherwise
const QObjectList * children()	Returns a pointer to the list of children of this object
QObjectList * queryList(const char * inherit=0, const char *name=0, bool regexMatch=TRUE, bool recursiveSearch=TRUE)	Permits regular expression searches for specific objects. It returns a pointer to the list of matching objects
virtual void insertChild(QObject *)	Inserts the specified argument as a child of this object
virtual void removeChild(QObject *)	Removes the specified object from this object's tree
void installEventFilter(const QObject *)	Installs an event filter for this object
void removeEventFilter(const QObject *)	Removes the event filter from this object

(continued)

Table 2.3   (Continued)

Public Members	Purpose

bool
connect(const QObject *sender,
  const char *signal,
  const char *member)
	Connects the signal from the sender object to the member slot. Returns true on success, false on failure

bool
disconnect(const char *signal=0,
  const QObject *receiver=0,
  const char *member=0)
	Disconnects the signal that is connected to the member slot of the receiver object. Returns true on success, false on failure

bool disconnect(const QObject *receiver, const char *member=0)	Disconnects all signals that are connected to the member slot of the receiver object. Returns true on success, false on failure
void dumpObjectTree()	Very useful for debugging. Dumps the object tree structure to the debugging output (stderr on Linux, application console on Windows (requires that Qt be built with debugging enabled)
void dumpObjectInfo()	Very useful for debugging. Dumps the object information (slot connections, etc.) to the debugging output (stderr on Linux, application console on Windows (requires that Qt be built with debugging enabled)
bool setProperty(const char *name, const QVariant &value)	Sets object's property name to the argument value. Returns true on success, false on failure
QVariant property(const char *)	Returns the specified property from the object
QObject * parent()	Returns a pointer to the object's parent object or NULL if no parent exists

Static Public Members	Purpose
QString tr(const char *)	Returns a translated version of the argument string or the argument string if no translation exists
const QObjectList * objectTrees()	Returns a pointer to all of the object's object trees

bool
connect(const QObject *sender,
  const char *signal,
  const QObject *receiver,
  const char *member)
	Connects the sender object's signal to the receiver object's member slot. Returns true on success, false on failure

(continued)

Table 2.3   (Continued)

Static Public Members	Purpose
bool disconnect(const QObject *sender, const char *signal, const QObject *receiver, const char *member)	Disconnects the sender object's signal from the receiver object's member slot. Returns true on success, false on failure

Protected Members	Purpose
QConnectionList * receivers(const char *)	Returns a pointer to an array of object/slot pairs for the argument signal or zero if the signal is not connected to anything
const QObject * sender()	Returns a pointer to the last object that sent a signal to this object
virtual void initMetaObject()	Enables the meta object associated with this object. This is performed on demand
virtual void timerEvent(QTimerEvent *)	Reimplement this method in a subclass to receive timer events
virtual void childEvent(QChildEvent *)	Reimplement this method in a subclass to receive child events (events are sent when child objects are inserted or removed)
virtual void connectNotify(const char *)	This method is called when the argument signal has been connected to a slot
virtual void disconnectNotify(const char *)	This method is called when the argument signal has been disconnected from a slot
virtual bool checkConnectArgs(const char *sig, const QObject *receiver, const char *member)	Returns true if the sig can be connected to the receiver object's member slot, false otherwise

Static Protected Members	Purpose
QMetaObject * staticMetaObject()	Enables the meta object associated with this object. This is performed on demand. Identical to initMetaObject() but reimplemented as a static method

Signals and Slots vs. Callbacks

Any GUI application that provides user interaction (as well as many applications that don't) relies to some extent on events or messages that will trigger the execution of code that will (hopefully) deal with the specific event or message. For X11 applications, these are commonly referred to as *events*, while the Windows-speak term is *messages*. The term is irrelevant but the concept is pretty much the same. The methods used to deal with them differ somewhat between the two architectures.

Applications based on the X11 Toolkit, Xt (Motif and friends), use *callback* functions that accept arguments specific to the widget or to the event they are intended to handle. These callback functions must be registered with Xt for each widget that will make use of the particular callback, and it's the programmer's responsibility to guarantee that the argument lists will match at runtime. Since there is very little (or no) type-checking performed at compile-time, there is no guarantee that the callback function's arguments will be set as the programmer intended. If you make a mistake and if you are very lucky, the program will crash and you will have a core file or some debug information to help you find the problem in your code. More often than not, unfortunately, the program will behave erratically and you'll spend some time tracking it down. Whatever the result, a lot more time is spent debugging these applications than would otherwise be required if these connections were type-checked.

The Microsoft Foundation Class library, or *MFC*, uses compile-time macros and message maps to connect messages to C++ methods. Neither C nor C++ compilers can type-check a macro so MFC provides no benefits in this respect over the callback approach for Motif. MFC also requires the programmer to provide a rather complex message map that is as difficult to read as it is to write. This issue is usually dealt with by using the sophisticated Microsoft or Borland IDEs and their visual design tools. I won't speculate on Microsoft's reasons for creating a dependence on Microsoft tools and neither should you.

Qt addresses all these issues with an elegant alternative. Qt objects and objects that you create can *emit* (or send) signals without knowing what object(s) will receive them. Qt objects can also provide slots to receive signals emitted by other objects without knowing anything about the object that emitted the signal. This is a big improvement over the other methods discussed above, and presents some unique problems of its own that will be discussed a little later.

Signals   Don't confuse Qt signals with Linux or UNIX signals! They have nothing to do with one another.

Qt signals are sent by Qt objects or objects you create. The object emits the signal and doesn't care who, if anyone, receives the signal. An object may emit a signal to notify that the mouse has been moved or that a value has changed. Not having to know anything about who will use the object eliminates the need to anticipate the intended use of that object, and this supports a component model of development that encourages reuse of existing code.

Slots   Qt objects and objects you create can provide special functions known as *slots.* Slot functions are special because signals that are emitted by any Qt object can be connected to, or disconnected from, these slot functions using the QObject::connect() and QObject::disconnect() methods. The only constraint on these connections is that the type of the signal must match the type of the slot. If you have ever performed any electronic "breadboarding," a method of electronic prototyping that's very component-oriented, the advantages of the signal/slot architecture are immediately apparent as the two approaches to development are very similar.

While the compiler won't usually catch a mismatch between connected signals and slots, the toolkit will catch them at runtime, since that is when the actual connection occurs. The default behavior is to produce a warning message and proceed. The slot will only be called by connected signals having a matching, partial or complete, argument list (i.e., if a signal passes three arguments to a slot that matches the first two arguments, the connection will be made, and the third argument is discarded). That is only the default behavior, though. You can easily change the way Qt deals with these conditions to suit your specific need.

Defining Signals And Slots   Implementing signals and slots is easy, but there are a few considerations:

- Any object that implements signals or slots must inherit QObject, either directly or indirectly. All Qt user interface objects (widgets) inherit QObject.
- You must include the keyword Q_OBJECT at the top of the class definition.
- Signals and slots must always have a void return value.
- Signals are defined in a section of the class definition, called `signals:`. Access specifiers have no meaning for signals, so you must not provide one.
- Slots are defined by appending the new keyword, `slots`, to the desired access specifier as in: `public slots:`, `protected slots:`, or `private slots:`. Slots cannot be declared static.
- Any code containing the keyword Q_OBJECT must be precompiled with the Qt Meta-Object Compiler, which is called moc (moc.exe on Windows). The moc output must be compiled and linked with the final program.

The following is a completely useless example that demonstrates nothing more than possible declarations and implementations. It will execute—just don't expect an epiphany or a dazzling fireworks display.

```
Useless signals and slots
#include <qobject.h>
#include <stdio.h>

class DoLittle : public QObject
{
Q_OBJECT
public:
DoLittle();

signals:
    // Overloaded signals
void     callSlot( int );
void     callSlot( bool );
void     callSlot( const char * );
```

```
public slots:
    void     intSlot( int );

protected slots:
    virtual void boolSlot( bool );

private slots:
    void     asciiSlot( const char * );
};

DoLittle::DoLittle()
{
    connect( this, SIGNAL(callSlot( int )),
        SLOT(intSlot( int )) );
    connect( this, SIGNAL(callSlot( bool )),
        SLOT(boolSlot( bool )) );
    connect( this, SIGNAL(callSlot( const char * )),
        SLOT(asciiSlot( const char * )) );
}

void
DoLittle::intSlot( int v )
{
    if( v != 0 ) emit callSlot( true );
    else emit callSlot( false );
}

void
DoLittle::boolSlot( bool v )
{
    emit callSlot( (v == true) ? "true" : "false" );
}

void
DoLittle::asciiSlot( const char *p )
{
    printf("%s\n", p );
}
```

This example only demonstrates some possible declarations of signals of various types and some slots to connect them to. As you can see, the slots are written just like any other method and they can even be called in the same manner as normal class methods. A more useful example follows, and it is more representative of code that you are likely to write.

Consider the following example that modifies the behavior of the existing QLine-Edit widget by adding a new slot called copy2clip(). The program body will connect the clicked() signal (all QPushButtons emit this signal when the left mouse button is clicked while the mouse cursor is positioned over the widget) to our new slot, which copies any text that has been entered to the clipboard.

```
Line edit example demonstrating signal/slot usage
#include <qpushbutton.h>
#include <qlineedit.h>
#include <qapplication.h>

// A new type of QLineEdit that inherits all the behaviors
// of a QLineEdit. We add a new public slot called clear()
//
class MyEdit : public QLineEdit
{
    Q_OBJECT
public:
    // Standard widget constructor
    MyEdit( QWidget *p=0, const char *n=0 );

public slots:
    virtual void copy2clip();
};

MyEdit::MyEdit( QWidget *p, const char *n )
:QLineEdit( p, n )
{
}

void
MyEdit::copy2clip()
{
    copy();
}

// We'll use this class to present a MyEdit widget
// and a pushbutton, arranged vertically.
//
class MyWidget : public QWidget
{
public:
    MyWidget();

private:
    QPushButton *button;
    MyEdit      *lineedit;
};

MyWidget::MyWidget()
{
    QVBoxLayout *top = new QVBoxLayout( this, 5 );
    lineedit = new MyEdit( this );
    top->addWidget( lineedit );
    button = new QPushButton( "Copy", this );
    connect( button, SIGNAL(clicked()), lineedit,
        SLOT(copy2clip()) );
    top->addWidget( button );
}
```

```
// And a main() routine to drive it
int
main( int argc, char **argv )
{
    QApplication *app = new QApplication( argc, argv );
    MyWidget *mw = new MyWidget();
    app->setMainWidget( mw );
    mw->show();
    return( app->exec() );
}

// We need to include the moc-generated output in the
// compile…
#include "MyEdit.moc"
```

You need to preprocess this code with the moc tool to generate the MyEdit.moc file that is included at line 67 of the example. The method for doing this is the same on any platform:

```
moc MyEdit.cpp -o MyEdit.moc
```

You are now ready to compile and run the example. You should compile this code in the same manner as described in the previous example. Execute the program and type some text into the newly created MyEdit object and then click the pushbutton marked "Copy." You can now paste the contents of the MyEdit widget to anything you like.

When you press the left mouse button while the cursor is positioned over the QPushButton, the QPushButton receives a mouse event and emits the clicked() signal that we connected to our copy2clip() slot using the inherited connect() method of QObject. QObject is inherited by QWidget (our base class for MyWidget).

While it's not an absolute requirement that you understand the hierarchy of inheritance for each Qt object, it will certainly help you to anticipate behavior in your finished application. Without any understanding of the hierarchy, you will probably find yourself reimplementing methods that are already provided. This may sound like a somewhat daunting task, but the Qt reference documentation lends itself quite well to the task of tracking an object's ancestors.

The above example, while certainly useful, is not very exciting. When you begin applying the signal/slot concept to some of the more complex tasks that we all deal with every day, the advantages become apparent. You will see many such examples in following chapters.

If you have not already done so, now is a good time to work through the tutorial exercises provided with the Qt toolkit distribution. Pay careful attention to Troll's use of signals and slots and read the reference documentation for new widgets as they're introduced. If you trace each widget's inheritance using the reference documentation at each step, you will find your Qt programming skills are adequate to tackle most basic tasks.

Signal/Slot Disadvantages

Disadvantages of the signal/slot mechanism include the extra build step required to generate the moc output code. The most severe drawback is the inability to provide signals and
slots that are conditionally compiled via traditional macros. The following code will not
produce the expected results because the moc compiler doesn't interpret macros or macro
definitions:

```
Code that demonstrates a flaw in the moc compiler approach

#include <qobject.h>

class MyObject : public QObject
{
    Q_OBJECT
public:
    MyObject();

signals:
#ifdef WIN64 // Ignored by moc
    void    valueChanged( __int64 );
#else
    void    valueChanged( unsigned int );
#endif

public slots:
#ifdef WIN64 // Ignored by moc
    void    setValue( __int64 );
#else
    void    setValue( double );
#endif

private:
#ifdef WIN64
    unsigned __int64 value;
#else
    unsigned int     value;
#endif
};
```

The output from the moc compiler will produce both sets of signals and slots because the macro test for WIN64 is ignored by the Qt MOC compiler. If your compiler
does not yet support the __int64 data type, or if you try to compile this on any system
other than a Windows box, you will get errors at compile-time even though you took the
correct steps to prevent them—at least from a C++ perspective. Of course, you can get
around this problem by defining a type outside the class definition, but the example is just
an illustration.

The moc program *will* intercept two special comments that will make it easier to
block the moc compiler from processing large groups of code:

```
// MOC_SKIP_BEGIN
moc won't see this
// MOC_SKIP_END
```

I suppose a future implementation of the moc compiler will support full header parsing and conditional compile interpretation, but that will create a problem all by itself. The C++ language is not intended to be dependent on a preprocessor, and a preprocessing step is required to provide this type of compile-time support.

SUMMARY

In this chapter, I briefly discussed the basic concepts of the Qt toolkit that make it unique. When I first started using the toolkit, I found myself asking questions on the Qt-interest mailing list that I wouldn't have had to ask if I had taken the time to read the QWidget documentation. In retrospect, I realize the gurus on the list have unbounded patience.

If you have gotten this far in the book without reading the QWidget reference documentation, you should put this book down and do that right away. It will save you at least one e-mail to the gurus on the Qt-interest mailing list.

PART

II

Qt Widgets and Convenience Classes

User Interaction Objects

The following pages discuss the visual Qt objects, or widgets, that provide some mechanism(s) with which the user may interact. Some examples of possible uses are included where appropriate. Some simple modifications to the behavior of these objects are included as well, although purists may balk at some of my seeming deviations from "standard interface and style guidelines" (as if there *were* such a thing).

This is not intended as a comprehensive guide to all the Qt visuals. To attempt such a work could only serve to emulate the excellent online reference documentation. Instead, I have attempted to organize Qt's visual components into those widgets that support end-user interaction in some way. This classification is further divided into functionally related groups. Hopefully, this organization will make it possible to browse for needed functionality without having to read either this book, or the Qt online reference documentation, in their entirety. This should lessen the effort required to find the right widget for a given task, and should also make it easier for the less-experienced Qt programmer to visualize different approaches to solving real problems. Widget discussions include a brief discussion of the object's purpose or purposes. Some discussions include common or obvious modifications to existing behavior that you might find useful.

USER INTERACTION OBJECTS

I define *user interaction objects* as those objects that permit the end-user of an application to input information, to change operating parameters, or to trigger operations. This includes objects that permit a user to select something from a list.

Where it makes sense to do so, I have included supporting objects that don't directly provide an interface or interaction.

Buttons

These objects provide user interaction in the form of pushbuttons, radio buttons, toolbars, checkboxes, and classes that are used to manage them.

QCheckBox

A check box is a boolean indicator and input widget that consists of a graphic box that either provides a check mark or an "x" (depending on the style) and an optional text label. An example is shown in Figure 3.1.

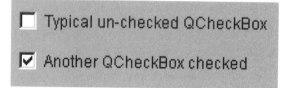

Figure 3.1   QCheckBox widgets

A Possible Instantiation

```
...
    QCheckBox *cb = new QCheckBox( "Option A", this );
...
```

Example Use

```
...
    cb->setChecked( true );
...
```

If your design requires a large number of checkboxes, or if the available screen real estate prevents creation of all the checkboxes required, consider using a QListView loaded with appropriate QCheckListItems instead.

QPushButton

Push buttons are used to trigger some sort of action, or to set a boolean value when used as a toggle button. Using the Qt push button is very simple—unless you come from a Motif background—in which case, you will miss the widget pointer that Motif passes to your callback. Of course, the only uses for that are related to button array handling, which is addressed a little differently in Qt. An example of a push button is shown in Figure 3.2.

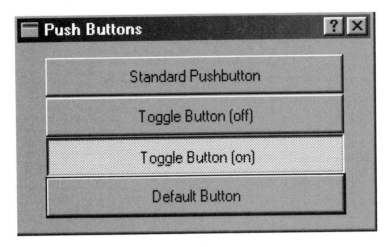

Figure 3.2   QPushButton widgets in a QDialog

A Possible Instantiation

```
...
    QPushButton *pb = new QPushButton( "&Quit", this );
...
```

Example Use

```
...
    connect( pb, SIGNAL(clicked()), qApp, SLOT(quit()) );
...
```

If you need to create an array of pushbuttons and need to discriminate between them within a single slot, you should either group the buttons using a QButtonGroup or you can create your own custom pushbutton that provides a signal that includes a pointer to itself as argument. Using a QButtonGroup is much easier (and potentially faster) than typical button array handling in Motif. The following example demonstrates a useless pushbutton array implementation:

```
Array of buttons

#include <qpushbutton.h>
#include <qbuttongroup.h>
#include <qlabel.h>
#include <qlayout.h>
```

```
#include <qstring.h>

class MyWidget : public QWidget
{
    Q_OBJECT
public:
    MyWidget( QWidget *p=0, const char *n=0 );

protected slots:
    virtual void onClick( int );

private:
    QLabel      *label;
};

MyWidget::MyWidget( QWidget *p, const char *n )
{
    QPushButton *pb[5];
    QString s;

    QVBoxLayout *top = new QVBoxLayout( this, 10 );
    QVButtonGroup *vbg = new QVButtonGroup( this );
    for(int a=0;a<5;a++) {
        s.sprintf( "Button %d", a );
        pb[a] = new QPushButton( s, vbg );
    }
    connect( vbg, SIGNAL(clicked( int )),
        SLOT(onClick( int )) );
    top->addWidget( vbg );
    label = new QLabel( "Click one.", this );
    top->addWidget( label );
}

void
MyWidget::onClick( int val )
{
    // val == index into push button array
    QString s;
    s.sprintf( "Button %d clicked.", val );
    label->setText( s );
}

#include "MyWidget.moc"
```

QRadioButton

Radio buttons combine a graphic indicator and input of boolean information with a text label, and are in many respects similar to a check box. Radio buttons differ from check boxes in that they are typically used in a group of two or more radio buttons, operating in an exclusive mode—only one radio button can be set at a time. You will normally use radio buttons with a QButtonGroup. Figure 3.3 represents three QRadioButtons in a QButton Group.

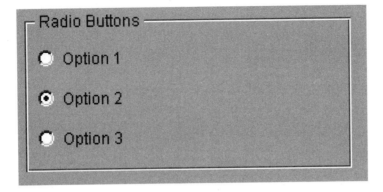

Figure 3.3   QRadioButton widgets in a QButtonGroup

A Possible Instantiation

```
...
    QButtonGroup *bg = new QButtonGroup( "Options", this );
    QRadioButton *rb = new QRadioButton( "Option A", bg );
...
```

Example Use

```
...
    if( rb->isChecked() == true ) {
        // User has selected Option A
    }
...
```

QToolBar

Toolbars (see Figs. 3.4 and 3.5) are a set of commonly used push/toggle buttons that provide for both an icon and a text label, arranged either horizontally or vertically. They are purely a convenience to the end-user and aren't always needed or useful. However, since nearly every new software package provides a toolbar (whether it makes sense to or not), you may find your latest project specification includes a section describing the toolbar.

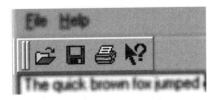

Figure 3.4   A "standard" QToolbar on a QMainWindow

Figure 3.5 QToolBar on a custom
QDialog. This provides a tear-off toolbar behavior

A Possible Instantiation

...

```
// Create a new toolbar on this QMainWindow
QToolbar *tools = new QToolbar( this );
```

...

Example Use

...

```
icon = QPixmap( idata );
toolb = new QToolButton( icon, "Save", "Save Changes",
                            this, SLOT(save()), tools, 0 );
toolb->setIconSet( QIconSet( idata ) );
```

...

Implementing a toolbar with Qt is fairly simple most of the time. It's certainly easier than finding or creating an icon that conveys the button's functionality to the user.

While QToolbars don't provide a way to create a free-floating toolbar, you can always add a toolbar to a borderless dialog and let the user drag that around—it looks the
same at any rate.

One odd behavior you will note is QMainWindow::usesBigPixmaps() and the or-
thogonal QMainWindow::setUsesBigPixmaps(bool) functions. Changing this setting
affects all QToolBars that are a child of that QMainWindow. There is no method in an
individual QToolBar to interrogate or set this. Maybe the next release. . . .

QToolButton

A tool button (see Fig. 3.6) is just a push button that is tailored for use in a QTool-
Bar. You can display a QPixmap on the button and an optional text label. You can (and
should) create and assign a QIconSet to tool buttons. QIconSet creates the appropriate en-
abled/disabled and large/small icons for the button.

Figure 3.6 A QToolButton on a
QToolBar

A Possible Instantiation

...

```
icon = QPixmap( idata );
```

```
toolb = new QToolButton( icon, "Save", "Save Changes",
                              this, SLOT(save()), tools, 0 );
```
...

Example Use
...
```
toolb->setIconSet( QIconSet( idata ) );
```
...

Predefined Dialogs

Qt provides a number of static dialogs for common functions such as file, font, and color selection. Since these dialogs are static, there is no need to instantiate them.

QColorDialog

As the name implies, this widget is a dialog that permits the user to select or specify a color value. (Fig. 3.7 is a grayscale screen shot of a QColorDialog.)

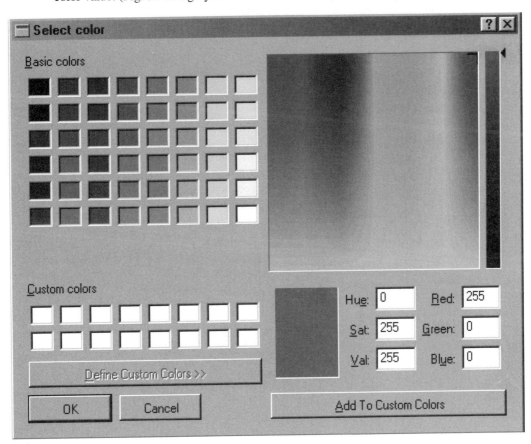

Figure 3.7   QColorDialog widget (in grayscale)

Example Use

```
...
    // Always start the dialog with red as default
    QColor face = QColor( "#ff0000" );
    // Get a user-defined color
    QColor newface = QColorDialog( face, qApp );
    // Make sure user didn't cancel—use default if so
    if(newface.isValid() == false) newface = face;
...
```

You don't need to instantiate this dialog as it is modal and provides static methods. A typical use would be as follows:

```
...
QColor userColor = QColorDialog::getColor();
myLabel->setPalette( QPalette( userColor ) );
...
```

QDialog   QDialog is the base class for all Qt dialogs. You can subclass the QDialog to provide virtually any conceivable form of popup window imaginable, from popup forms to splash screens. Of course, you can accomplish the same thing with a QWidget, but QDialog adds some convenient functionality appropriate for typical dialog behavior.

The parent/child relationship of QDialog widgets (and QSemiModal discussed below) has an effect on the appearance of the dialog on the screen. Passing a valid widget parent to a dialog will cause the dialog to center over the parent widget, while a dialog that has no parent will center itself on the screen itself.

The following example is a "Splash Screen" widget based on QDialog. (I don't approve of splash screens, but recognize that they are *sometimes* necessary.)

```
Splash.h

#ifndef _SPLASH_H
#define _SPLASH_H

#include <qdialog.h>
#include <qpixmap.h>
#include <qstring.h>
#include <qprogressbar.h>
#include <qlabel.h>

class Splash : public QDialog
{
  Q_OBJECT
public:
  Splash( const QPixmap &p, const char *title,
```

```
const char *cpyr, bool pbar=false );

  bool     isProgressSplash()    { return( isps );  }
  int      progressValue()       { return( progr );  }

public slots:
  void     setProgressValue( int );
  void     setProgressText( const QString & );

private:
  bool          isps;
  int           progr;
  QProgressBar *pbar;
  QLabel       *plabel;
};
#endif // _SPLASH_H




splash.cpp

#include <Splash.h>
#include <qlayout.h>
#include <qlabel.h>
#include <qprogressbar.h>

Splash::Splash( const QPixmap &pix,
  const char *mmsg, const char *cpyr, bool isp )
 : QDialog( 0, "Splash", false,
  WStyle_DialogBorder|WStyle_Customize )
{
  isps = isp;
  progr = 0;

  QVBoxLayout *top = new QVBoxLayout( this, 10 );
  QHBoxLayout *hb = new QHBoxLayout();
  top->addLayout( hb, 5 );
  hb->addSpacing( 10 );

  // Add Pix
  QLabel *l = new QLabel( this );
  l->setPixmap( pix );
  hb->addSpacing( 10 );

  // Add Product name/Main message
  QVBoxLayout *vb = new QVBoxLayout();
  hb->addLayout( vb );
  if(mmsg != 0) {
    l = new QLabel( this );
    l->setAlignment( AlignVCenter|AlignHCenter );
    l->setFont( QFont( "helvetica", 18,
    QFont::Bold|QFont::Italic ) );
    l->setText( mmsg );
```

```
    vb->addWidget( 1, 2 );
  }


  // Add copyright info
  if(cpyr != 0) {
    l = new QLabel( this );
    l->setAlignment( AlignVCenter|AlignHCenter );
    l->setText( cpyr );
    vb->addWidget( 1, 3 );
  }


  // Maybe add progressbar
  if(isps == true) {
    hb = new QHBoxLayout();
    top->addLayout( hb );

    // A text label
    plabel = new QLabel( this );
    plabel->setAlignment( AlignVCenter|AlignRight );
    plabel->setFixedHeight(fontMetrics().height()
      + 6 );
    hb->addWidget( plabel );

    // A progress bar
    pbar = new QProgressBar( 100, this );
    pbar->setFixedHeight(fontMetrics().height(
      + 6 );
    pbar->setValue( 0 );
    hb->addWidget( pbar );
  }
  top->activate();
  show();
}

void
Splash::setProgressValue( int v )
{
  if(isps == false) return;
  pbar->setValue( v );
  progr = v;
}

void
Splash::setProgressText( const QString &s )
{
  if(isps == false) return;
  plabel->setText( s );
}


#include <Splash.moc>
```

QFileDialog

QFileDialogs (see Fig. 3.8) are used to allow an end-user to select a file for open or save functionality, or to select or create a subdirectory.

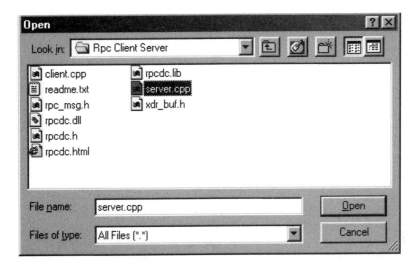

Figure 3.8   QFileDialog widget

This is another static dialog, so it will typically be used in the following manner:

Example Use

```
...
// Get a filename from the user to save to
QString s = QFileDialog::getSaveFileName( "*.txt" );
if(!s.isnull()) { // Save it
    ...
} // else user cancelled
...
```

QFontDialog

The font dialog (see Fig. 3.9) is used to prompt the user for a text font and typeface. As is the case with most Qt dialogs, QFontDialog has no constructor. A typical use goes something like:

Example Use

```
...
bool ret;
QLabel *l = new QLabel( "Altered Font", this );
QFont f = QFontDialog::getFont( &ret, this );
```

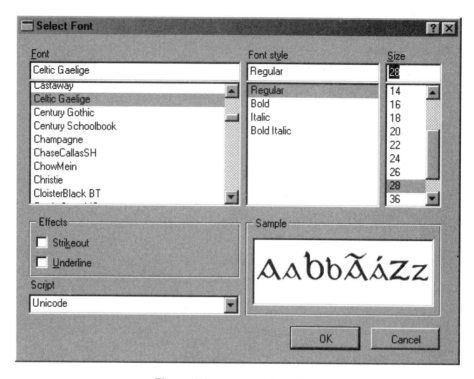

Figure 3.9   QFontDialog widget

```
if( ret == true) {
l->setFont( f );
    }
...
```

QInputDialog

This dialog was a new addition in Qt 2. It provides a number of convenient methods for inputting a single value, either as a text string, an integer, a floating point value, or from a combo box. Fig. 3.10 is an example of a QInputDialog's getText() Dialog.

Figure 3.10   QInputDialog::getText() dialog

The following example produces the dialog displayed in Figure 3.10:

Example Use

...

```
bool retry = FALSE;
QString svr = QInputDialog::getText( "Enter Hostname",
    "Hostname or IP Address:",
    "ftp.kahuna.surf.org",
    &retry, this );
if( retry == true && !svr.isEmpty() )
    // Deal with a retry attempt
else
    // No hostname or user pressed cancel
```

...

QMessageBox

This is the standard message box widget for Qt. It consists of a dialog box, an optional icon, a dialog caption, a label for some text, and up to three buttons with customizable labels.

Figure   3.11   QMessageBox::warning() dialog widget

It provides the usual warning() (see Fig. 3.11 for an example), critical(), and information() methods that determine the icon displayed with the message box text that you supply and they're very simple to use:

Example Use

...

```
QMessageBox::information( this, "Info", "Details" );
```

...

QProgressDialog

A QProgressDialog (Fig 3.12) provides progress feedback to the end-user. (See Fig. 3.12.)You may want to implement these for operations that take a long time to complete.

Figure 3.12   QProgressDialog widget

Example Use

```
...
QProgressDialog progress( "Copying...",
    "Cancel", num, this, "PD_1", TRUE );
for (int a=0; a<num; a++) {
    progress.setProgress( a );
    if( progress.wasCancelled() == true ) break;
    // Make one copy
    myCopy( a );
}
progress.setProgress( num );
...
```

QSemiModal

This is the base class for all semimodal dialogs. Dialogs created with this widget differ from those created with QDialog in that they have no event loop and have no concept of a default button.

QSemiModal provides very little of the functionality that QDialog does. As a result, subclasses (like QProgressDialog) must provide all the code for periodically updating the dialog contents.

QTabDialog

The tab dialog (see Fig. 3.13) provides a stack of tabbed widgets. These are commonly used to present a set of easily navigated property pages in configuration dialogs, but they can be used for other purposes just as effectively.

You will normally subclass QTabDialog, as in the following example:

```
...
class SDialog : public QTabDialog
{
    Q_OBJECT
public:
    SDialog( QWidget *p=0, const char *n=0 );

protected slots:
    void  ok();
    void cancel();
};
```

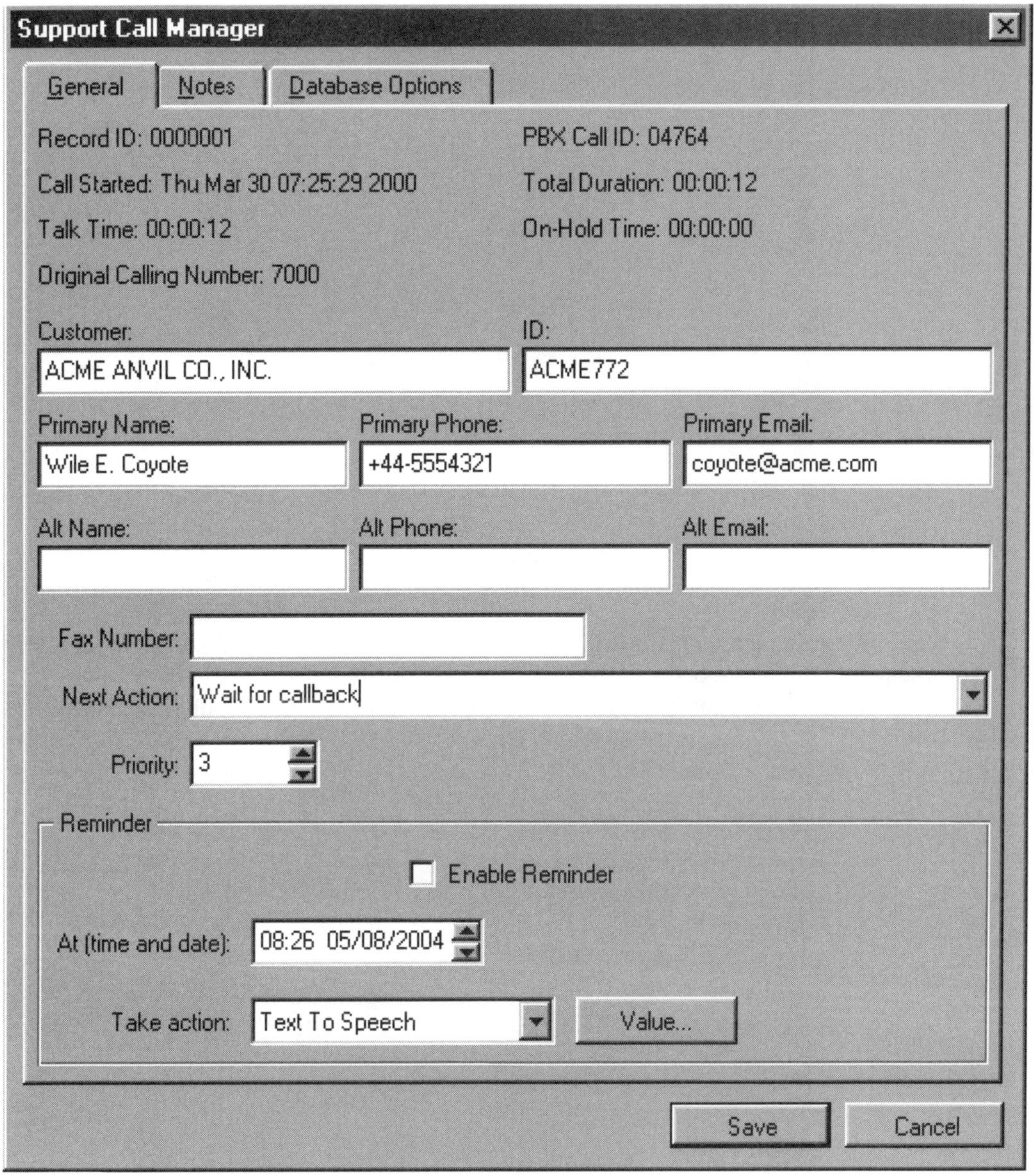

Figure 3.13   QTabDialog widget

```
SDialog::SDialog( QWidget *p, const char *n )
: QTabDialog( p, n )
{
    // Single "General" tab
    QWidget *w = new QWidget( this );
```

```
setOkButton( "Save" );
connect( this, SIGNAL(applyButtonPressed()), SLOT(ok()) );
setCancelButton( "Cancel" );
connect( this, SIGNAL(cancelButtonPressed()), SLOT(cancel()) );

// Vertical Layout
QVBoxLayout *top = new QVBoxLayout( w, 5 );

QHBoxLayout *hb = new QHBoxLayout();
top->addLayout( hb );

QLabel *l = new QLabel( "Useless Label", w );
hb->addWidget( l, 1 );
QLineEdit *e = new QLienEdit( w );
hb->addWidget( e, 2 );

top->activate();
addTab( w, "&General" );
}
...
```

Simple TabDialog

QWizard

Wizards are a carryover from the Microsoft Windows family. They're typically provided with install or configure functionality and can be used to guide even the most naïve user through a series of (possibly complex) sequential steps, using individual "pages" for each step and by providing "Forward," "Back," "Finish," and "Cancel" buttons. Figure 3.14 is the first "page" of a simple wizard.

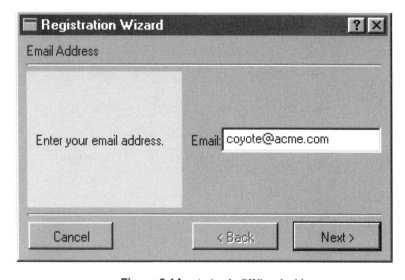

Figure 3.14   A simple QWizard widget

FUNCTIONAL GROUPING

A complex form can be made more intuitive by grouping related tasks together and giving the end-user a visual queue that some distinction exists between this set of widgets and that set of widgets. End-user visual queues aside, there are programmatic reasons you may want to create a group of widgets, such as widget arrays. Qt provides a reasonably comprehensive set of abstractions, and many of the more frequently needed grouping mechanisms.

QGroupBox

Group boxes (Fig 3.15) provide a frame and a text label. They're commonly used to present the user with a logical grouping of related features or functionality. A complex form can be very confusing to a user who may not be familiar with how the information fits together. Group boxes and tabbed forms are two ways to address this potential confusion.

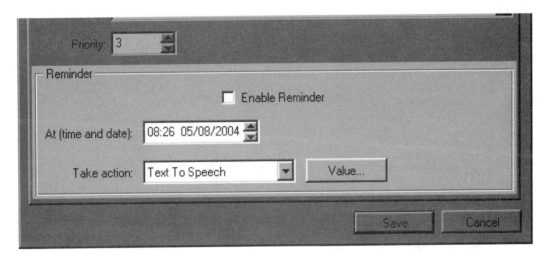

Figure 3.15   QGroupBox widget with a complex layout

A Possible Instantiation

```
...
    QGroupBox *gb = new QGroupBox( "Detail Info", this );
...
```

Example Use

```
...
    // Reminder box
    QGroupBox *box = new QGroupBox( "Reminder", this );
    QVBoxLayout *vb = new QVBoxLayout( box, 10 );
    vb->addSpacing( 10 );
```

```
// Add a line to the overall layout
QHBoxLayout *hb = new QHBoxLayout();
vb->addLayout( hb );

////
// First line in the box
// Add an empty label for spacing
l = new QLabel( box );
hb->addWidget( l, 2 );
// Add a enable/disable checkbox
enabled = new QCheckBox( "Enable Reminder", box );
enabled->setChecked( was_enabled );
hb->addWidget( enabled, 0 );
// Add another empty label
l = new QLabel( box );
l->setFixedHeight( fh+10 );
hb->addWidget( l, 2 );

////
// Second line in layout—add a SpinTime_T widget
hb = new QHBoxLayout();
vb->addLayout( hb );
l = new QLabel( "At (time and date):", box );
hb->addWidget( l );
spintime = new SpinTime_T( 0, 0x7fffffff, r->alert, box );
connect(spintime, SIGNAL(valueChanged( time_t )),
            SLOT(deltaTime( time_t )) );
hb->addWidget( spintime );
l = new QLabel( box );
hb->addWidget( l, 10 );
...
```

It is usually necessary (unless you enjoy hard-coding widget sizes and positions—a practice I despise) to add a set of layouts to your group box so that the contained widgets are not on top of one another. The following code fragment demonstrates how this is accomplished:

```
...
QGroupBox *box = new QGroupBox( "Status", this );
// Add a vertical layout
QVBoxLayout *boxtop = new QVBoxLayout( box, 10 );
boxtop->addSpacing( 10 );
// Add a button
QPushButton *pb = new QPushButton( "Update", box );
connect( pb, SIGNAL(clicked()), SLOT(update()) );
boxtop->addWidget( pb );
// Add an indicator/label pair horizontally
QHBoxLayout *boxhb = new QHBoxLayout( boxtop );
iconLabel = new QLabel( box );
iconLabel->setPixmap( QPixmap( "statOK.xpm" ) );
boxhb->addWidget( iconLabel );
```

```
QLabel *boxl = new QLabel( "Current State", box );
boxhb->addWidget( boxl, 1 );
...
```

QHGroupBox   A convenience subclass of QGroupBox, QHGroupBox organizes widgets in a group with a single horizontal row.

QVGroupBox   Another convenience subclass of QGroupBox, QVGroupBox organizes widgets in a group with a single vertical column.

QButtonGroup   This class provides a way to manage multiple QButton widgets as a logical group. This widget is commonly instantiated in one of two ways; either with the optional frame and text label, or without any visual component. If you need to manage an array of buttons, this class will probably be useful. Fig 3.16 represents six push buttons within a button group. The QbuttonGroup widget will emit a clicked (int) signal when any one of the buttons is clicked.

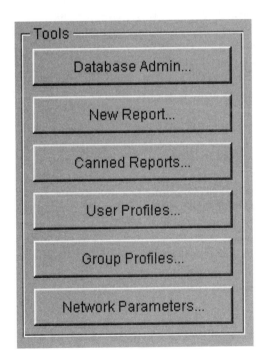

Figure 3.16   QButtonGroup with QPushButton children

A Possible Instantiation

```
...
    QButtonGroup *bg = new QButtonGroup( "Options", this );
...
```

Example Use

```
...
QButtonGroup *bg = new QButtonGroup( "Options", this );
QRadioButton *rb = new QRadioButton( "Option A", bg );
if( rb->isChecked() == true ) {
   // User has selected Option A
}
...
```

While no default layout is provided by the QButtonGroup class, there are two sub-classes, QHButtonGroup and QVButtonGroup, that provide horizontal or vertical layouts, respectively. It's very easy to create a custom layout, but you need to understand the QLayout classes to do so—or you can provide hard-coded widget geometry specifications. There's an example of adding a custom layout in the QGroupBox discussion and the same methods apply to QButtonGroup.

QHButtonGroup   A subclass of QButtonGroup, the QHButtonGroup organizes QButton widgets in a group with a single horizontal row, appropriate for a small number of checkboxes, radio buttons, and the like.

QVButtonGroup   Another subclass of QButtonGroup, the QVButtonGroup organizes QButton widgets in a group with a single vertical column, appropriate for a small number of checkboxes, radio buttons, and so forth.

LAYOUT AND GEOMETRY MANAGEMENT

The design of an interface—especially data entry forms—is probably the most critical and time consuming part of the GUI development process. The most useful or best-behaved application is virtually worthless if the interface is so confusing that the end-user can't learn to use it quickly and efficiently. The interface design process almost always involves multiple iterations because we, the programmers, have a totally different perspective of workflow than the end-user. Like any customer, the end-user is always right (except when the beta-test guinea pigs start using terms like "bigger," "smaller," or other purely subjective terms).

Just as with any GUI toolkit, Qt provides for two approaches to interface layout: hard-coded widget geometry specification, and relative layout. There are drawbacks and advantages to each, but it is my opinion that the relative layout approach is the better of the two; it is more maintainable, and permits sensible, predictable, and less complicated resizing of the application.

If you have ever used a WYSIWYG (what you see is what you get) dialog or form editor, you probably noticed that these tools almost always use the hard-coded geometry approach to form layout, and almost never provide tools for relative layout. This is because the editor can easily translate your widget positioning and sizing information into hard-coded x, y coordinates and width, height sizing. It's not easy (sometimes it's impossible) to accurately represent an abstract layout scheme that can be dramatically affected by each widget's runtime properties such as font size or contents.

A good understanding of, and a lot of experience with, the QLayout based classes will allow you to quickly implement complex forms with only a preliminary sketch of what the form should look like. It takes practice, but a programmer with that skill can implement a complex dialog using relative layout just about as quickly as a programmer who uses a WYSIWYG dialog editor can generate a less elegant, hard-coded interface that doesn't resize nearly as well. Most Motif programmers already know this quite well.

QHBox, QVBox, and QGrid   These classes manage the geometry of widgets in rows, columns, or both, and display each managed widget in a separate frame. These classes are of little practical use—with the possible exception being state/status indicators on a status bar, as frequently seen in many Microsoft Windows applications. However, they can be used to provide simple management in "quickie" applications that don't have strict layout requirements.

QLayoutItem, QWidgetItem, and QSpacerItem   QLayoutItems are the abstract items on which QLayout operates. QWidgetItems are QLayoutItems specific to QWidgets. A QSpacerItem is simply an empty QLayoutItem you can use for spacing purposes.

QLayout   The base class for all layouts, QLayout provides an abstraction of the functions that are common to QBoxLayouts and QGridLayouts.

The online reference documentation provides an example of a custom layout based on QLayout. If you have a need for special layouts that can't be easily implemented using combinations of the provided layout classes, this is the obvious place to begin.

QBoxLayout, QHBoxLayout, and QVBoxLayout   QBoxLayout manages widgets in either a horizontal or vertical direction. QHBoxLayout and QVBoxLayout are convenience implementations that provide horizontal or vertical layouts, respectively.

A Possible Instantiation

...

```
// Create a toplevel layout with a spacing of ten pels
QHBoxLayout *top = new QHBoxLayout( this, 10 );
```

...

Example Use

...

```
QVBoxLayout *top = new QVBoxLayout( this, 10 );
QHBoxLayout *hb = new QHBoxLayout();
```

```
top->addLayout( hb );
...
```

The layout direction, horizontal or vertical, is determined at the point of instantiation, via the *Direction* argument to the constructor. You will note (perhaps with a bit of disappointment) that this value can be interrogated after instantiation, but cannot be changed.

As widgets (or other layouts) are added to the QBoxLayout, a cell is created within the layout to manage its geometry. It's important to provide appropriate minimumSize() and maximumSize() methods for widgets you add. This will prevent the layout from resizing your widget to an inappropriate value. While most widgets you add will provide this automatically, you will undoubtedly run into at least one instance where the widget does not size correctly.

QBoxLayouts have two margin values associated with them. The first is the margin between the layout itself and surrounding objects, and is referred to as the *border width*. The second is the margin between each cell of the layout itself, and is referred to as the *intra widget width*. These margins are set via arguments to the constructor.

A term you need to be familiar with regarding QLayouts is *stretch*. The stretch of a given cell determines how that cell will resize, relative to other cells in the layout. As an example, consider the extremely common scenario in which you create several, vertically arranged pairs of labels and text fields. You probably want the text fields to resize more than their accompanying labels. You *may not* want the labels to resize at all, but that usually produces an undesirable "cramped" appearance. The following code fragment demonstrates a possible approach that will cause the labels to align with their text fields and horizontally resize in a manner that creates an overall spaciousness as the width is increased:

```
...
int a;
QLabel *labs[10];
QLineEdit *fields[10];
QString str;
int StdA = AlignVCenter|AlignRight;

// A toplevel layout with 10 pel border-width and
// 5 pels of intra-widget spacing
QHBoxLayout *fTop = new QHBoxLayout( this, 10, 5 );
// Two vertical layout children that the toplevel
// layout will horizontally resize in a 2:5 ratio
QVBoxLayout *lVbox = new QVBoxLayout();
fTop->addLayout( lVbox, 2 );
QVBoxLayout *fVbox = new QVBoxLayout();
fTop->addLayout( fVbox, 5 );
for(a=0;a<5;a++) {
str.sprintf( "Data Field %d", a+1);
labs[a] = new QLabel( str, this );
labs[a]->setAlignment( StdA );
```

```
lVBox->addWidget( labs[a] );
fields[a] = new QLineEdit( this );
fVbox->addWidget( fields[a] );
    }
...
```

QGridLayout   Grid layouts are two-dimensional layouts arranged in rows and columns. The same behavior can be achieved using QBoxLayouts—at the expense of a lot more coding.

A Possible Instantiation

```
...
    QGridLayout *gl = new QGridLayout( this, 2, 3 );
...
```

Example Use

```
...
    int a, b;
    QString s;
    QLabel *l;

    QGridLayout *gl = new QGridLayout( this, 2, 3 );
    for(a=0;a<2;a++) {
        for(b=0;b<3;b++) {
            s.sprintf( "%d, %d", a, b );
            l = new QLabel( s, this );
            gl->addWidget( l, a, b );
        }
    }
...
```

QRect, QPoint, and QSize   These classes encapsulate screen coordinates and size information and provide convenient conversion methods to support most requirements likely to be encountered. Most of the Qt widgets (and QWidget itself) accept these classes for geometry specifiers.

A Possible Instantiation

```
...
    // get the current desktop size
    QRect r_wsSize = QApplication::desktop()->rect();

    // Convert to a QSize
    QSize s_wsSize( r_wsSize.width(), r_wsSize.height() );
...
```

QSizeGrip   This widget provides the resize grip graphic for a top-level window. Since QStatusBar (provided by QMainWindow) already incorporates a QSizeGrip, it is unlikely that you'll need to create an instance of this explicitly.

A Possible Instantiation

...

```
QSizeGrip *sg = new QSizeGrip( this );
```

...

QSizePolicy   This is the attribute object that determines how horizontal and vertical resizing is to be performed. Use this attribute to set an appropriate resize behavior for your widgets if the default is not acceptable.

Aspect ratio control and controlled resizing based on a widget's dynamic sizeHint() value are two possible reasons why you might customize this attribute.

LISTS, TABLES, AND LIST ITEMS

Many applications (not all) require the display of, or selection from, a list of items. When the list is static (never changes), it is sometimes best to provide an array of checkboxes, pushbuttons, toggle buttons, and so on. When the list is dynamic, subject to frequent or infrequent change, or when the list is large, it usually makes more sense to provide a scrolling list of these items and let the user pick the ones to use.

Every serious toolkit provides a list box, and so does Qt. The Qt lists are a bit faster, a little more efficient, and the class methods make a lot more sense. Other than that, you will notice very little difference in appearance or behavior from MFC, Motif, Lesstif, and others.

QHeader   QHeader (Fig 3.17) provides a heading for tables, such as those provided by the QListView widget. They allow the end-user to rearrange columns, resize columns of tabular data, or toggle the sorting order.

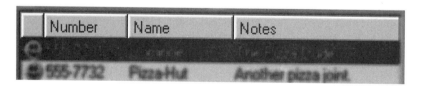

Figure 3.17   QHeader widgets in a QListView

Example Use

...

```
// Create a list and implied header—3 cells
QListView *theView = new QListView( this );
```

```
theView->addColumn( "Employees" );
theView->addColumn( "Salary" );
theView->addColumn( "Raise" );

// If profits were uninspired...
if( profits < ideal ) {
   theView->header()->setLabel( 2, "Pay Cut" );
}
```
...

QListBox   QListBox (Fig 3.18) provides typical list box functionality. It presents a list of read-only items and provides signals when a user selects an item or changes her selection. Vertical and horizontal scrollbars are displayed if the size of the displayed data is greater than the list box's viewport.

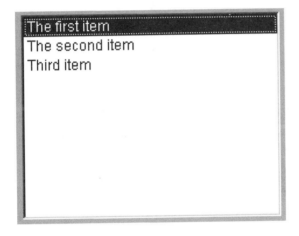

Figure 3.18   QListBox widget

A Possible Instantiation

...
```
QListBox *lb = new QListBox( this );
```
...

Example Use

...
```
QString s;
QListBox *lb = new QListBox( this );
for(int a=0;a<1000;a++) {
    s.sprintf( "List Item %d", a );
    lb.insertItem( s );
}
```
...

Qt list boxes use QListBoxItems for displayed content. This is a little different from other toolkits' implementations, but provides much greater flexibility in controlling the contents of the list.

QListBoxItem   This is the base class for all QListBox line items. It is subclassed by QListBoxPixmap and QListBoxText, which are discussed below.

While it is certainly a matter of preferences and style, I feel it is confusing to provide multiple objects in a list item (e.g., a pixmap *and* a text item). This is only because a listbox does not provide column headers that provide a clue as to what the user is supposed to be looking at. Aren't opinions useful?

QListBoxPixmap   This is a list box item that provides only a pixmap.

QListBoxText   This is a list box item that provides only a text label.

QListView   List views (Fig 3.19) provide a tabular view with optional tree behavior. List views display QListViewItems, which can contain a limited number of pixmap or text label items. The Qt examples included with the Qt software distribution adequately demonstrate the many uses for list views, so I won't bore you with detailed examples.

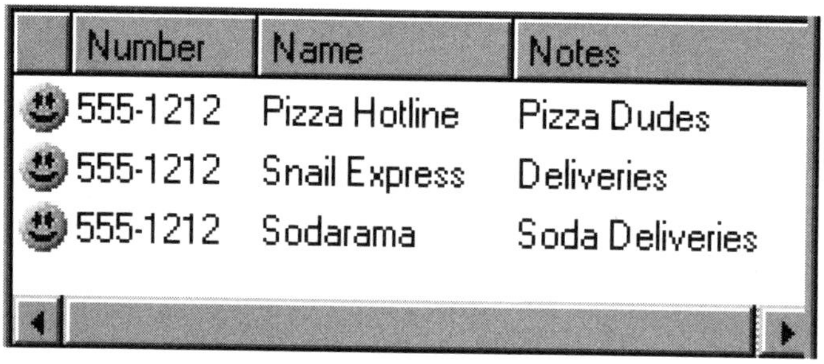

Figure 3.19   QListView widget with four columns and three QListViewItems

A Possible Instantiation

...
```
QListView *theView = new QListView( this );
```
...

Example Use

```
// Create a list and implied header-3 cells
QListView *theView = new QListView( this );
```

```
theView->addColumn( "Employees" );
theView->addColumn( "Salary" );
theView->addColumn( "Raise" );

// If profits were uninspired...
if( profits < ideal ) {
   theView->header()->setLabel( 2, "Pay Cut" );
}
QCheckBox *cb = new QCheckBox( "Option A", this );
QListViewItem *li = new QListViewItem( theView,
   "Billy", "$0.14/week", "$0.02" );
...
```

Data sets, or line-items, in a Qt list view are encapsulated by the QListViewItem or its descendents. QListViewItems can be tracked or enumerated with a QListViewItem-Iterator.

Tree behavior and appearance in a Qt list view is a function of QListViewItem parenting; a QListViewItem whose parent is the QListView itself will have top-level appearance in the list view, while a QListViewItem that has one of these top-level widgets for a parent will appear as a second-level child of the list view, and so on.

QListViewItem   A QListView displays information using QListViewItems (see Fig. 3.20) and QListViewItems can manage very large data sets quite well. The parenting of QListView-Items determines QListView tree appearance and behavior.

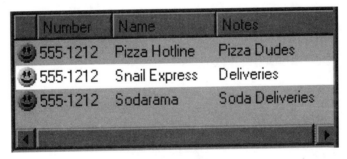

Figure 3.20   Three QListViewItem widgets. The center item is selected.

A Possible Instantiation

```
...
QListViewItem *li = new QListViewItem( parent_lView,
   "Column0", "Column1", "Column2" );
...
```

You will quickly discover that the provided constructors for QListViewItems won't permit more than eight columns, although you can obtain more by reimplementing the class.

QListViewItems maintain a parent/child relationship that affects their appearance in a QListView. QListView will display QListViewItem trees in an intuitive tree-browser manner similar to most file system browsers.

QListViewItemIterator   This class is provided to ease the task of iterating collections of QListViewItems, or iterating items within a QListView. Refer to the online reference for practical examples.

Example Use

```
...
QListViewItem *
MyWidget::checkSelected( QListView *theView )
{
    // We already have a loaded QListView. See if an item
    // is selected...
    QListViewItemIterator it( theView );
    for( ;it.current();++it) {
       if( it.current()->isSelected() == true ) break;
    }
    return( it.current() );
}
...
```

QCheckListItem

This is a subclass of QListViewItem that provides some added functionality that supports a list of checkable list items with optional tree behavior.

You can iterate these classes using QListViewItemIterator. Fig. 3.21 represents a number of QCheckListItem widgets in a QListView.

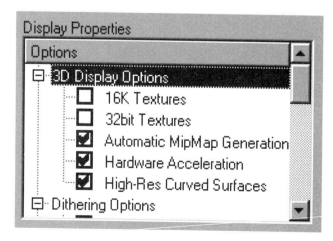

Figure 3.21   QCheckListItem widgets in a QListView

QTableView   An abstraction of tabular data display, QTableView provides most of the features you're likely to use for a table widget. The online reference documentation and the examples that come with the Qt distribution demonstrate some basic uses for this widget. If your requirements are more than basic, however, you will need to understand the provided QTableView::paintCell() method, as you will almost certainly have to reimplement it for your project. Unfortunately, that's a topic that is entirely dependent on what you need to accomplish, so examples won't help you much. Remember that the gurus of the Qt-interest mailing list will usually help you out if you get stuck.

The Qt distribution includes an example of a simple, scrolling table.

COMPOSITE WIDGET SUPPORT

This section describes the composite widgets (my own definition) of the Qt toolkit. For clarity, a *composite widget* is any widget that integrates two or more widgets that can be used by themselves outside that composite widget, and that provide no event loop such as that provided by the convenience dialogs. This is (currently) a very short list, as you will notice. The next release (or maybe the one after that) will provide others, I'm sure.

QMainWindow   A QMainWindow (Fig 3.22) provides most of the functionality that you will typically need for a given application including a menu bar, tool bar support, and a status bar. You will typically subclass QMainWindow. See the Qt example programs for many variations.

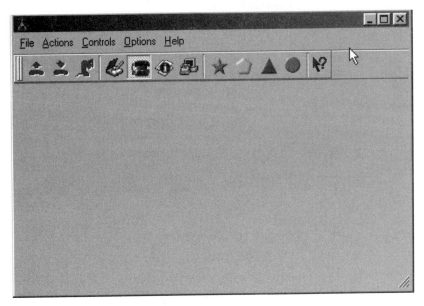

Figure 3.22   Custom QMainWindow widget. Shaded area is the central widget.

A Possible Instantiation

...

```
QMainWindow *mw = new QMainWindow();
```

...

Example Use

...

```
QApplication app( argc, argv );
QMainWindow *mw = new QMainWindow();
QPushButton *pb = new QPushButton( "Push Me", mw );
mw->setCentralWidget( pb );
app.setMainWidget( mw );
mw->show();
return( app.exec() );
```

...

It's worth noting that a lot of programmers don't always approve of this type of application interface.

QMenuBar   This class provides the functionality for horizontal menu bars as Figure 3.23 depicts.

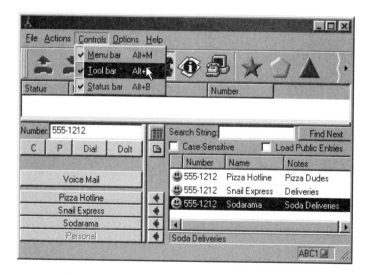

Figure 3.23   A QMenuBar with a popup menu

A Possible Instantiation

...

```
QMenuBar *menu = new QMenuBar( this );
```

...

Example Use

...

```
QMenuBar *menu = new QMenuBar( this );
QPopupMenu *file = new QPopupMenu();
file->setFont( orgfont );
menu->insertItem( "&File", file );
file->insertItem( "&Quit", this, SLOT(quit()), CTRL+Key_Q );
```
...

QMenuBar sets its own geometry to position itself at the top of its parent widget. The layout classes provide a method to address the layout issues that would otherwise be created by this behavior.

QMenuData   The base class for QMenuBar and QPopupMenu, QMenuData provides the functionality required to manage menu items.

QPopupMenu   Popup menus (Fig. 3.24) are used for drop-down menus on menu bars and combo boxes, as well as for the context menus you may need to provide for list items or other widgets.

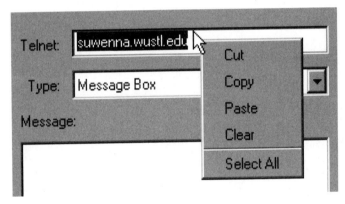

Figure 3.24   A QLineEdit widget with custom QPopupMenu

A Possible Instantiation

...
```
QPopupMenu *file = new QPopupMenu();
```
...

TEXT INPUT

Practically every application requires that a user input text at some point. This is usually limited to a single line of text such as the user's name. This type of input is often called a line edit.

Some applications must accept multiple lines of text—word processors are a good example—and the widget that accepts this type of data is generally referred to as a multiline edit. I expect a full-featured editor widget in a future release. For now, we use the basics.

Obviously, these two examples of text input are supported by the Qt toolkit, but there are other ways to accept user text input as well. The following widgets describe the widgets provided with the toolkit and some possible variations on their default behaviors.

QComboBox   QComboBoxes (Figs. 3.25 and 3.26) are a blending of text field and popup menu functionality. There are two flavors: read-only and read-write. The read-only variety provides only a popup menu of possible values from which the user may choose. The read-write variety permits the user to input whatever value he wishes, or can be constrained by a validator.

Figure 3.25   A QLabel widget and a QComboBox widget

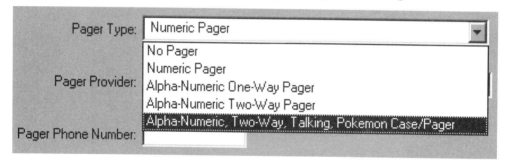

Figure 3.26   The QComboBox from Figure 3.25, with its popup menu displayed

A Possible Instantiation

...
```
QComboBox *cb = new QComboBox( this );
```
...

Example Use

...
```
QComboBox *box = new QComboBox( true, this );
box->setAutoCompletion( true );
box->insertItem( "Log Off" );
box->insertItem( "Reboot" );
box->insertItem( "Shut Down" );
```
...

They are used (primarily) in two types of situations:

- The user *must* select from a list of predefined (possibly hard-coded) values
- The user may enter a free-form or validated value *or* select a predefined value from a list

Another possible use for combo boxes is to preserve previous text input in the form of a text field history. Enabling automatic completion with the setAutoCompletion(bool) slot can further simplify editing of tedious forms for a user.

QLineEdit   This class provides a single line of user-editable text and all the functionality you are likely to require for this basic task. Fairly simple, right? Wrong. There are many special considerations for user input of text. Fig. 3.27 depicts two QLineEdit widgets, each with a QLabel.

Figure 3.27   Two QLabel/QLineEdit pairs

A Possible Instantiation

...

```
QLineEdit *le = new QLineEdit( this );
```

...

Example Use

...

```
QLineEdit *le = new QLineEdit( this );
connect( le, SIGNAL(textChanged( QString & )),
    SLOT(validate( QString & )) );
```

...

Since the provided object accepts any Unicode text, you'll usually have to verify that what the user enters is valid in the particular context. The unaltered object provides for attaching a QValidator object to the widget. That is sufficient for most purposes, but not all.

You can usually get exactly what you need from this widget by subclassing it and adding the desired changes. The following example demonstrates a fictitious part number widget that is a simple subclass of QLineEdit. Our design specification for this data item is:

- Accepts a five-character identifier in the range A0000 to Z9999
- The first character is an alpha value between "A" and "Z"

- The remaining characters are numeric in the range 0 to 9
- Provides a Boolean test for validity
- Produces a notification when validity changes state, suitable for connect to a QButton::setEnabled(bool) slot (e.g., an OK button)
- Value can be set programmatically
- Invalid input is not accepted
- A lowercase leading alpha will be capitalized automatically

```
#ifndef _PARTNUMH
#define _PARTNUMH

#include <qlineedit.h>
#include <ctype.h>

class PartNum : public QLineEdit
{
    Q_OBJECT
public:
    PartNum( QWidget *p=0, const char *n=0 );
    virtual   Partnum();

    bool      isValid() { return( _valid ); }

signals:
    // We'll emit this whenever the validity
    // changes
    void      valid( bool );

protected slots:
    // This slot will perform all the input
    // validation
    virtual void verify( const QString & );

private:
    bool      _valid;
};
```

PartNum.h

```
#include <PartNum.h>

PartNum::PartNum( QWidget *parent,
    const char *name )
: QLineEdit( parent, name )
{
    _valid = false;
    connect( this,
      SIGNAL(textChanged( const QString & )),
      SLOT(verify( const QString & )) );
```

```
}

PartNum::~PartNum()
{
}

void
PartNum::verify( const QString &s )
{
    static bool busy = false;
    char bp[6];   // OK—range invalid for i18n
    int i;

    if(busy == true) return;
    memset(bp, 0, 6);
    strncpy(bp, s, 5);
    if(strlen(s) > 5) {
        busy = true;
        setText( bp );
        busy = false;
    }
    if(bp[0] >= 'a' && bp[0] <= 'z') {
        bp[0] = toupper(bp[0]);
        busy = true;
        setText( bp );
        busy = false;
    }
    if(bp[0] >= 'A' && bp[0] <= 'Z') {
        for(i=1;i<5;i++) {
                if(!isdigit(bp[i])) break;
        }
        if(i == 5) {
                if(_valid == false) {
                _valid = true;
                        emit valid( _valid );
                }
                return;
        } else {
                bp[i] = '\0';
                busy = true;
                setText( bp );
                busy = false;
        }
    }
    if(_valid == true) {
    _valid = false;
    emit valid( _valid );
}
    return;
}
#include <PartNum.moc>
```

PartNum.cpp

The busy flag in the verify routine is to prevent the recursion (and the subsequent stack overflow) that you can expect when you cause a slot to call itself as the verify routine does by calling the setText() method.

The following is a very useful and reusable modification to QLineEdit that provides a popup menu for the right mouse button. The menu provides some common clipboard or cutbuffer operations that PC users will recognize from Microsoft products like Office 2000 and others. Features provided are *copy, paste, cut, select all, clear all, clear all and paste,* and *select all and copy.* Note that the same modification can be applied to a subclass of QMultiLineEdit. This functionality is present in Qt 2.1 and above, so this modification should not be necessary.

```
#ifndef _LINEEDIT_H
#define _LINEEDIT_H

#include <qlineedit.h>
#include <qevent.h>
#include <qpopupmenu.h>

class LineEdit : public QLineEdit
{
    Q_OBJECT
public:
    LineEdit( QWidget *p=0, const char *n=0 );

protected slots:
    virtual void mousePressEvent( QMouseEvent * );
    virtual void doCut();
    virtual void doCopy();
    virtual void doPaste();
    virtual void doSelect();
    virtual void doClear();
    virtual void doClearPaste();
    virtual void doSelectCopy();

private:
    int          pmid[7];
    QPopupMenu  *pop;
};

#endif // _LINEEDIT_H
```

LineEdit.h

```
1.  #include <Lineedit.h>

LineEdit::LineEdit( QWidget *parent,
    const char *name )
: QLineEdit( parent, name )
{
    pop = new QPopupMenu();
```

```
        pmid[0] = pop->insertItem( "Cut", this,
            SLOT(doCut()) );
        pmid[1] = pop->insertItem( "Copy", this,
            SLOT(doCopy()) );
        pmid[2] = pop->insertItem( "Paste", this,
            SLOT(doPaste()) );
        pmid[3] = pop->insertItem( "Clear All",
            this, SLOT(doClear()) );
        pop->insertSeparator();
        pmid[4] = pop->insertItem( "Select All",
            this, SLOT(doSelect()) );
        pop->insertSeparator();
        pmid[5] = pop->insertItem(
            "Select All & Copy", this,
            SLOT(doSelectCopy()) );
        pmid[6] = pop->insertItem(
            "Clear All & Paste", this,
            SLOT(doClearPaste()) );
}


void
LineEdit::mousePressEvent( QMouseEvent *e )
{
    if(e->button() != RightButton) {
        QLineEdit::mousePressEvent( e );
        return;
    }
    int n = strlen(text());
    pop->setItemEnabled( pmid[0],
        hasMarkedText() );
    pop->setItemEnabled( pmid[1],
        hasMarkedText() );
    pop->setItemEnabled( pmid[3],
        (n > 0) ? true : false );
    pop->popup( e->globalPos() );
}


void
LineEdit::doCopy()
{
    copy();
}


void
LineEdit::doCut()
{
    cut();
}


void
LineEdit::doPaste()
{
```

```
        paste();
}

void
LineEdit::doSelect()
{
    selectAll();
}

void
LineEdit::doClear()
{
    setText( "" );
}

void
LineEdit::doClearPaste()
{
    setText( "" );
    paste();
}

void
LineEdit::doSelectCopy()
{
    selectAll();
    copy();
}

#include <Lineedit.moc>
```

Lineedit.cpp

This final modification provides for selecting and highlighting existing contents of a QLineEdit widget whenever the widget obtains keyboard focus:

```
LineEdit.h
#ifndef LINEEDIT_H
#define LINEEDIT_H
#include <qevent.h>
#include <qlineedit.h>

class LineEdit : public QLineEdit
{
    Q_OBJECT
public:
    LineEdit( QWidget *parent=0,
    const char *name=0 );

protected slots:
    void           focusInEvent( QFocusEvent * );
```

```
        void                focusOutEvent( QFocusEvent * );
};
#endif
LineEdit.cpp
#include <LineEdit.h>

LineEdit::LineEdit( QWidget *parent,
    const char *name )
: QLineEdit( parent, name )
{
}

void
LineEdit::focusInEvent( QFocusEvent *e )
{
    QLineEdit::focusInEvent( e );
    selectAll();
    repaint( false );
}

void
LineEdit::focusOutEvent( QFocusEvent *e )
{
    QLineEdit::focusOutEvent( e );
    setSelection( 0, 0 );
    repaint( false );
}

#include <LineEdit.moc>
```

QMultiLineEdit   This is a very basic text editor widget. While it provides most of the low-level functionality required for the simplest text editing, it lacks much of the higher-level functionality that is required for most editing tasks. Fig. 3.28 is an example of a QMultiLineEditwidget with a QLabel

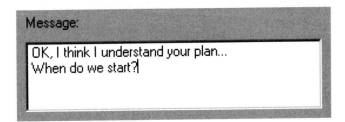

Figure 3.28   A QLabel widget and a QMultiLineEdit widget

A Possible Instantiation

...
```
    QMultiLineEdit *me = new QMultiLineEdit( this );
```
...

Example Use

```
...

me->setText( "The quick brown fox\njumped over the"
             "slow lazy dog" );

...
```

One very simple enhancement is to add the cut and paste menu described in the discussion of QLineEdit.

NUMERIC INPUT

Sometimes an application needs to acquire a numeric value from the user. You can provide a standard line edit and assign a validator to only accept numbers but, even with tooltip help, this is not always intuitive. Other methods have been devised and tested over the years and more will come. Here are the widgets provided with Qt.

QSlider   QSlider (Fig. 3.29) provides an intuitive way to acquire numeric user input. Bounds checking is provided via QSlider's QRangeControl parent.

Figure 3.29   QSlider widget

A Possible Instantiation

```
...

QSlider *s = new QSlider( QSlider::Horizontal, this );

...
```

Example Use

```
...

QSlider *s = new QSlider( QSlider::Horizontal, this );
s->setRange( -180, 180 );
s->setValue( 0 );

...
```

QSpinBox   A spin box (Fig. 3.30) is a text field that accepts (usually) integer data. It includes a pair of pushbuttons that permit the user to increment or decrement the displayed value. The step rate and range are programmable.

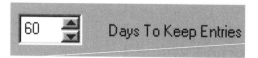

Figure 3.30   QSpinBox widget

A Possible Instantiation

...
```
QSpinBox *sb = new QSpinBox( this );
```
...

Example Use

...
```
// Create a spinbox for invoice payment
// period allowance.
// Minimum = 10, Maximum = 90, step = 10
// Default to COD, (-1 from sb->value())
QSpinBox *sb = new QSpinBox( 10, 90, 10, this );
sb->setSuffix( " days net" );
sb->setSpecialText( "C.O.D." );
```
...

Methods are provided to interpret value types other than integer values, but the value must eventually be evaluated as an integer. To make dramatic changes to QSpin-Box's functionality usually requires a reimplementation of the widget. An example of a spinbox that operates on time t values is included on the CD-ROM.

SCROLLING

Just like all other GUI toolkits, Qt provides scrollbars. They're easier to use than other toolkit implementations.

QScrollBar   Scrollbars (Fig. 3.31) are common graphic widgets that permit a user to scroll or pan a clipped view of a potentially very large visual component. The QScroll-Bar widget provides a feature-rich implementation.

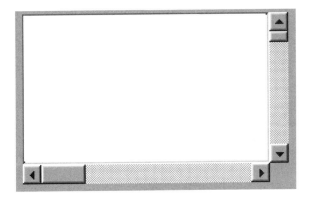

Figure 3.31   QLineEdit widget with vertical and horizontal QScrollBar widgets

A Possible Instantiation

```
...

QScrollBar *sb = new QScrollBar( QScrollBar::Vertical,
    this, "MyScroll" );

...
```

Example Use

```
...

QScrollBar *sb = new QScrollBar( 1, num_lines, 20, 1,
    QScrollBar::Vertical, this, "MyScroll" );
connect(sb, SIGNAL(valueChanged( int ),
    SLOT(handleScroll( int )) );

...
```

The most common complaint would seem to revolve around the use of integer values for positioning information. However, since the maximum integer value matches (or even exceeds) the coordinate system limitations of the supported platforms, the arguments for using a larger data value are not very compelling.

QScrollView   A scroll view is just a generic, scrollable area that provides appropriate vertical and horizontal scrollbars as they are needed.

A Possible Instantiation

```
...

QScrollView *sv = new QScrollView( this );

...
```

Example Use

```
...

// Create a huge array of push buttons
QPushButton *pb;
QScrollView *sv = new QScrollView( this, "SV1",
    WPaintClever );
QVButtonGroup *vbg = new QVButtonGroup( sv );
for( int a=0; a<1000; a++ ) {
    pb = new QPushButton( "Yet Another Button", vbg );
}

...
```

The scroll view is very useful for the display of large quantities of visual data, but you will run into platform integer limitations that are mentioned in the discussion of QScrollBars. Again, the platform integer meets or exceeds the display coordinate system on all the supported platforms, and while some architectures (Windows 2000-Win64, for instance) will very likely accommodate 64-bit (63, really) screen coordinates once 64-bit processors are commonly available, it would be a waste of system resources to actually create a display that exceeds the current limitations.

Virtual viewports of an arbitrarily large data set are not a new idea, and can be easily implemented within the current limitations—even data sets that require 64- or 128-bit coordinate systems *internally* can be displayed very effectively, and rapidly, with as few as 11 bits of QScrollView coordinate resolution if you approach the problem with some common sense.

SPLIT PANES AND TABS

Many applications can benefit from a visible partition to subdivide the application interface into logical groupings of features. There are several ways to do this. The first is to divide the interface into separate panes that can be moved around or resized by the user. Another method is to provide a row of "tabs" that the user can select to display different "pages" of information or features. There are other methods that are less direct from a programmatic standpoint, but the following methods are provided with the Qt toolkit.

QSplitter   A QSplitter provides split-pane resizing functionality to its child widgets. Virtually any number of child widgets can be added, although at some point, the results will become visually unappealing, not to mention confusing to the end-user.

A Possible Instantiation

```
...
    QSplitter *s = new QSplitter( this );
...
```

Example Use

```
...
    // Create a split-pane with a listbox on the left
    // and a listview on the right
    QSplitter *s = new QSplitter( this );
    QListbox *lb = new QListBox( s );
    QListView *lv = new QListView( s );
...
```

QTab   QTabs are the class used to implement the individual tabs in QTabBars. If you want to customize the appearance of your application's tabs, this is where you should start.

QTabBar   A tab bar provides a visual interaction with the end-user that creates an effect similar to a card-file or tabbed dividers in a notebook. The user selects a tab and a "page" of widgets is presented.

A Possible Instantiation

```
…
    QTabBar *tb = new QTabBar( this );
…
```

Example Use

```
…
    QTab *t[3];
    t[0] = new QTab();
    t[0]->label.setText( "&General" );
    t[1] = new QTab();
    t[1]->label.setText( "&Advanced" );
    t[2] = new QTab();
    t[2]->label.setText( "&Basic" );
    QTabBar *tb = new QTabBar( this );
    tb->addTab( t[2] );
    tb->addTab( t[0] );
    tb->addTab( t[1] );
…
```

By default, the tabs have only a text label. You can change the default by reimplementing the QTab class to provide what your specification requires.

QTabWidget   QTabWidget provides a stack of tabbed widgets. This is very useful for preserving screen real estate, but lacks some important functionality, such as the ability to set the displayed page.

A Possible Instantiation

```
…
    QTabWidget *tabs = new QTabWidget( this );
…
```

Example Use

```
…
    // Create a QTabWidget
    QTabWidget *tabs = new QTabWidget( this );
    // An instance of a custom widget that performs its
    // own geometry management
    SoundProperties *sp = new SoundProperties( this );
    // Add a tab and an accelerator
    tabs->insertTab( sp, "&Sound Properties" );
    // Add more tabs…
…
```

You may find it more worthwhile to implement similar functionality using a QWidgetStack and a QToolBar.

TOOLTIPS AND WHAT'S THIS SUPPORT

The more help you provide the end-user, the fewer support calls you're likely to get from users who were confused. Qt provides two forms of direct end-user help in the forms of per-widget popup help called tooltips, and a more formal popup help called What's This?. Tooltip help will popup when the mouse hovers over a widget to which you assign a help message, while WhatsThis help usually requires a trigger widget such as a toolbutton or a popup menu item to display the help.

QToolTip   A tooltip is a popup window that displays very simple (usually a single, short line) help for any widget.

A Possible Instantiation

```
...
    QPushButton *pb = new QPushButton( "Exit", this );
    connect( pb, SIGNAL(clicked()), qApp, SLOT(quit()) );
    QToolTip::add( pb, "Exit this application." );
...
```

QToolTipGroup   QToolTipGroups tie the popup tooltip for a widget to an optional (possibly different) tooltip that can be displayed in the status bar or some other widget. This is most commonly seen in QToolButton widgets constructed using a group text argument that displays in a status bar.

A Possible Instantiation

```
...
    QToolTipGroup *tg = new QToolTipGroup( this );
...
```

Example Use

```
...
    QPushButton *pb = new QPushButton( "OK", this );
    QToolTipGroup *tg = new QToolTipGroup( this );
    QLabel *helpline = new QLabel( this );

    connect( tg, SIGNAL(showTip(const QString &)),
        helpline, SLOT(setText(const QString &)) );
    connect( tg, SIGNAL(removeTip()),
        helpline, SLOT(clear()) );
    QToolTip::add( pb, "OK", tg,
        "Press this button to proceed." );
...
```

QWhatsThis   The QWhatsThis class provides a collection of widget descriptions (that you must provide) that is accessed either when the user first clicks a WhatsThis button on a toolbar and then clicks on the widget they're curious about, or by explicitly calling QMainWindow::whatsThis(). Several methods of customizing the default behavior are provided.

Example Use

```
...
    QPushButton *pb = new QPushButton( "OK", this );
    QWhatsThis::add( pb, "Press this button to continue." );
...
```

SUMMARY

It's important to keep in mind that all the widgets discussed above, and all the widgets discussed in the following chapters, can be combined, subclassed, and modified to create completely new widgets—with a minimum of coding effort. It is my experience that the basic line edit, as provided by the QLineEdit widget, is the most common widget to require modification, as the supplied modification examples attest.

It is equally important to maintain a consistent feel and behavior throughout your application to avoid confusing the user. Qt makes it very easy to "play" with different ways to achieve a single result. This sometimes leads to a confusing interface, creeping functionality, or both.

4

Program Output Objects

Program output objects are classes that are typically used to display information. Unlike the widgets discussed in the previous chapter, these objects provide no default user interaction functionality or behavior by themselves. They provide no keyboard or mouse handling functionality, although you can easily add either if the need arises.

COLOR AND PALETTE SUPPORT

The details of color management are highly platform-dependent. Microsoft Windows does not allocate colors in the same way that an X11 application allocates colors, and the X11 color allocation model is extremely complicated, especially when high-end graphics adapters and their accompanying X server extensions must be taken into account by a given application.

Qt greatly simplifies the vast majority of the issues involved in selecting and displaying color elements—in most applications. Highly specialized programs geared toward the high-end graphics user will, of course, require a finer level of control than the Qt classes provide by default. That alone is a topic for an entire book.

QColor and QColorGroup   The QColor class provides an abstraction of color attributes. The class handles dynamic intelligent allocation and deallocation, and provides constructors for RGB or HSV color specification.

Color groups are an encapsulation of the common set of color attributes that a widget is likely to use. If you want to change the default foreground color, background color, etc., of a widget, you will also need to read about QPalette.

A Possible Instantiation

...

```
QColor text( "blue" );
QColor bgd( "#e0e0e0" );
QColorGroup *lc = new QColorGroup();
lc->setColor( QColorGroup::Foreground, text );
lc->setColor( QColorGroup::Background, bgd );
```

...

Example Use

...

```
QLabel *l = new QLabel( "Color Label", this );
QColor text( "blue" );
QColor bgd( "#e0e0e0" );
QColorGroup lc = l->palette().active();
lc.setColor( QColorGroup::Foreground, text );
lc.setColor( QColorGroup::Background, bgd );
QPalette *pal = new QPalette( lc );
l->setPalette( pal );
```

...

QPalette   QPalette encapsulates the QColorGroups that are used to represent different widget states: normal, disabled, and active.

A Possible Instantiation

...

```
QPalette *pal = new QPalette( QColor( "red" ) );
```

...

Example Use

...

```
QPalette pal( QColor( "red" ) );
QPushButton *pb = new QPushButton( "Stop!", this );
pb->setPalette( pal );
```

...

GRAPHIC IMAGE OUTPUT SUPPORT

The following classes provide the necessary support for outputting graphic picture data to a widget that supports the use of QPainter, or to a graphics output device.

QBitmap   The QBitmap class provides an off-screen, monochrome (single-bit depth) painting mechanism.

A Possible Instantiation

```
...

   QBitmap bm;

...
```

Example Use

```
...

   QBitmap bm;
   bm.load( "arrow.xbm", "XBM" );

...
```

QBitmap's uses include:

- Cursors and cursor masks
- Brushes
- Widget masks

Cursors and cursor masks are covered in the online reference documentation for QCursor. Brushes are discussed later in the chapter. An example of widget masking (an elliptical, 3D, animated pushbutton) can be found in the QBitmap directory, under the chapter-examples on the CD that comes with this book. I disapprove of "gimmicks" such as this, but it makes a good visual demonstration nonetheless.

QCursor   QCursor is the encapsulation of mouse cursor attributes. Virtually any valid QBitmap can be used to create a new mouse cursor and sensible platform-dependent defaults are predefined.

A Possible Instantiation

```
...

   QCursor wait( QCursor::WaitCursor );

...
```

Example Use

```
...

   setCursor( QCursor( QCursor::WaitCursor ) );

...
```

QIconSet   This class provides a set of icons of various sizes and provides icons that present an enabled or disabled visual queue. You will normally use icon sets for QToolButton icons.

A Possible Instantiation

```
...
    QPixmap p = QPixmap( "pix.bmp" );
    QIconSet ico( p );
...
```

Example Use

```
...
#include "myicon.xpm"
...
    QPixmap p = QPixmap( (const char **)myicon );
    toolb = new QToolButton( p, "Save",
       "Save this document",
       this, SLOT(save()),
       mytools, 0 );
    toolb->setIconSet( QIconSet( myicon ) );
    connect( this, SIGNAL(pixmapSizeChanged( bool )),
       toolb[0], SLOT(setUsesBigPixmap( bool )) );
...
```

QImage   QImages are platform-independent image representations that provide direct access to the per pixel image data.

A Possible Instantiation

```
...
    // Create a 640x480 monochrome image
    QImage i( 640, 480, 1, 2 );
...
```

Example Use

```
...
    QImage i, mirror;
    if(i.load( "Pix.bmp", "BMP" ) == true) {
       mirror = i.mirror( true, false );
    } else {
       mirror = i;
    }
...
```

QMovie   QMovie incrementally loads animated images and provides methods to deal with their display on a widget that provides a paint device. Typically, you will implement a movie on a QLabel, but a QPushButton will work just as well.

A Possible Instantiation

```
...
    QMovie *m = new QMovie( "flix.gif" );
...
```

Example Use

```
...
#include "world.h"
...
    // Create a label containing a QMovie
    movielabel = new QLabel( this );
    // Load a QByteArray with the raw GIF data
    barray.setRawData((const char *)world, world_len);
    movie = QMovie( barray );
    movie.setSpeed( 100 );
    movie.connectStatus( this,
        SLOT(animStat(int)) );
    movielabel->setMovie( movie );
    movielabel->setMargin( 0 );
    movielabel->setFixedSize( 64+movielabel->frameWidth()*2,
                              64+movielabel->frameWidth()*2 );
    movie.pause();
...
```

Note that built-in GIF support is not automatically provided, and requires specific inclusion at the time you configure your Qt installation. This is because the GIF image format is proprietary and because the GIF compression algorithm requires licensing in some countries (the U.S. being one in particular). Unisys will, no doubt, appreciate any feedback you may have on the subject of software patent law.

To implement a QMovie without purchasing a Limpel-Ziv-Welch software license from Unisys, you can use any good paint program to create animation frames in PNG format, then use the QPNGImagePacker to create compressed animated images.

QPaintDevice and QPaintDeviceMetrics   A QPaintDevice is an abstraction of a two-dimensional space that you can paint to using a QPainter class.

A QPaintDeviceMetrics class encapsulates the physical dimensions information of a QPaintDevice.

QPainter   This class provides some very fast methods for painting on a QPaint-Device.

A Possible Instantiation

```
...
    QPainter p( this );
...
```

Example Use

```
...
    QPushButton *pb = new QPushButton( this );
    QPixmap pm = QPixmap( "ButtonBgd.bmp" );
    pb->setPixmap( pm );
    QPainter p( &pm, pb );
    p.begin();
    p.drawText( pb->rect(), AlignCenter, "Click Me" );
    p.end();
...
```

Many commonly needed drawing shapes are provided (including text). The Qt documentation contains many examples.

QPen and QBrush   QPen defines QPainter outline drawing style and color. QBrush defines QPainter fill style and color.

QPicture   A QPicture is a class that captures QPainter commands in an off-screen paint device and serializes the commands for platform-independent playback. Windows programmers will recognize these as meta-files. The serialized data can be saved and restored.

A Possible Instantiation

```
...
    QPicture *pic = new QPicture();
...
```

Example Use

```
...
    // Create and save a new picture
    QPicture *pic = new QPicture();
    QPainter p;
    p.begin( pic );
    p.drawText( pb->rect(), AlignCenter, "Some Text" );
    p.end();
    pic->save( "some_text.pic" );

    // Load and display the picture
    QLabel *1 = new QLabel( this );
    QPicture newpic;
    newpic.load( "some_text.pic" );
    QPainter np;
    np.begin( 1 );
    np.drawPicture( newpic );
    np.end();
...
```

QPixmap   QPixmap is an off-screen paint device. Most Qt widget methods that accept an image or icon as an argument assume that the argument is a QPixmap.

A Possible Instantiation

```
...
    QPixmap pix = QPixmap( "forest.bmp" );
...
```

Example Use

```
...
    QPixmap pix = QPixmap( "forest.bmp" );
    QLabel *l = new QLabel( this );
    l->setPixmap( pix );
...
```

Because I spend a lot of time coding for Windows 2000, I usually create icons with a Windows paint program and save them in Windows Bitmap format (.bmp). While that format is not directly useful for embedded graphics, you can make use of the provided load() and save() methods to convert the image to XPM format. Then, you can embed the XPM image in your code, something like this:

```
#ifndef NEED_CVT
#include "pixmaps/new_icon.xpm"
#endif
...
QPixmap new_ico;
#ifdef NEED_CVT
new_ico.load( "new_icon.bmp" );
new_ico.save( "pixmaps/new_icon.xpm", "XPM" );
#else
new_icon = QPixmap( (const char **)new_icon );
#endif
...
```

This approach makes it very easy to mass-convert an entire new set of toolbar icons with only a conditional compile, greatly simplifying a project deployment.

QPNGImagePacker   This class is useful for creating compressed PNG animated images.

A Possible Instantiation

```
...
    QFile f( "anim.png" );
    f.open( IO_WriteOnly );
    QPNGImagePacker p( f, 8, 0 );
...
```

Example Use

```
...
    QFile f( "anim.png" );
    f.open( IO_WriteOnly );
    QPNGImagePacker p( f, 8, 0 );
    QImage img = myLabel->pixmap().convertToImage();
    p.packImage( img );
...
```

Given Unisys Corporation's attitude regarding the use of LZW compression, I recommend using the PNG image format for animations to avoid the licensing that is required in some countries.

QPrinter   QPrinter is a paint device for use on printers. On Microsoft Windows systems, QPrinter uses the existing printer drivers and the native spooler. On Linux systems, QPrinter generates PostScript output and sends it to a spooler of your choosing.

A Possible Instantiation

```
...
    QPrinter *p = new QPrinter();
...
```

The online documentation provides a detailed example.

QRegion   QRegions define the clipping area of a QPainter.

A Possible Instantiation

```
...
    QRegion r( QRect(10, 10, 50, 50), QRegion::Ellipse );
...
```

Example Use

```
...
    QLabel *l = new QLabel( this );
    QPixmap pic = QPixmap( "my_square_pic.bmp" );
    QRegion r( QRect(0, 0, pic.width(), pic.height()),
        QRegion::Ellipse );
    QPainter p;
    p.begin( l );
    p.setClipRegion( r );
    p.drawPixmap( 0, 0, pic );
    p.end();
...
```

TEXT SUPPORT

The following classes provide the data and methods needed to support text display.

QFont, QFontInfo, and QFontMetrics QFont provides the encapsulation for platform-dependent text fonts. QFontInfo provides general information about a specified font. QFontMetrics provides metrics information about a font.

Example Use

```
...
    QFont f( "Helvetica", 10 );
    setFont( f );
    int fw = fontMetrics().width( "Hello" );
    int fh =
    QLabel *l = new QLabel( "Hello", this );
    l->setFixedWidth( fw );
...
```

QSimpleRichText QSimpleRichText encapsulates the Qt simplified implementation of rich text. You will use this primarily to add rich-text drawing support to custom widgets.

A Possible Instantiation

```
...
    QSimpleRichText rt( "<b>Boldly</b> going", font() );
...
```

Example Use

```
...
    QLabel *l = new QLabel( this );
    QSimpleRichText rt( "<b>Boldly</b> going", font() );
    QPainter p;
    p.begin( l );
    rt.draw( &p, 0, 0,
        QRegion( QRect( 0, 0, rt.widthUsed(), rt.height() ),
            QRegion::Rectangle ),
        palette() );
    p.end();

    // It's much easier to simply:
    l->setText( "<b>Boldly</b> going" );
...
```

As the above example implies, a limited subset of Qt widgets provide support for the Qt rich-text implementation. This will undoubtedly change over time. In the meantime, you can implement Qt rich text on any paint device using QSimpleRichText.

QStyleSheet   QStyleSheet provides a basic collection of styles for use by the Qt simple rich-text rendering mechanisms.

A Possible Instantiation

```
...
QStyleSheet *ns = QStyleSheet::defaultSheet();
...
```

By adding QStyleSheetItems to a style sheet, you are adding new tag support to that style sheet.

OUTPUT WIDGETS

The following widgets are used only for output or display purposes.

QFrame   A frame is a graphic border around a widget, or it can appear as a vertical or horizontal line. QFrame is the base class for widgets that either have a frame or have an optional frame such as QLabel.

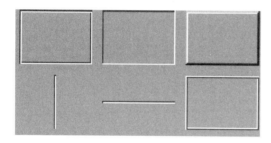

Figure 3.32   Various QFrame widgets

A Possible Instantiation

```
...
QFrame *f = new QFrame( this );
...
```

Example Use

```
...
QFrame *f = new QFrame( this );
f->setFrameStyle( QFrame::HLine | QFrame::Sunken );
f->setLineWidth( 2 );
...
```

If you are from a Motif background, you'll probably assume that pushbuttons inherit QFrame somewhere—but they don't.

QLabel   QLabels are used to display a text string or a pixmap image.

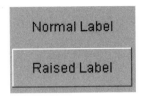

Figure 3.33   QLabel widgets

A Possible Instantiation

...
```
QLabel *l = new QLabel( "Hello", this );
```
...

Example Use

...
```
QLabel *status = new QLabel( this );
status->setFrameStyle( QFrame::WinPanel|QFrame::Sunken );
status->setText( "Status bar created." );
```
...

Embedded simple rich text is recognized and painted accordingly. Example:

...
```
QLabel *l = new QLabel( "<b>Bold</b> text", this );
```
...

QLCDNumber   This class displays a decimal number in a manner similar to an LCD display. Fig. 3.34 depicts a digital clock using QLCDNumbers.

Figure 3.34   QLCDNumber widgets from the *dclock* example in the distribution

A Possible Instantiation

...
```
QLCDNumber *lcd = new QLCDNumber( 3, this );
```
...

Example Use

...
```
countdown = new QLCDNumber( 2, this );
countdown->display( 30 );
```

```
    mytimer = new QTimer( this );
    connect( t, SIGNAL(timeout()), SLOT(count()) );
    t->start( 1000, false );
...
void
MyWidget::count()
{
    int a;
    a = countdown->intValue();
    if(a <= 0) {
        mytimer->stop();
        // Blast off
    } else {
        countdown->display( a-1 );
    }
}
...
```

QProgressBar   A QProgressBar (Fig. 3.35) provides a horizontal progress indicator.

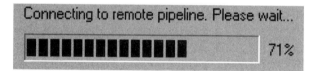

Figure 3.35 QLabel widget and QProgressBar widget

A Possible Instantiation

```
...
    QProgressBar *bar = new QProgressBar( 100, this );
...
```

Example Use

```
...
    QProgressBar *bar = new QProgressBar( 100, this );
    bar->setProgress( 0 );
...
```

QStatusBar   This widget provides a horizontal bar that can be used to display temporary messages to the end-user. Fig. 3.36 is a QStatusBar widget on a QMainWindow widget.

Figure 3.36   QStatusBar on a QMainWindow widget

A Possible Instantiation

...

```
QStatusBar *b = new QStatusBar( this );
```

...

Example Use

...

```
QMainWindow *mw = new QMainWindow();
mw->show();
QStatusBar *status = mw->statusBar();
status->message( "Starting up. Please Wait." );
```

...

```
status->clear();
```

...

QStyle   QStyle encapsulates many common elements of a GUI look and feel. It isn't always possible (or sensible) to capture all the elements that make a GUI appear the way it does, but many of the visual elements are common. A pushbutton has a frame or border, and that frame or border may change when the user clicks it with a mouse. It is these common elements that QStyle captures.

Many of the Qt widgets use their inherited style to present their visual appearance to the user, so it is relatively easy to change the overall appearance of your applications by changing the QStyle that the widgets inherit.

Qt provides four predefined styles for your use:

- QCDEStyle captures many elements of the CDE interface.
- QMotifStyle provides a Motif look and feel.
- QPlatinumStyle provides a very different appearance that is not *too* awful.
- QWindowsStyle encapsulates the Windows 9x or NT4 look and feel.

It is not very difficult to create a new style, but making the new style attractive and intuitive requires a considerable time investment.

QTextBrowser   QTextBrowser (see Fig. 3.37) provides a very basic simple rich-text viewer with some of the functionality needed for browsing.

A Possible Instantiation

...

```
QTextBrowser *b = new QTextBrowser( this );
```

...

Example Use

...

```
QTextBrowser *b = new QTextBrowser( this );
```

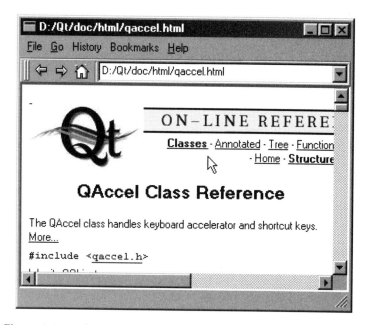

Figure 3.37 QTextBrowser as implemented in the Qt *helpviewer* example

```
b->setSource( "file://mytext.html" );
...
```

QTextBrowser inherits QTextView. As a result, you can couple QTextBrowser's browsing support with QTextView's MIME content support to create a browsing viewer for nearly any form of data over almost any transport (local file system, network, etc.).

QTextView   This widget provides sophisticated and highly customizable rich-text viewing capability, limited to a single page. Scrollbars are provided as necessary. Fig. 3.38 shows a QTextView widget on a dialog.

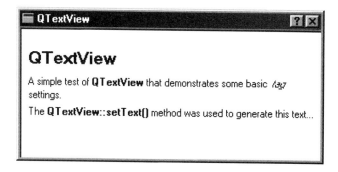

Figure 3.38   QTextView widget on a dialog

A Possible Instantiation

···

```
QTextView *tv = new QTextView( this );
```

···

Example Use

···

```
QTextView *tv = new QTextView( this );
tv->setText( "<p>Some text.</p>" );
tv->append( "<p>Yet more text.</p>" );
```

···

Any tag parsing limitations are inherited from the base QStyleSheet implementation. You will almost certainly need to add some custom QStyleSheetItems to address anything more than very basic rich-text display.

QWidgetStack   QWidgetStack manages a "stack" of widgets in which only the top widget is visible at any given time. This is an excellent way to present multiple views of information in a limited real estate environment, when only one view is needed or pertinent at a time.

A Possible Instantiation

···

```
QWidgetStack *cards = new QWidgetStack( this );
```

···

Example Use

···

```
QWidgetStack *cards = new QWidgetStack( this );
// Create an instance of our new Gizmo Widget
myCustomWidget = new CustomWidget( this );
// Add it to the 'top' of the stack
cards->addWidget( myCustomWidget, 0 );
// Create an instance of the Cosmos Widget
myCosmos = new Cosmos( this );
// Add it to the stack
cards->addWidget( myCosmos, 1 );
// Make Cosmos the one on top (visible)
cards->raiseWidget( 1 );
```

···

No visual widget-queuing mechanism is provided, but a toolbar or tab bar is an intuitive solution that can be easily added.

SUMMARY

In this chapter, I glossed over the Qt widgets that are primarily intended to provide output mechanisms for your applications. The widgets provided are adequate by themselves for most applications. With a minimum of work, they can be combined or enhanced to provide most functionality you're likely to require.

Trolltech pulled some of the output-only widgets just prior to the 2.1 release. This was done to alleviate some of the creeping-bloat and its associated buginess that had begun to appear in the toolkit snapshot releases. The most exciting of these objects is the QCanvas widgets that manage animated sprites. I hope these will reappear in a future release.

CHAPTER

5

Qt Convenience Objects

No useful application was ever created from visual code alone. The following pages attempt to organize descriptions of those Qt classes that provide no direct user interaction, or are provided for convenience's sake. The organization appears as follows:

- Event handling classes and parameters
- Input/Output related classes
- Collection, array, and linked-list classes
- Text and internationalization classes

As in the previous chapter, these descriptions are not intended to provide a reference to the various classes and parameters—they are more than adequately documented by the Qt online reference material and examples. This is intended as a possible "shopping list" of available Qt functionality, and nothing more.

EVENTS AND EVENT PARAMETERS

Since Qt always uses the underlying window system's mechanisms for receiving input or using timers and other such event-generating phenomena, and because all the supported window systems are event-driven, Qt is also event-driven and relies on the parameters passed to it by the underlying window system to receive keyboard input, mouse input, etc. An event is an asynchronous message that your application receives during normal processing of the Qt event loop. Qt provides default event loops in the QApplication::exec() and the QDialog::show() methods. These loops simply call the QApplication::process-NextEvent() method repeatedly. As events occur, the underlying window system's platform-dependent event parameters are translated to the appropriate Qt platform-independent event format and then passed to your application as a Qt event. Your application can make use of the default "reaction" to those events, or you can create custom event handlers to alter your application's behavior.

This section discusses the standard event types, what causes those events to occur, and a few possible modifications.

QChildEvent

When you insert or remove a child object from a QObject, a QChildEvent is passed to the parent QObject. You must reimplement the QObject::childEvent(QChildEvent *) method in order to make use of it.

QCloseEvent

The QWidget class provides a method QWidget::closeEvent(QCloseEvent *) that is called when either the window menu (a function of the window manager) is used to close the widget or the widget's QWidget::close() method is explicitly called from within the program. The QCloseEvent parameter contains an *accept* flag that can be used for cleanup functionality. The following example illustrates a typical use of QCloseEvent:

```
...
void
MyMainWin::closeEvent( QCloseEvent *e )
{
    if( modified == true ) {
        int v = QMessageBox::information( this,
            "Whoa, Big Fella!",
            "You have changed the drawing!",
            "Save...", "Cancel", "Exit", 0, 1 );
        switch( v ) {
         case 0: // Save!
            save();
            e->accept();
            break;
         case 1: // Cancel
            e->ignore();
            break;
         default: // Exit
            e->accept();
            break;
        }
    } else {
```

```
                e->accept();
        }
}
```

QCustomEvent

This class provides support for user-defined events. You can generate events using the provided QApplication::postEvent() and QApplication::sendEvent() methods. Any QWidget subclass can provide a handler by implementing a QWidget::customEvent (QCustomEvent *) method.

QDragEnterEvent

This event is sent to a QWidget when a drag and drop object is first dragged over this QWidget. This event will be followed by one or more QDragMoveEvents, so it's only necessary to provide an implementation of one or the other. See QDragMoveEvent below.

QDragLeaveEvent

When a drag and drop object leaves the current QWidget's "airspace," that QWidget will receive this event.

QDragMoveEvent

This event is sent to the QWidget under the mouse while a drag and drop action is in progress. If the QWidget accepts drag and drop events via QWidget::acceptAcceptDrops (bool) and the widget accepts the event via QDragMoveEvent::accept(bool), it is eligible to receive a QDropEvent.

QDropEvent

This event is sent to a QWidget when the drag and drop operation is completed.

QEvent

This is the base class of all other event classes and only contains an event type parameter. These event types are enumerated values that are documented in the QEvent reference. Since the enumerated values are subject to change, you should never use the hard-coded values to refer to, or test for, a specific event.

QFocusEvent

QFocusEvents are generated for QWidgets as a change in focus occurs. Only the two obvious methods are provided by the class, gotFocus() and lostFocus(). The following example demonstrates a modification to QLineEdit that will select all text when the line edit receives the keyboard focus. It will also deselect the text when focus is lost:

```
SLineEdit.h

#ifndef _SLINEEDIT_H
#define _SLINEEDIT_H

#include <qlineedit.h>

class SLineEdit : public QLineEdit
{
    Q_OBJECT
public:
    SLineEdit( QWidget *p=0, const char *n=0 );

protected slots:
    virtual void focusInEvent( QFocusEvent * );
    virtual void focusOutEvent( QFocusEvent * );
};

#endif // _SLINEEDIT_H

SLineEdit.cpp

#include "SLineEdit.h"

SLineEdit::SLienEdit( QWidget *parent, const char *name )
: QLineEdit( parent, name )
{
}

void
SLineEdit::focusInEvent( QFocusEvent *e )
{
    QLineEdit::focusInEvent( e );
    selectAll();
    repaint( false );
}

void
SLineEdit::focusOutEvent( QFocusEvent *e )
{
    QLineEdit::focusOutEvent( e );
    setSelection( 0, 0 );
    repaint( false );
}

#include "SLineEdit.moc"
```

QHideEvent

This event is sent to a QWidget *after* it is hidden using the QWidget::hide() method, but *before* the hide() method returns. This event is also generated whenever a top-level widget is iconified by the window manager.

QKeyEvent

Any time a QWidget has the keyboard focus, it is eligible to receive QKeyEvents. This class provides the basic information needed to process most keystrokes, and can be easily tailored to provide additional information. The default QWidget implementation provides event handlers for keyPressEvent() and keyReleaseEvent().

QMouseEvent

Surprisingly, the QMouseEvent class is the parameter that describes mouse events. The QWidget class provides handlers for mousePressEvent(), mouseReleaseEvent(), mouse-DoubleClickEvent(), and mouseMoveEvent().

QMoveEvent

When a widget is moved (relative to its parent) it receives a QMoveEvent. You can make use of the event by reimplementing the QWidget::moveEvent(QMoveEvent *) method.

QPaintEvent

Motif programmers will recognize this as an *expose* event. The event is generated when a widget needs to redraw itself. You can use QPaintEvent::rect() to obtain the QRect that represents the area that needs to be repainted.

QResizeEvent

When a widget is resized, it receives a QResizeEvent via its QWidget::resizeEvent() method.

QShowEvent

Show events can be generated by the underlying window system (external show events) or when the QWidget::show() method is called (internal show events), and are handled by the widget's showEvent() method. In the case of internal show events, the event is received *before* the widget is made visible.

QTimerEvent

QTimerEvent describes a timer event as received by QObject::timerEvent() whenever the QObject has activated one or more timers. Currently, the only useful value is the timer ID of the particular timer that triggered this event. See the QTimer documentation.

QWheelEvent

QWheelEvents are generated when the mouse wheel is rotated while the widget has focus. A special accept() method is provided by QWheelEvent to allow you to prevent the parent widget from receiving the same event.

INPUT AND OUTPUT CLASSES

Every interactive application performs I/O. The input could be from a keyboard, a mouse, a file or a network socket. The output could be to a display widget, a file, or yet another network socket. Qt provides a number of useful classes to help perform these normally platform-dependent operations in a platform-independent manner.

QAccel

This class provides handling for accelerator and shortcut keystrokes. Note that QAccel handles key events for the top-level widget that contains the QAccel parent widget, and for all children of that top-level widget.

A Possible Instantiation

```
...
    QAccel *a = new QAccel( this );
...
```

Example Use

```
...
    QAccel* a = new QAccel(this);
    a->connectItem( a->insertItem( ALT+Key_M ),
        this, SLOT(toggleMenuBar()) );
    a->connectItem( a->insertItem( ALT+Key_T ),
        this, SLOT(toggleToolBar()) );
    a->connectItem( a->insertItem( ALT+Key_B ),
        this, SLOT(toggleStatusBar()) );
...
```

QAsyncIO

QAsyncIO provides an abstract mechanism for performing lengthy or slow I/O operations without blocking the user interface. See QDataPump below.

QBuffer

This class provides buffered QByteArray I/O functionality. You can use QBuffer's internal QByteArray or provide your own.

A Possible Instantiation

```
...
    QBuffer b();
...
```

Example Use

```
...
```

```
    // A roundabout variable initializer
    int a, b;
    QByteArray s;
    QBuffer b( s );
    QTextStream ts( &b );
    ts << "456 123" << '\0';
    QTextIStream tis( &arr ) >> b >> a;
...
```

Note that this class is not appropriate for creating streams of Unicode text. QTextStream provides a QString implementation for that purpose.

QDataStream

QDataStream provides some basic methods for serializing binary data to a QIODevice. A data stream is independent of platform-dependent byte ordering.

A Possible Instantiation

```
...
    QFile f( "some_data.dat" );
    f.open( IO_ReadOnly );
    QDataStream s( f );
...
```

Example Use

```
...
    float myfloat;

    // Open a file for writing
    QFile f( "data.dat" );
    f.open( IO_WriteOnly );
    // Associate the file's QIODevice with a stream
    QDataStream s( f );
    // Write data into the stream
    s << 0x0102030405;
    s << (double)3.1416;
    myfloat = 0.01120113;
    s << myfloat;
    // Close the file
    f.close();
...
```

Note that QDataStream allows you to specify the byte ordering of the output (the default is MSB first, or big-endian) but changing the default will break the portability.

QDataPump

A QDataPump moves data from a QDataSource to a QDataSink during normal event processing (interleaved) by examining the QDataSource::readyToSend() and QDataSink::readyToReceive() methods of its arguments, and responding to the ASyncIO::activate() signals of the QDataSource and QDataSink. QDataPump is used by the Qt toolkit to asynchronously "feed" animated image data to QMovie objects.

QDataSink

QDataSink is an asynchronous consumer of data. It is normally used with a QDataPump and a QDataSource to move asynchronous data from point A to point B. See QDataPump above and QDataSource below.

QDataSource

QDataSource is an asynchronous producer of data and will typically be used with a QDataPump and a QDataSink to read asynchronous data from an ASIC port or a network socket. See QDataPump above.

QDir

QDir encapsulates the concept of a filesystem directory (on Windows systems, these are frequently called "folders") in a platform-independent manner.

A Possible Instantiation

```
...
    QDir d( "/etc/ppp" );
...
```

Example Use

```
...
    QDir d( "/etc/ppp" );
    QFile f( d.filePath( "options" ) );
    if(f.open( IO_ReadWrite ) == true ) {
        // Modify PPP options
    } else {
        QMessageBox::warning( 0, "Whoops!",
                "Can't open /etc/ppp/options..." );
    }
...
```

QFile

QFile encapsulates file I/O functionality in a platform-independent manner. Windows programmers should learn to use a forward-slash (/) as a directory delimiter. This will ease porting to other platforms.

A Possible Instantiation

```
…
QFile f( "/Windows/system.ini" );
…
```

Example Use

```
…
QFile f( "/Windows/win.ini" );
f.open( IO_ReadWrite );
if(f.size()) {
   QString s;
      f.readLine( s, 256 );
      // Do stuff
} else {
      // Do other stuff
}
f.close();
…
```

QFileInfo

QFileInfo provides file information in a platform-independent manner.

A Possible Instantiation

```
…
QFile f( "/vmlinuz" );
QFileInfo fi( f );
…
```

Example Use

```
…
QFile of( "/usr/src/linux/archi386/vmlinuz" );
QFileInfo ofi( of );
QFile f( "/vmlinuz" );
QFileInfo fi( f );
if( fi.lastModified() < ofi.lastModified() ) {
      // /vmlinuz is older or the same…
}
…
```

QIODevice

This is the base class for all Qt I/O devices and provides much of the common functionality required by platform I/O devices. QBuffer and QFile are subclasses of QIODevice.

QIODeviceSource

This class is a subclass of QDataSource, whose data is provided by any QIODevice or QIODevice subclass (such as a QFile). It provides an asynchronous source of data with a QIODevice as the source.

QTextIStream

This subclass of QTextStream is a convenience class that provides a text input stream.

A Possible Instantiation

...
```
QCString s = "1234567";
int n;
QTextIStream( &s ) >> n;
```
...

QTextOStream

This subclass of QTextStream is a convenience class that provides a text output stream.

QTextStream

QTextStream provides typical C++ IOstream functionality that is required for reading or writing text (ASCII or Unicode) from or to a QIODevice.

QSocketNotifier

QSocketNotifier provides the mechanisms needed for event-driven socket communications. Since the Linux/X11 implementation of this class uses a single select() system call for all QSocketNotifiers, it may be possible to use the class to monitor objects other than network sockets—a named pipe, for example.

A Possible Instantiation

...
```
QSocketNotifier *qsn = new QSocketNotifier( sock,
    QSocketNotifier::Read );
```
...

Example Use

...

```
Socket.h
#ifndef SOCKET_H
#define SOCKET_H
#include <stdio.h>
#include <stdlib.h>
#ifndef WIN32
#include <unistd.h>
#include <stdarg.h>
#endif
#include <qapplication.h>
#include <qsocketnotifier.h>
#include <sys/types.h>
#ifndef WIN32
#include <sys/socket.h>
#include <netinet/in.h>
#include <sys/ioctl.h>
#include <fcntl.h>
#include <netdb.h>
#include <sys/param.h>
#else
#include <winsock.h>
#endif
#include <errno.h>

// For Linux, we define a common type
#ifndef WIN32
#define INVALID_SOCKET -1
typedef int SOCKET;
#endif

class Socket : public QObject
{
    Q_OBJECT
public:
    //Create on existing descriptor
    Socket( SOCKET _sock );

    // Create and connect
    Socket( const char *_host, unsigned short _port );

    // Destroy - closing if still open
    ~Socket();

    // Retrieve the descriptor
    SOCKET socket() const { return sock; }

    // Enable read - If true, emit readEvent on socket input
    void enableRead( bool );

    // Enable write - If true, emit writeEvent on socket input
    void enableWrite( bool );

    // Retrieve the address
```

```
    unsigned long getAddr();

    // Formatted print()
    void print( const char *fmt, ... );

    // Retrieve one 'line' of data up to 'len' bytes or
    // EOF or newline
    char *line(char *p, int len);

signals:
    // Data is available for reading (if enableRead( true ) called)
    void readEvent( Socket * );

    // Socket is ready for writing (if enableWrite( true ) called)
    void writeEvent( Socket * );

    // Raised when connection is broken
    void closeEvent( Socket * );

public slots:
    // Connected to the Notifiers
    void slotWrite( int );
    void slotRead( int );

protected:
    bool connect( const char *_host, unsigned short _port );
    bool init_sockaddr( const char *hostname, unsigned short port );

    struct sockaddr_in name;
    SOCKET sock;
    in_addr addr;

    QSocketNotifier *readNotifier, *writeNotifier;
};

class ServerSocket : public QObject
{
    Q_OBJECT
public:
    ServerSocket( int _port );
    ~ServerSocket();

    // Retrieve the descriptor
    SOCKET socket() const { return sock; }

    // Retrieve the port being monitored
    unsigned short getPort();

    // Retrieve the current address
    unsigned long getAddr();

public slots:
    // Called when someone connects to our port
    virtual void slotAccept( int );
```

```
signals:
    // A connection has been accepted
    // don't forget to delete the Socket when no longer needed
    void accepted( Socket * );

protected:
    bool init( unsigned short );

    QSocketNotifier *notifier;
    SOCKET sock;
};

#endif



Socket.cpp
#include <Socks.h>

#ifdef WIN32
static bool isinited = false;
// Here's where we initialize Winsock (goofy, huh?)
static void
initWinSock()
{
    if(isinited == true) return;
    WORD wVersionRequested;
    WSADATA wsaData;
    int r;

    wVersionRequested = MAKEWORD( 1, 1 );

    r = WSAStartup( wVersionRequested, &wsaData );
    if ( r == 0 ) {
          isinited = true;
    }
}
#endif

// Socket ctor with existing platform socket
Socket::Socket( SOCKET _sock )
{
#ifdef WIN32
    initWinSock();
#endif
    sock = _sock;
    readNotifier = 0L;
    writeNotifier = 0L;
}

// Socket ctor from host/port info
Socket::Socket( const char *_host, unsigned short int _port )
{
#ifdef WIN32
    initWinSock();
```

```
#endif
    sock = INVALID_SOCKET;
    readNotifier = 0L;
    writeNotifier = 0L;
#ifdef WIN32
    if(isinited == false) return;
#endif
    connect( _host, _port );
}

// print() - print formatted to stream, same syntax as printf
void
Socket::print( const char *fmt, ...)
{
    char p[4096];
    va_list ap;

#ifdef WIN32
    if(isinited == false) return;
#endif

    memset(p, 0, 4096);
    va_start(ap, fmt);
#ifdef _HPUX_SOURCE  // Old 9.0x stuff
    vsprintf(p, fmt, ap);
#endif
#ifdef WIN32
    vsprintf(p, fmt, ap);
#endif
#ifdef LINUX
    vsnprintf(p, 8191, fmt, ap);
    va_end(ap);
#endif
    send( sock, p, strlen(p), 0 );
}

// Enable/Disable the read QSocketNotifier
void
Socket::enableRead( bool state )
{
    if ( state ) {
        if ( !readNotifier ) {
            readNotifier = new QSocketNotifier( sock,
                QSocketNotifier::Read );
            QObject::connect( readNotifier,
                SIGNAL( activated(int) ), this,
                SLOT( slotRead(int) ) );
        } else readNotifier->setEnabled( true );
    } else if ( readNotifier )
        readNotifier->setEnabled( false );
}

// Enable/Disable the write QSocketNotifier
```

```
void
Socket::enableWrite( bool state )
{
    if ( state ) {
        if ( !writeNotifier ) {
            writeNotifier = new QSocketNotifier( sock,
                QSocketNotifier::Write );
            QObject::connect( writeNotifier,
                SIGNAL( activated(int) ), this,
                SLOT( slotWrite(int) ) );
        } else {
            writeNotifier->setEnabled( true );
        }
    } else if ( writeNotifier )
        writeNotifier->setEnabled( false );
}

// The read slot - argument notifier is ignored
void
Socket::slotRead( int )
{
    char buffer[2];

#ifdef WIN32
    if(isinited == false) return;
#endif
    if(sock == INVALID_SOCKET) return;
    int n = recv( sock, buffer, 1, MSG_PEEK );
#ifndef WIN32
    if ( n <= 0 )
        emit closeEvent( this );
    else
        emit readEvent( this );
#else
    // Winsock is verbose...
    if(n > 0) {
        emit readEvent( this );
        return;
    }
    switch(n) {
    case 0:
        emit closeEvent( this );
        break;
    case SOCKET_ERROR:
        n = WSAGetLastError();

        switch(n) {
        case WSANOTINITIALISED:
            break;
        case WSAENETDOWN:
            emit closeEvent( this );
            break;
        case WSAEFAULT:
```

```
                          break;
              case WSAENOTCONN:
                      emit closeEvent( this );
                      break;
              case WSAEINTR:
                      break;
              case WSAEINPROGRESS:
                      break;
              case WSAENETRESET:
                      emit closeEvent( this );
                      break;
              case WSAENOTSOCK:
                      emit closeEvent( this );
                      break;
              case WSAEOPNOTSUPP:
                      break;
              case WSAESHUTDOWN:
                      emit closeEvent( this );
                      break;
              case WSAEWOULDBLOCK:
                      break;
              case WSAEMSGSIZE:
                      break;
              case WSAEINVAL:
                      break;
              case WSAECONNABORTED:
                      emit closeEvent( this );
                      break;
              case WSAETIMEDOUT:
                      emit closeEvent( this );
                      break;
              case WSAECONNRESET:
                      emit closeEvent( this );
                      break;
              default:
                      break;
              }
              break;
       }
#endif
}

void Socket::slotWrite( int )
{
    emit writeEvent( this );
}

// Initialize the platform-level socket
// Note that this will even work with dotted IP on
// Win95 platforms...
bool
Socket::init_sockaddr( const char *hostname, unsigned short int port )
{
```

```
        struct hostent *hostinfo;
        int oa, ob, oc, od;

        name.sin_family = AF_INET;
        name.sin_port = htons( port );
        // Tacky - should use QString
        if(sscanf(hostname, "%d.%d.%d.%d", &oa, &ob, &oc, &od) == 4) {
            addr.S_un.S_addr = inet_addr( hostname );
            name.sin_addr = addr;
        } else {
            if((hostinfo = gethostbyname( hostname )) == NULL) {
                return( false );
            }
            name.sin_addr = *(struct in_addr*) hostinfo->h_addr;
        }
    return true;
}

bool
Socket::connect( const char *_host, unsigned short int _port )
{
    sock = ::socket(PF_INET,SOCK_STREAM,0);
    if (sock == INVALID_SOCKET) {
        return false;
    }

    if ( !init_sockaddr( _host, _port) ) {
#ifdef WIN32
        ::closesocket( sock );
#else
        ::close( sock );
#endif
        sock = INVALID_SOCKET;
        return false;
    }

    if ( ::connect(sock, (struct sockaddr*)(&name), sizeof( name )) < 0 )
{
#ifdef WIN32
        ::closesocket( sock );
#else
        ::close( sock );
#endif
        sock = INVALID_SOCKET;
        return false;
    }

    return true;
}

unsigned long
Socket::getAddr()
{
```

```
    struct sockaddr_in name; int len = sizeof(name);
    getsockname(sock, (struct sockaddr *) &name, &len);
    return ntohl(name.sin_addr.s_addr);
}


char *
Socket::line( char *p, int len )
{
    unsigned char c;
    int a;

#ifdef WIN32
    if(isinited == false) return( NULL );
#endif
    memset(p, 0, len);

    for(a=0;a<len;a++) {
        if(recv(sock, (char *)&c, 1, 0) <= 0) {
            if(a == 0) return(NULL);
            else return(p);
        }
        p[a] = c;
        if(c == '\n') return(p);
    }
    return(p);
}


Socket::~Socket()
{
    if ( readNotifier ) {
        delete readNotifier;
    }
    if ( writeNotifier ) {
        delete writeNotifier;
    }
#ifdef WIN32
    if(isinited == false) return;
#endif
    if(sock != INVALID_SOCKET) {
#ifdef WIN32
        ::closesocket( sock );
#else
        ::close( sock );
#endif
        sock = INVALID_SOCKET;
    }
}


ServerSocket::ServerSocket( int _port ) :
    sock( -1 )
{
```

```
        sock = INVALID_SOCKET;
#ifdef WIN32
    initWinSock();
    if(isinited == false) return;
#endif
    if ( !init ( _port ) ) {
            return;
    }

    notifier = new QSocketNotifier( sock, QSocketNotifier::Read );
    connect( notifier, SIGNAL( activated(int) ), this,
        SLOT( slotAccept(int) ) );
}

bool
ServerSocket::init( unsigned short int _port )
{
    struct sockaddr_in name;

    sock = ::socket( PF_INET, SOCK_STREAM, 0 );
    if (sock == INVALID_SOCKET) {
            return false;
    }

    name.sin_family = AF_INET;
    name.sin_port = htons( _port );
    name.sin_addr.s_addr = htonl(INADDR_ANY);

    if ( bind(sock, (struct sockaddr*) &name,sizeof( name )) < 0 ) {
#ifdef WIN32
            ::closesocket( sock );
#else
            ::close( sock );
#endif
            sock = INVALID_SOCKET;
            return false;
    }

    if ( listen(sock, 1000) < 0 ) {
#ifdef WIN32
            ::closesocket( sock );
#else
            ::close( sock );
#endif
            sock = INVALID_SOCKET;
            return false;
    }

    return true;
}

unsigned short
ServerSocket::getPort()
```

```
{
    struct sockaddr_in name; int len = sizeof(name);
    getsockname(sock, (struct sockaddr *) &name, &len);
    return ntohs(name.sin_port);
}

unsigned long
ServerSocket::getAddr()
{
    struct sockaddr_in name; int len = sizeof(name);
    getsockname(sock, (struct sockaddr *) &name, &len);
    return ntohl(name.sin_addr.s_addr);
}

void
ServerSocket::slotAccept( int v )
{
    struct sockaddr_in client;
    SOCKET new_sock;

    int size = sizeof(client);

    if ( (new_sock = ::accept(sock,
        (struct sockaddr *) &client,
        &size)) < 0 ) {
            return;
    }

    emit accepted( new Socket( new_sock ) );
}

ServerSocket::~ServerSocket()
{
    if ( notifier )
    delete notifier;

#ifdef WIN32
    if(isinited == false) return;
    ::closesocket( sock );
#else
    ::close( sock );
#endif
    sock = INVALID_SOCKET;
}

#include "Socket.moc"
...
```

The example above provides *extremely* basic TCP socket-level support. A protocol-based network extension will be available for Qt someday. Until then, hacks like this will be a necessary evil.

The CD-ROM contains this code plus an example (bare-bones) e-mail client and SMTP class. (Don't get rid of your e-mail client yet—these classes are the absolute minimal functionality required.)

COLLECTIONS, ARRAYS, AND LINKED-LISTS

The Qt toolkit provides some very flexible classes for maintaining collections, arrays, and linked lists of objects. These classes comprise nearly half the overall value of the toolkit in my opinion. You will have to exercise a bit of caution when selecting a specific class, as Troll often provides two flavors of a given class; one that operates on values and another that operates on references to values. Unlike most other Qt classes, the naming conventions are not always a good clue as to which classes are value- or reference-based. I have tried to make it a little more obvious in the descriptions that follow.

QArray

QArray is a value-based template class that can maintain arrays of simple objects, where "simple" means that there is no constructor, destructor, or virtual functions.

A Possible Instantiation

...
```
    QArray<int> nums( 10 );
```
...

Example Use

...
```
    QArray<int> so( 100 );
    for(int a=0;a<100;a++) so[a] = a;
```
...

QArray uses bit-level copy and compare operations. See the QVector class for reference-based implementations of an array.

QAsciiCache

QAsciiCache is a template class that provides caching functionality based on character pointer keys. Keys are stored in least-recently used order. Note that this class is not appropriate for Unicode cache implementations. QCache provides a QString-based caching mechanism with full Unicode support, and since there is no performance difference between the two, QAsciiCache is only useful for legacy coding purposes.

QAsciiCacheIterator

This class provides an iterator for QAsciiCache objects.

QAsciiDict

QAsciiDict provides a dictionary that is based on character pointer keys. This class provides no Unicode support, while QDict does. This class is provided for support of legacy code that is not Unicode compatible.

QAsciiDictIterator

This class provides an iterator for QAsciiDict objects.

QBitArray

This class maintains an array of single bit values and provides methods for performing bit-level operations on the array elements.

A Possible Instantiation

```
...
    QBitArray b( 4 );
...
```

Example Use

```
...
    // New array, initialize to 010
    QBitArray first( 3 );
    first[0] = 0;
    first[1] = 1;
    first[2] = 0;
    // Another, initialize to 011
    QBitArray second( 3 );
    second.clearBit( 0 );
    second.setBit( 1 );
    second.setBit( 2 );
    // New array == 010 | 011 == 011
    QBitArray third = first | second;
...
```

QByteArray

QByteArray is implemented from QArray and provides an explicitly shared array of byte values.

QCache

QCache is a template class that provides a simple caching mechanism based on QString keys. Two optional parameters to the constructor will affect performance. These are the *maxcost* and *size* parameters.

Maxcost specifies the maximum size to use for the caching mechanism. When storage of a new item will cause this parameter to be exceeded, the least-recently used item will be discarded to make room for it.

The size parameter specifies how many hash slots will be used. This should be a prime number that meets or exceeds the total number of expected entries. Every implementation will require some tuning to achieve the optimal balance between performance and resource utilization.

QCacheIterator

This class provides an iterator for the QCache collection class.

QCollection

QCollection is the base class of all Qt collection classes.

QDict

QDict is a template class that provides a dictionary based on QString keys. QDict operates on references to its elements. See QMap for a value-based implementation.

A Possible Instantiation

```
...
    QDict<char> d;
...
```

Example Use

```
...
class myType
{
public:
    myType( int s=0, int v=2 ) ( _sal = s, _vac = v; }
    int salary() { return( _sal ); }
    int vacation() { return( _vac ); }

private:
    int _sal;
    int _vac;
};
...
    QDict<myType> d( 23, FALSE );

    d.insert( "Bob", new myType( 40000, 2 ) );
    d.insert( "George", new myType( 54000, 3 ) );
...
    cout << "Bob's Salary: " << d["Bob"].salary() << "\n";
...
```

QDictIterator

This class provides an iterator for the QDict collection class.

QIntCache

QIntCache provides a caching mechanism based on integer keys.

QIntCacheIterator

QIntCacheIterator is an iterator for the QIntCache collection class.

QIntDict

QIntDict provides a dictionary of integer values.

QIntDictIterator

QIntDictIterator is an iterator for the QIntDict collection class.

QIntValidator

QIntValidator provides upper and lower range checking for integer values.

QList

QList is a template class that implements doubly linked lists. QList operates on references to its elements. See QValueList for a value-based implementation.

A Possible Instantiation

```
...
    QList<myItem> *theList = new QList<myItem>(;
...
```

Example Use
```
...
// Matches a word to a database offset
class ref
{
public:
    ref( unsigned long offset=0L );
    virtual ~ref();

    QStrList           &retrieve( const QString & );

private:
    unsigned long      offset;
};
...
```

```
// Construct a new DB list
QList<ref> *index = db.wordlist();
// Check for a match
QStrList sl = index->retrieve( keywords->text() );
```
...

QListIterator

QListIterator is an iterator for QList collections.

QMap

QMap is a template class that provides collections and dictionary lookup. The most significant difference between QMap and QList or QDict is that QMap is value-based. It maintains discrete copies of its collection. QList and QDict are reference-based.

QMapConstIterator

QMapConstIterator is one of two iterators for QMap collections. As the name "const" implies, iterating a QMap collection using this class will not permit the collection values to be modified.

QMapIterator

QMapIterator is one of two iterators for QMap collections. Also see QMapConstIterator.

QPtrDict

QPtrDict provides a dictionary based on void pointer keys.

QPtrDictIterator

This class provides an iterator for QPtrDict collections.

QQueue

This template class implements a first-in, first-out (FIFO) queue. See QStack for LIFO behavior.

QSortedList

This is a subclass of QList that provides the extra functionality needed for sorting, based on operators < and ==.

QStack

QStack is a reference-based template class that provides a last-in, first-out (LIFO) stack. See QQueue for FIFO behavior. See QValueStack for a value-based implementation.

QStrList and QStrIList

QStrList provides a doubly linked list of character pointer values. QStrIList adds case-insensitive comparison.

QStrListIterator

This is an iterator for QStrList or QStrIList collections.

QStringList

This class manages a list of QString objects and provides methods for searching.

QValueList

QValueList is a *value*-based template class that provides doubly linked lists. See QList for a reference-based implementation.

QValueListConstIterator

This is one of two iterators for QValueList collections. It will not permit the QValueList values to be modified.

QValueListIterator

This is one of two iterators for QValueList collections. See QValueListConstIterator.

QValueStack

This is a *value*-based template class that implements a LIFO stack. Use QStack for reference-based implementations.

QVector

QVector is a *reference*-based template class for implementing an array. QVector has an advantage over a QArray in that the complexity of the array elements does not suffer the restrictions that QArray's value-based implementation imposes.
    See QArray for a value-based implementation.

TEXT HANDLING

Qt provides classes to encapsulate text objects and concepts in a platform-independent and, in several instances, a language-independent manner. The following discussions provide a brief overview of these classes and their intended purposes.

QChar

QChar encapsulates Unicode characters and provides test, classification, and conversion methods much like those provided for ASCII characters by ctype.h.

QClipboard

QClipBoard provides methods to access the underlying window system's clipboard.

QConstString

This class provides the functionality of the QString class, optimized for existing Unicode data. By eliminating copy operations (the primary overhead of the QString class) the QConstString class can provide a significant performance increase. If any modification is attempted on the data, however, the class will make a copy of the data so that it will persist unmodified.

QCString

This class is an abstraction of typical zero-terminated strings. QCString inherits QArray, so its contents are explicitly shared. Also see QString.

QDoubleValidator

QDoubleValidator provides range checking for double precision floating point numbers. See QValidator and QIntValidator.

QRegExp

QRegExp provides pattern matching using regular expressions in a manner similar to the GNU regex implementation. Support is provided for Unicode support and case-insensitive matching except for non-ASCII Latin-1 characters.

QString

QString is an abstraction of Unicode text and character strings. QString implicitly shares text strings.

QTextCodec

This abstract class provides conversions between text encodings and encapsulates the common elements of Qt text encodings.

QTextDecoder

QTextDecoder provides a single method, toUnicode(), that is used to convert an array of bytes into Unicode text. The class maintains prior state information for continued processing in subsequent calls, making QTextDecoder useful in data streams. See QText-Encoder.

QTextEncoder

QTextEncoder converts from Unicode to another format (you have to provide the target format of course), maintaining prior state information for processing in subsequent calls. This makes the class suitable for use with data streams. See QTextDecoder.

QTranslator

QTranslator provides internationalization support for text output. A QTranslator object contains a set of translations from the reference language to a target language, and provides methods to add, find, or remove such translations. Methods are also provided to save the current object to a file or load a previously saved file.

QValidator

QValidator is a base class for validating input text. See QIntValidator and QDouble-Validator.

DATE AND TIME

While all the supported platforms provide the time t standard value as a representation of time plus all the associated library functions, Qt provides its own encapsulation of date and time that is not quite as limited as the platform representations are.

QDate

QDate is an abstraction of date values. The implementation is a platform-independent calculation of Gregorian dates, valid from September 14, 1752, to the eighth millennium. I expect the resolution to change significantly in future releases of Qt as 64-bit CPU architectures become more prevalent. The native *time_t* value on these systems is valid to BSN (Beyond Solar Nova).

QDateTime

QDateTime combines the functionality of the QDate and QTime classes. The class also adds some convenience routines to permit interfacing to the native time_t values supplied by the platforms that Qt is available for.

QTime

The QTime class is an abstraction of time in hours, minutes, seconds, and milliseconds since midnight. QTime provides methods for comparison and conversion.

MISCELLANEOUS

Most of the following classes belong in no specific category, but are extremely useful, nonetheless.

QRangeControl

This class provides the means to bound integer values within a specific range. This is much more intuitive than letting the user input an integer with a text field and in some circumstances, is even more intuitive than a spin box (it depends on the context).

Likely Instantiation

```
...
    QRangeControl *rc = new QRangeControl( 0, 100, 1, 10, 0 );
...
```

Common Use

```
...
    QRangeControl *rc = new QRangeControl( 0, 100, 1, 10, 0 );
    int n = rc->pageStep();
...
```

There are five concepts covered by the class which make its use in QScrollBar widgets rather apparent:

- A current value as a bounded integer which is retrieved via the QRangeControl::value() method and set using the QRangeControl::setValue() method.
- The minimum value.
- The maximum value.
- A line-step value that can be used to determine the preferred number of lines to scroll.
- A page-step value that can be used to determine the appropriate number of lines to scroll for a page-forward or page-backward scroll.

QGuardedPtr

This template class provides guarded pointers to QObjects. A guarded pointer behaves like any other C++ pointer except that its value is set to NULL when the object it references is deleted. I have not been able to measure any significant performance hit as a result of using guarded pointers, and they can improve product reliability. Using guarded pointers does increase coding time and complexity, of course.

QMimeSource

QMimeSource encapsulates an abstract piece of data. It is used by the drag and drop classes and by QClipBoard.

QMimeSourceFactory

QMimeSourceFactory provides an interface to a collection of abstract data.

QPoint

QPoint is an abstraction of a point within a plane.

QPointArray

QPointArray maintains an explicitly shared array of QPoint objects.

QRect

QRect provides an abstraction of a rectangular area of a plane.

QSignal

QSignal provides a very simple way to send a signal with no parameters to a slot that accepts no parameters. This is typically used by classes that don't inherit QObject to send signals.

QSignalMapper

QSignalMapper provides mechanisms to map signals that don't provide a parameter to signals that provide either an integer or QString parameter. This is very useful for managing multiple popup menu items from a single slot. You can also use this class to map an array of pushbuttons to a single slot.

QSize

QSize defines the size (in pixels) of two dimensional objects and provides methods and operators for comparison and value modifications.

QTimer

QTimer provides periodic and single-shot timing signals.

Likely Instantiation

...

```
            QTimer *t new QTimer( this, false );
...


        Common Use


...
// We need a flashing text label, so we subclass QLabel and
// add a QTimer. We tried to tell the customer it uses a lot
// of resources...
class Blinky : public QLabel
{
        Q_OBJECT
public:
        Blinky( QWidget *p=0, const char *n=0 );
        Blinky( const QString &s, QWidget *p=0, const char *n=0 );

public slots:
        void   setValue( const QString &s );

protected slots:
        void   myTimeout();

private:
        QLabel *1;
        QString &str;
        bool showing;
};

// Convenience ctor sets the label text and saves a copy
Blinky:: Blinky ( const QString &s, QWidget *p, const char *n )
: QLabel( s, p, n )
{
        str = s;
}

// Standard constructor adds the timer
Blinky:: Blinky ( QWidget *p, const char *n )
{
        Blinky( "", p, n );
        showing = true;
        tmr = new QTimer( this );
        connect( tmr, SIGNAL(timeout()), SLOT(myTimeout()) );
        t->start( 500 );
}

// A slot to set the text value
void
Blinky::setValue( const QString &s )
{
        setText( s );
        str = s;
}
```

```
// This is called by our QTimer every 500ms
void
Blinky::myTimeout()
{
    // Toggle text every 500ms...
    if(showing == true) {
    showing = false;
    setText( "" );
    } else {
    showing = true;
  setText( str );
    }
}
...
```

QVariant

QVariant behaves like a union of many commonly used Qt data types.

QWMatrix

QWMatrix performs 2D transformations of a coordinate system. The result can be applied to a graphic image to translate, scale, shear, or rotate the image. See QPainter in the previous chapter.

SUMMARY

While Qt doesn't provide a class for every conceivable programming need outside the purely visual interface component arena, it certainly covers a wide range of common tasks, from the obvious timesavers to the dauntingly complex linked-list handlers. I expect great things in future releases.

CHAPTER

6

The Qt Namespace and Qt Extensions

There are a couple of topics that bear discussing but are not so paper-consuming that they deserve an entire chapter. The first topic covered is the Qt class, which provides some commonly used enumerated constant values. The second topic discusses the Trolltech extensions to the Qt toolkit, which have evolved to a degree that the Trolls have moved the extensions out of the second release of the toolkit itself.

QT CLASS

Providing global values is tacky and frowned on by almost every OO programmer. There are a lot of good reasons for this. The most compelling reason to avoid using global definitions is to avoid pollution of the development name space. The Microsoft development environment is a good example of a polluted environment—it is becoming increasingly difficult with every new release of VC++ to create a unique identifier name that doesn't conflict with some macro in an included header file. As an example, consider the following macro definitions:

```
...
#define AlignLeft          0x01
#define AlignRight    0x02
...
```

These macro definitions, which appear at first glance to be harmless, will cause interesting things to happen during compilation of code for almost any graphic toolkit, not just Qt. Creating global variables, macros, and constant values causes trouble. Even if you assign unlikely names, there is a possibility that it will cause a conflict with someone else's code later on.

A better way to address the need for "global" constants is to declare them within a class and simply inherit that class. This is the purpose served by the Qt class.

Many of the Qt widgets and classes accept constant flags, modifiers, and data values that are common across nearly all the widgets and many of the convenience classes. Rather than further pollute the name space, the Qt toolkit defines a class called Qt that exposes these common values to its subclassed objects. Since QObject—and many classes that are not based on QObject—inherit the Qt class, these enumerated constants are directly accessible from any class that is derived from one of these subclasses of Qt. Of course, there is nothing wrong with accessing one of these values explicitly; for example:

```
...
    QColor r( Qt::red );
...
```

For any subclass of QObject or one of the other Qt subclasses, it is much easier to simply access the values as follows:

```
...
    QColor r( red );
...
```

The classes QBrush, QCustomMenuItem, QEvent, QIconViewItem, QListViewItem, QObject, QPainter, QPen, QPixmap, QStyleSheetItem, QToolTip, and QWhatsThis all inherit the Qt class, so the constants are directly accessible by the methods of these subclasses and their subclasses in turn.

Table 6.1 lists the data type and constant name pairs.

Table 6.1   Data Type and Constant Name Pairs

Value Type	Constant
ButtonState	NoButton, LeftButton, RightButton, MidButton, MouseButtonMask, ShiftButton, ControlButton, AltButton, KeyButtonMask
Orientation	Horizontal, Vertical
AlignmentFlags	AlignLeft, AlignRight, AlignHCenter, AlignTop, AlignBottom, AlignVCenter, AlignCenter = AlignVCenter | AlignHCenter, SingleLine, DontClip, ExpandTabs, ShowPrefix, WordBreak, DontPrint
WidgetState	WState_Created, WState_Disabled, WState_Visible, WState_ForceHide, WState_OwnCursor, WState_MouseTracking, WState_CompressKeys,

(continued)

Table 6.1   (Continued)

	WState_BlockUpdates, WState_InPaintEvent, WState_Reparented, WState_ConfigPending, WState_Resized, WState_AutoMask, WState_Polished, WState_DND, WState_Modal, WState_Reserved1, WState_Reserved2, WState_Reserved3, WState_Reserved4, WState_TranslateBackground, WState_ForceDisabled, WState_Exposed
WidgetFlags	WType_TopLevel, WType_Modal, WType_Popup, WType_Desktop, WType_Mask, WStyle_Customize, WStyle_NormalBorder, WStyle_DialogBorder, WStyle_NoBorder, WStyle_Title, WStyle_SysMenu, WStyle_Minimize, WStyle_Maximize, WStyle_MinMax = WStyle_Minimize | WStyle_Maximize, WStyle_Tool, WStyle_StaysOnTop, WStyle_Dialog, WStyle_ContextHelp, WStyle_NoBorderEx, WStyle_Mask, WDestructiveClose, WPaintDesktop, WPaintUnclipped, WPaintClever, WResizeNoErase, WMouseNoMask, WNorthWestGravity, WRepaintNoErase, WX11BypassWM
ImageConversionFlags	ColorMode_Mask, AutoColor, ColorOnly, MonoOnly, AlphaDither_Mask, ThresholdAlphaDither, OrderedAlphaDither, DiffuseAlphaDither, NoAlpha, Dither_Mask, DiffuseDither, OrderedDither, ThresholdDither, DitherMode_Mask, AutoDither, PreferDither, AvoidDither
BGMode	TransparentMode, OpaqueMode
PaintUnit	PixelUnit, LoMetricUnit, HiMetricUnit, LoEnglishUnit, HiEnglishUnit, TwipsUnit
GUIStyle	MacStyle, WindowsStyle, Win3Style, PMStyle, MotifStyle
Modifier	SHIFT, CTRL, ALT, MODIFIER_MASK, UNICODE_ACCEL, ASCII_ACCEL = UNICODE_ACCEL
Key	Key_Escape, Key_Tab, Key_Backtab, Key_BackTab = Key_Backtab, Key_Backspace, Key_BackSpace = Key_Backspace, Key_Return, Key_Enter, Key_Insert, Key_Delete, Key_Pause, Key_Print, Key_SysReq, Key_Home, Key_End, Key_Left, Key_Up, Key_Right, Key_Down, Key_Prior, Key_PageUp = Key_Prior, Key_Next, Key_PageDown = Key_Next, Key_Shift, Key_Control, Key_Meta, Key_Alt, Key_CapsLock, Key_NumLock, Key_ScrollLock, Key_F1, Key_F2, Key_F3, Key_F4, Key_F5, Key_F6, Key_F7, Key_F8, Key_F9, Key_F10, Key_F11, Key_F12, Key_F13, Key_F14, Key_F15, Key_F16, Key_F17, Key_F18, Key_F19, Key_F20, Key_F21, Key_F22, Key_F23, Key_F24, Key_F25, Key_F26, Key_F27, Key_F28, Key_F29, Key_F30, Key_F31, Key_F32, Key_F33, Key_F34, Key_F35, Key_Super_L, Key_Super_R, Key_Menu, Key_Hyper_L, Key_Hyper_R, Key_SpaceKey_Any = Key_Space, Key_Exclam, Key_QuoteDbl, Key_NumberSign,

(continued)

Table 6.1   (Continued)

	Key_Dollar, Key_Percent, Key_Ampersand, Key_Apostrophe, Key_ParenLeft, Key_ParenRight, Key_Asterisk, Key_Plus, Key_Comma, Key_Minus, Key_Period, Key_Slash, Key_0, Key_1, Key_2, Key_3, Key_4, Key_5, Key_6, Key_7, Key_8, Key_9, Key_Colon, Key_Semicolon, Key_Less, Key_Equal, Key_Greater, Key_Question, Key_At, Key_A, Key_B, Key_C, Key_D, Key_E, Key_F, Key_G, Key_H, Key_I, Key_J, Key_K, Key_L, Key_M, Key_N, Key_O, Key_P, Key_Q, Key_R, Key_S, Key_T, Key_U, Key_V, Key_W, Key_X, Key_Y, Key_Z, Key_BracketLeft, Key_Backslash, Key_BracketRight, Key_AsciiCircum, Key_Underscore, Key_QuoteLeft, Key_BraceLeft, Key_Bar, Key_BraceRight, Key_AsciiTilde, Key_nobreakspace, Key_exclamdown, Key_cent, Key_sterling, Key_currency, Key_yen, Key_brokenbar, Key_section, Key_diaeresis, Key_copyright, Key_ordfeminine, Key_guillemotleft, Key_notsign, Key_hyphen, Key_registered, Key_macron, Key_degree, Key_plusminus, Key_twosuperior, Key_threesuperior, Key_acute, Key_mu, Key_paragraph, Key_periodcentered, Key_cedilla, Key_onesuperior, Key_masculine, Key_guillemotright, Key_onequarter, Key_onehalf, Key_threequarters, Key_questiondown, Key_Agrave, Key_Aacute, Key_Acircumflex, Key_Atilde, Key_Adiaeresis, Key_Aring, Key_AE, Key_Ccedilla, Key_Egrave, Key_Eacute, Key_Ecircumflex, Key_Ediaeresis, Key_Igrave, Key_Iacute, Key_Icircumflex, Key_Idiaeresis, Key_ETH, Key_Ntilde, Key_Ograve, Key_Oacute, Key_Ocircumflex, Key_Otilde, Key_Odiaeresis, Key_multiply, Key_Ooblique, Key_Ugrave, Key_Uacute, Key_Ucircumflex, Key_Udiaeresis, Key_Yacute, Key_THORN, Key_ssharp, Key_agrave, Key_aacute, Key_acircumflex, Key_atilde, Key_adiaeresis, Key_aring, Key_ae, Key_ccedilla, Key_egrave, Key_eacute, Key_ecircumflex, Key_ediaeresis, Key_igrave, Key_iacute, Key_icircumflex, Key_idiaeresis, Key_eth, Key_ntilde, Key_ograve, Key_oacute, Key_ocircumflex, Key_otilde, Key_odiaeresis, Key_division, Key_oslash, Key_ugrave, Key_uacute, Key_ucircumflex, Key_udiaeresis, Key_yacute, Key_thorn, Key_ydiaeresis, Key_unknown
ArrowType	UpArrow, DownArrow, LeftArrow, RightArrow
RasterOp	CopyROP, OrROP, XorROP, NotAndROP, EraseROP= NotAndROP, NotCopyROP, NotOrROP, NotXorROP, AndROP, NotEraseROP=AndROP, NotROP, ClearROP, SetROP, NopROP, AndNotROP, OrNotROP, NandROP, NorROP, LastROP=NorROP

(continued)

Table 6.1   (Continued)

PenStyle	NoPen, SolidLine, DashLine, DotLine, DashDotLine, DashDotDotLine, MPenStyle
PenCapStyle	FlatCap, SquareCap, RoundCap, MPenCapStyle
PenJoinStyle	MiterJoin, BevelJoin, RoundJoin, MPenJoinStyle
BrushStyle	NoBrush, SolidPattern, Dense1Pattern, Dense2Pattern, Dense3Pattern, Dense4Pattern, Dense5Pattern, Dense6Pattern, Dense7Pattern, HorPattern, VerPattern, CrossPattern, BDiagPattern, FDiagPattern, DiagCrossPattern, CustomPattern=24
WindowsVersion	WV_32s, WV_95, WV_98, WV_DOS_based, WV_NT, WV_2000, WV_NT_based
TextFormat	PlainText, RichText, AutoText

QT EXTENSIONS

The Qt extensions lie outside the core functionality supported by the vendor. This does not mean that Troll won't support the extensions if you spot a bug, but Troll offers no formal warranties to their portability or functionality on a given platform. The following information provides an overview of the extensions, and brief examples of how they are used.

OpenGL Extension

OpenGL is a 3D rendering API from Silicon Graphics, Inc. (SGI). OpenGL or similar APIs, are available for all the platforms that Qt is available on, but OpenGL provides very little functionality for providing 2D user interface support. Historically, an OpenGL application would have some Motif or MFC code for that purpose. The Qt OpenGL extension serves the same function and permits the Qt programmer to add a 3D rendering view his application—or it permits the OpenGL programmer to add a nice user interface to his rendering application—depending on which side of the 2D/3D fence you're marking territory at the moment.

The Qt OpenGL extension will work quite well with OpenGL, Mesa, GLX, and others, and several useful examples are supplied. As with all of the extensions, you will have to explicitly build the source, and you'll have an extra library to link with if you use the extension.

The following classes are provided by the extension:

- *QGLWidget*—an easy-to-use Qt widget that supports an OpenGL rendering context.
- *QGLContext*—an encapsulation of an OpenGL rendering context.
- *QGLFormat*—specifies the display format and operating parameters of the rendering viewport.

Networking Support

While no formal network protocol support is provided with the Qt toolkit itself, a separate Qt extension is in development at this time. Check the Trolltech Web site for availability.

SUMMARY

The topics covered in this chapter are unrelated to the material in prior or subsequent chapters, and so they received a chapter of their own.

The Qt class defines a large number of constants that would, traditionally, have been relegated to global variables or global constants. Since the Qt class is inherited by most Qt classes, those classes and their subclasses can use these values directly.

While the Trolls have reduced the number of available extensions in the toolkit in favor of making the extensions available as separate libraries, there appears to be a desire on their part to continue the tradition for a little while longer. The only extension that remains from the 1.X and 2.0 releases is the OpenGL widget class.

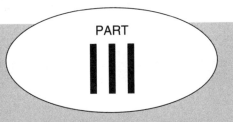

PART

III

Developing Professional Qt Applications

Qt Development Considerations

There is a great deal more to application development than widgets positioned just-so and classes that encapsulate an algorithm or programming concept with grace and style. Most enterprise development projects are driven, at the front-end at least, by a marketing specification that lists features and functions that must appear in the product. That specification is frequently used to create a prototype. After the marketing people "Oooo" and "Ahhh"over the prototype at innumerable dog-and-pony shows (be thankful that programmers usually don't have to attend these), a revised marketing specification is generated.

There are usually two paths followed from this part of the cycle; either a detailed specification is chiseled into a stone tablet or a set of Microsoft PowerPoint presentation slides (I hate these), or a repeated cycle of create, test, review and revise begins. This latter approach is sometimes referred to as the "iterative approach" (named for the numerous iterations projects evolve through) and is usually the most productive. Either way, you'll have a set of goals for the end product that probably include international distribution criteria, target platform restrictions, size and performance targets, all in addition to the functional requirements.

The following subjects attempt to discuss some of these topics in a Qt-relevant manner.

INTERNALIZATION

There are many reasons to add internationalization support (I18N) to a new or existing project. The project may have a written requirement for support of U.S. English and Canadian French, or perhaps you can foresee a future requirement for distribution in countries other than your own. Whatever the reason, the Qt toolkit provides some I18N mechanisms that are so easy to use it makes sense to implement an internationalized application whether the specification calls for it or not, simply because it expands the useable audience for your application. Existing Qt applications can be retrofitted to include I18N support with relatively little difficulty.

You've probably seen examples of source code with embedded strings. These embedded strings can take several different forms. For example, the following code fragments demonstrate two very common methods of embedding a hard-coded string into an application:

```
...
// I've actually seen this error message:
#define EMSG0001 "Bad treeout in do_relop"
...
    fprintf( stderr, "%s\n", EMSG0001 );
...
    QLabel *l = new QLabel( "Enter Password:", this );
...
```

These methods of embedding strings in an application are very common. Conventional methods of internationalizing code like this example are tedious and time-consuming. The programmer must add calls to (platform-dependent!) translator methods, as in the following code fragment:

```
...
    /*** Set up for I18N support ***/
    setlocale( LC_ALL, "" );
    if( XSupportsLocale() ) {
        XtSetLanguageProc(NULL, (XtLanguageProc)myProc, NULL);
    }
    msgCatalog = catopen( CATALOG_NAME, 0 );
...
    char *msg = catmsg( S_HELLO, "Hello World" );
...
```

Adding translation support to an existing project can be more than time-consuming, it can be downright discouraging, especially when schedules are being pushed back, deadlines are being missed, and your marketing department is asking for hourly progress reports.

Qt's QObject and QApplication classes provide functions that simplify the output translations portion of the internationalization effort, either at the point of implementation or for legacy Qt applications. Consider the following example of noninternationalized and internationalized implementations of a simple QLabel widget:

```
...
    // Non I18N label
    QLabel *l = new QLabel( "Hello World", this );
...
    // I18N-enabled label
    QLabel *l = new QLabel( tr("Hello World"), this );
...
```

This is not all there is to it, of course, and it doesn't address the complications revolving around user input, but it helps to demonstrate the ease of converting legacy Qt applications and the ease of adding I18N support during the initial implementation.

The following rules will help ensure that your application is as language-independent as possible.

Use QString

Since Qt's QString class implements text internally as Unicode, and since all Qt objects (except for those that explicitly operate on char * values) accept QString arguments, an internationalized application should experience no performance hit as a direct result of having added I18N support.

Always use QString objects to store all user-visible text. QString stores its text as Unicode text internally and can therefore handle virtually any encoding currently in use. It is easy to use, and it provides shared string storage, automatic storage, and more. Examples:

```
...
    QString *s = new QString( tr("Last Name:") );
...
```

Although a more practical example is:

```
...
    // Open a file—who knows what's in it
    QFile f( "/Program Files/Acme/Anvil/config.nfo" );
    f.open( IO_ReadOnly );

    // Associate the file with a stream
    QTextStream *stream = new QTextStream( &f );

    // Read one line (strips whitespace)
    QString s = stream->readLine();

    // Loop to EOF
    while( s.isNull() == false ) {
        // add it to our listBox if not a blank line
        if( s.isEmpty() == false ) myList->insertItem( s );
```

```
            // Read another line
            s = stream->readLine();
    }
    // Close the file
    f.close();
    delete stream;
...
```

You don't need to use QString for string literals that the user will never see, such as those you provide for class names or object instance names. To do so offers no advantages.

QObject::tr()

Qt provides simple translation of a text object from the native (reference) language to some other corresponding text object. This is accomplished via the QApplication::translate() method or, more conveniently, using the QObject::tr() method. Qt uses a proprietary format for the translated message files, and utilities are provided to make the process of adding language support painless. An example is probably the fastest way to demonstrate just how easy it is to add new language support.

Use QObject::tr() for string literals or QApplication::translate() directly. Here are some examples:

```
    // If this is a member function of a class derived
    // from QObject
    QLabel *l = new QLabel( tr("Customer Number:"), this );
...
    // If this is a member function of a class that is NOT
    // derived from QObject, use another object that is
    QLabel *l = new QLabel( myWidget::tr("Enter ID:"), this );

    // Or use QApplication::translate() directly
    QLabel *ll = new QLabel( this );
    ll->setText( QApplication::translate("Enter ID:"), this );
```

The following example is a "Hello World" program example, written in U.S. English but hard-coded to use a Spanish translation. We'll take the example, a step at a time, beginning with the actual source code:

```
#include <qapplication.h>
#include <qtranslator.h>
#include <qlabel.h>

class HiLabel : public QLabel
{
public:
    HiLabel( QWidget *p=0, const char *n=0 );
};
```

```
HiLabel::HiLabel( QWidget *p, const char *n )
: QLabel( p, n )
{
    // Hard-coded default string, translated text
    setText( tr( "Hello World" ) );
}

int
main( int argc, char **argv )
{
    QApplication *app = new QApplication( argc, argv );

    // Create a new translator
    QTranslator xlat = QTranslator( 0 );

    // Load the Spanish translation
    xlat.load( "Hello_sp.qm", "." );

    // Install the new translator
    app->installTranslator( xlat );

    // Create a translated label
    HiLabel *l = new HiLabel();

    app->setMainWidget( l );
    return( app->exec() );
}
```

The above call to QObject::tr() is where the actual translation takes place. A translation table file that contains an appropriate translation from our U.S. English example is still required and will be loaded at runtime by the QTranslator instance created in main().

Three utilities are provided with Qt to assist in creating the translation table files. These are *findtr*, *msg2qm*, and *mergetr*. The .po translation files can be created by hand, but it's much easier to use the utilities. Each is discussed below.

findtr UTILITY

The *findtr* program (actually a Perl script) can locate all calls to tr(const char *) within the named input files and will generate a text table that can be hand-edited to include the string translations. Typically, you will create a single translation file using a syntax something like:

```
findtr hello.cpp > hello_sp.po
```

This creates a baseline translation file that can be copied to sensibly-named files for each of the target languages (e.g., hello_sp.po for a Spanish file). Using the hello program above, *findtr* will generate some header information which helps to identify the translation file and the version of the *findtr* utility that was used to generate it. It will also generate the following entry:

```
...

#: hello.cpp:15
msgid "HiLabel::Hello World"
msgstr ""
```

The actual table entries are made up of a *msgid* and *msgstr* pair. You can easily identify the required translation from the *msgid* value, but don't translate the entire text of the *msgid* value, as the scoping information (required by the QApplication::translate() method) is included. Assuming our target language is Spanish, the following fragment of hello_sp.po is a hand-edited Spanish translation for the example:

```
...

#: hello.cpp:15
msgid "HiLabel::Hello World"
msgstr "Hola Mundo"
```

We are now ready to create the platform-independent binary message file with the *msg2qm* utility.

msg2qm UTILITY

Once you have used the *findtr* utility to create the baseline translation table and completed the task of translating all the strings, you are ready to create the platform-independent Qt message files for the target languages. This is done using the *msg2qm* utility that can be found under the src/util directory in the Qt distribution. For some bizarre reason, the default Qt build process will compile the *findtr* utility (which you don't need) and install it in the bin directory of the Qt distribution—but the *msg2qm* (which you *do* need) and *mergetr* utilities must be explicitly compiled from their source directory, src/util.

To create the Spanish message file for the preceding example, simply execute the utility as follows:

```
msg2qm hello_sp.po hello_sp.qm
```

The *msg2qm* utility converts the human readable translation file into an internal format that can be read more quickly. When you execute the example program, it will now display in Spanish.

mergetr UTILITY

As you make changes or additions to your application, you will probably need to change your translation files accordingly. To do so, you can simply run the *findtr* utility again to create a new baseline translation file, then use the *mergetr* utility to merge the changes into your existing language-specific translation files. This will recreate the target translation file with comments about the changes.

Once you've edited the new translation files, you can use the *msg2qm* utility to create the Qt message files that QTranslator expects.

```
findtr hello.cpp > hello.po  # create a new base
```

(Edit hello.po, making any required changes or additions.)

```
mergetr hello.po hello_sp.po
msg2qm hello_sp.po hello_sp.qm
```

It's a good idea to maintain the translation files with a good version control system such as RCS, CVS, Microsoft VSS, or whatever you prefer. This is especially true during the initial implementation, when the project is subject to major feature changes. It is very easy to lose track of which translation files are appropriate for a given release of the application.

INPUT METHODS

Of course, Qt doesn't address *all* the complex issues involved in internationalized application development. The underlying window system must take responsibility for much of the low-level functionality. This is especially true in the case of keyboard input methods. Very few companies have the resources that are required to provide a comprehensive set of input methods, but because Qt is so widely accepted by the Linux community, there are an ever-increasing number of freely available implementations.

Those languages with unidirectional single-byte encodings (European Latin1 and KOI8-R, etc.) and the unidirectional multibyte encodings (East Asian EUC-JP, EUC-KR, etc.) are directly supported. Support for "complex" encodings—those that may require right-to-left input or complex character composition (e.g., Arabic, Hebrew, and Thai script)—will probably be implemented in a later release.

The following list is the (more or less) current state of encodings support (assuming your OS doesn't provide the support already, as is the case with Linux):

- Microsoft Windows—The local encoding is always supported.
- ISO standard encodings—ISO 8859-1, ISO 8859-2, ISO 8859-3, ISO 8859-4, ISO 8859-5, ISO 8859-7, ISO 8859-9, and ISO 8859-15 are fully supported.

- Arabic (ISO 8859-6-I) and Hebrew (ISO 8859-8-I) encodings are not supported, but are under development by third parties.
- KOI8-R is fully supported.
- EUC-JP is fully supported.
- EUC-KR is fully supported (thanks to Mizzi Research, Inc.).
- Big5—Qt contains a Big5 codec developed by Ming Che-Chuang. Testing is under way with the xcin (2.5.x) XIM server.
- "Simplified" Chinese—currently unsupported.
- EUC-TW—Under external development.

You should have no trouble working with the proprietary input methods such as those provided with HP/UX locale packages, unless you require the functionality of XIM protocol revision 4.0, as HP still provides version 3.5.

Qt makes it much easier to code internationalization support into any application— even existing Qt projects that weren't originally coded "properly." Having added language translation support to an existing medium-scale project (there is virtually no input other than via mouse), I learned an important lesson: Add language translation support (at least) whether the specification calls for it or not. It's easy; there is no noticeable performance hit, and you just might save yourself a few hours of future time, because you never know when you'll be told your project is going to ship to a foreign country.

At the cost of "plugging" my employer's products, I think it's worth noting that Hewlett-Packard and most other large UNIX vendors market PS/2 keyboards (with mini-DIN connectors) that sport language-specific keycaps. At the expense of plugging a competitor's products, IBM sells PS/2 keyboards with detachable keycap sets for various languages. These will work on most Intel-based Linux implementations, although you will still need to provide some form of input method, or maybe just a custom keyboard configuration for your X server. Contact your favorite vendor for pricing on specialized keyboards, but don't expect a lot of vendor support for that keyboard on Linux.

PLATFORM-INDEPENDENT PROJECTS

There are several schools of thought regarding the creation and maintenance of project build scripts. On Linux (or other UNIX-like) platforms, developers are already comfortable with the Makefile format. These Makefiles are often created on demand by a configure script that is either a highly customized shell, Perl, or Tcl script, or the product of a GNU *autoconf* script. Developers on Microsoft Windows platforms are usually more comfortable with a Visual C++ project or workspace file. This creates yet another platform-dependency barrier that is separate from other platform dependencies.

Tmake UTILITY

Trolltech has addressed this issue with a free utility called *Tmake*. *Tmake* is a Perl script that reads a platform-independent project description file (usually with a .pro suffix) and creates a platform-dependent Makefile or Visual C++ project (.dsp suffix) file. The *Tmake* utility is provided as a binary for Windows platforms, so as a developer you don't need to be a Perl expert to use it. *Tmake* comes bundled with HTML documentation, some commonly needed template files, and another utility, *progen*, that will automatically create a very simple *Tmake* project file from C++ source and header files it finds in the current directory and its subdirectories.

Copies of the October 1999 snapshot of *Tmake* 1.4 for Linux (other Un*xes as well) and Microsoft Windows are included on the CD that comes with this book. It should take you about thirty minutes to become fluent in its use. You will probably consider those thirty minutes well spent as this utility makes any development project easier to manage.

Tmake can be modified to suit a specific need, but Windows developers will need to get a copy of Perl for Windows to do so.

OBJECT REUSE CONSIDERATIONS

Veteran C++ programmers can probably skip this chapter—it is little more than a brief overview of basic design considerations for programmers who will be creating reusable tools based on Qt.

One of the most common reasons for using an object-oriented language is the object reuse implications associated with polymorphic mysticism. The Trolls have demonstrated a consistent policy of making the Qt toolkit objects recyclable in a predictable manner (i.e., you don't usually need to look at the documentation or the headers to determine what you need to override to accomplish a given task).

Most C++ developers eventually acquire a skill for spotting the reusable pieces of code they produce. A much smaller subset of these developers can actually make their code reusable *by other developers*. This is no small accomplishment to be certain. It is the nature of almost every developer to declare "This would be so much better if only. . . ." There is certainly nothing wrong with that attitude, but if the developer takes it so far as to reimplement the entire platform SDK, their projects will never be completed!

There are entire books and even courses of study devoted to this topic. While there is no magic rule that will guarantee immediate adoption of your new XYZ widget, there are some simple guidelines that will help you produce consistent results that your users feel comfortable in using.

Keep It Simple and to the Point

A good object design exposes only those methods required to make it perform all its intended functions. Adding extra or off-topic features, especially features that are not likely to be used very often, will result in an unprofessional, "hacked" appearance. A simple interface often implies a simple—and therefore *reliable*—implementation.

An object's methods should accept a simple and obvious set of arguments. A user of the object should never have to scratch his head, wondering why a method needs a particular piece of unrelated information.

Default values should be used whenever a known value will be used more than half the time. Don't provide a default value if any combination of all the arguments, combined with your default value, can break the implementation. When in doubt, provide no default value.

Always Consider Performance . . .

. . . but avoid *obsession* with performance.

A large number of projects have been scrapped in their entirety because little or no regard was given to performance in the early design stages. Virtual functions are great, but there is a very real performance and resource cost associated with their runtime management. Careful consideration of how an object will be used can help prevent unnecessary performance (or even resource) issues later on in the development cycle.

If you can see no reason to ever change the behavior of a particular method, don't declare it virtual. Your users will let you know whether you need to revisit that part of your design.

If a given method can be implemented in one or two lines, doesn't need to be virtual, and doesn't need to hide the implementation from the users, consider making it an inline function. (I point this out because I just realized a seventy percent performance increase in an old utility program—just by inlining one of the frequently called methods.)

Know Your Compiler

While not exactly necessary, and somewhat difficult to acquire, a solid understanding of what the compiler is going to do with the code you write will almost certainly result in a product that is well behaved and robust. At the very least, a fundamental understanding of what will happen at compile-time vs. what will happen at runtime is essential.

If you've ever seen a library routine that accepts the *value* of a (possibly large) structure as an argument, then you have seen code written by someone who doesn't understand what the compiler will do with the code. While more advanced compilers can compensate for some of these errors in judgment, no compiler is completely foolproof. Any book on compiler design is a wise investment.

Assume Nothing

Always initialize private and global data to reasonable values. Just because your *Acme Millennium Edition, Deluxe C++ Compiler* will guarantee that all uninitialized pointers will be NULL at runtime doesn't mean that this same compiler will be used throughout the lifetime of the product.

Always check the return from the *new* operator with a subsequent call to the Qt CHECK_PTR() macro. A bug in an object's constructor or a resource or quota problem can be very difficult to locate otherwise. The following example demonstrates a possible convention to use.

```
...
Qlabel *l = new QLabel( this );
CHECK_PTR( l );
...
```

Use Slots For Exposed void-return Methods

Declaring an access specifier on a class method as "<access> slots:" has no associated performance cost if the method is called as a normal class method. There is a very small resource cost incurred within the text (or code) segment, and a very minor performance cost if the method is invoked via emit. Since the signal/slot mechanism is totally independent of the GUI event loop, the use of signals and slots doesn't mean your object must be used in a GUI application.

Consider the following code fragment:

```
class MyObject : public QObject
{
Q_OBJECT
public:
MyObject( QObject *p=0 );
const QString &text();
void nonSlotSetText( const QString &s ) { data = s; }

public slots:
void setText( const QString &s ) { data = s; }
private:
QString data;
};
```

In this example, the nonSlotSetText() method will perform no better (or worse) than the setText() slot method, when called as a normal class method. The only real difference is that the nonSlotSetText() method cannot be connected to another object's signal. Therefore, it makes sense to expose reusable components' public or protected void-return methods as slots, whether you can foresee a need to connect them to a signal or not.

DYNAMIC AND STATIC LINKAGE

Almost every modern operating system has adopted the concept of *dynamic* (or shared) libraries of routines. On Linux platforms, these are usually denoted by a .so.Major.Minor suffix on an executable file, reminiscent of the Sun Microsystems naming convention. On other UNIX-like platforms, a .sl suffix, or a trailing _s.a convention is used. On Microsoft Windows, a .dll suffix is in fashion.

Whatever the naming convention used for your shared library mechanisms, the concept is the same: A single text segment (code segment on Windows) image of each library routine is loaded into memory and shared by all applications that make use of the routines. Each application will have a private stack and heap segment, so local variables within the library routines are safe from modification by another process using the same libraries. This mechanism can save a great deal of memory when compared with the *static* linkage model, in which every copy of an application that uses the library routines has a completely separate copy of each library routine. The choice seems obvious, and many developers don't look beyond the obvious disk-image size difference of the linked executable. There are some serious considerations that need to be made, however, before committing to a shared library deployment of a project.

Big Programs

A statically linked program will be *big*. It will have a much larger filesystem footprint, and it will use a lot more memory when executed. With few exceptions, each successive invocation will use just as much memory as the first. Some compilers will permit runtime sharing of certain sections of an application, completely aside from the shared library mechanisms, but these are uncommon.

Static programs are very compatible. A well-behaved, static application will yield very few support calls.

Compatibility

As almost every Microsoft Windows user, IT professional, or developer will testify, version conflicts between releases of a shared library are a serious support headache. Most Linux developers have experienced shared library incompatibilities as well, though Linux has traditionally maintained an advantage in addressing this issue, and a developer usually won't panic when she sees an error message, as end-users often do. Windows 2000 greatly reduces the risk of incompatibility problems—for Windows 2000-specific projects. Legacy projects may still experience problems, however.

Trolltech frequently releases new versions of the Qt toolkit—about every six months or so. These releases are not always binary-compatible, although Troll is very good about warning the consumer of potential conflicts. Even so, your dynamically linked application, with its small memory and filesystem footprint, is dependent on specific library routines that may (or will) one day be replaced with a version that is going to break your application.

Possible Solutions

These two problems can be managed in a number of ways. Each has advantages and disadvantages, and you are left to decide what is best for your unique circumstances.

Configuration Management

Within production environments, a conscientious IT management staff can institute comprehensive configuration management (CM) policies that prevent the installation of shared material until it has passed an approved battery of compatibility testing. This will prove sufficient in most cases, but introduces severe limitations on the installation of new or updated software since all changes have to be approved by the IT department. That usually takes a very long time.

Development environments should match the end-user environment as closely as possible to avoid costly delays that result from oversights in shared resource version control. This implies the same restrictions on installation of new software and updates as the production environment, although a development team usually has more flexibility in this regard.

The testing and quality-control environments should be maintained by the IT staff, with all the restrictions of the production environment. There may be additional restrictions imposed by the IT staff, relating to network access, access to critical production data repositories, and other critical resources.

Total Static Linkage

Total static linkage is achieved by linking only to the static versions of all the libraries an application uses. While complete static linkage of an application is usually frowned on by developers and IT professionals alike, there are some clear advantages that should be weighed against the resource costs:

- A statically linked application will never experience a shared library version mismatch failure or a library incompatibility issue. Ever.
- A completely static linkage application can be run on any binary-compatible system without installing additional support libraries, so dependency tracking is a simple task, and little regard need be given to target environment.
- When your application is the only application that will use its library's routines, and only one instance of that application is likely to execute at a time, a statically linked version will use *fewer* system resources than a dynamically linked version, and startup time will be significantly reduced. Remember, there is system overhead involved in shared library management.

Mixed Static/Dynamic Linkage

This is a fairly common tradeoff, used by many vendors to reduce the risk of compatibility issues, while providing some of the benefits associated with dynamic linkage. It involves statically linking the application with any libraries that aren't *guaranteed* to be present on the target platform, and dynamically linking with libraries that can safely be assumed to exist on the target platform. The Netscape product family uses this approach with a large degree of success. Communicator was traditionally provided in two varieties for many flavors of UNIX systems: dynamic or static Motif linkage. The base C library was dynamically linked in either.

The tradeoff is, of course, increased compatibility and decreased interdependency for a corresponding increase in system resource utilization.

Nobody will be able to tell you which model is best or appropriate for your targeted end-users. You must determine that for yourself with existing infrastructures playing a key role in the determination process. If your target audience is a "shareware" or "freeware" release of a product, compatibility should be your primary concern. If your users live in a shielded, IT "bubble," you can likely try to save as many resources as possible.

DEBUGGING PROJECTS

A safe definition for "software bug" is: *any behavior of the software that deviates from the end-user's expectation.* That's a very broad statement, but it embodies the only aspect of the entire software development cycle that really matters—meeting or exceeding your end-user's expectations. Any software—be it a GUI CD player, a system administration utility, a network service daemon, or a power grid control application—is created to serve some purpose. That purpose may have been mandated by a detailed and well-planned specification, or it may have been the result of a half-baked, chocolate and caffeine-induced epiphany, implemented to the chainsaw harmonies of Nine Inch Nails. Whatever the source of the software's purpose, an end-user will have some expectations regarding the behavior of the software based almost entirely on her perception of its purpose. If those expectations are not met, your software has a bug. It may be a documentation bug, or it may be a software logic flaw that causes a total power blackout in New York City. Either way, the end-user's expectation has not been met.

As a software developer, you will eventually become involved in the support process that is associated with every software project. Not every developer is a skilled or experienced troubleshooter, and there is no short path to becoming one. However, if you follow these basic steps when attempting to solve an end-user problem, the chances that you will be successful are greatly improved:

- Get an accurate description of the problem. This is the most important and usually the most difficult step. It is especially difficult to get a good problem description when dealing with users who have little or no technical training. Please remember, the use of torture in extracting a problem description violates several international treaties.

- Once the user has given you a description that you feel may be adequate, repeat his description back to him and ask him to confirm or correct your version of his description. This will eliminate almost all communication problems.

- If you are not certain how this impacts his work, ask him. This has two goals: it will help you prioritize the tasks involved in a solution, and it indicates to the user that you understand his entire problem—the way *he* sees it. If you already know the impact to the user, tell the user what you believe the impact to be and ask him to verify it. The user may add you to his Last Will and Testament or send you a case of beer—at the very least, he will be more cooperative.

- Try to determine whether the user can reproduce the problem he has described. If possible, get the user to write the procedure down or send it to you via e-mail.
- If it's a complex problem, or the user is unable to describe the problem, try to reach a mutual agreement with the end-user as to what the solution will "look like." The purpose is to get an accurate description of what this user *expects*.

Obviously, this is a rather formal approach to support methodology, and many developers will never speak to an end-user because these developers are lucky enough to have a separate end-user support organization—or they develop only for other developers, who will quietly solve the problem themselves and later take full credit for all the work.

Documentation and Training Bugs

I define *documentation defects* as any visual cue associated with the software that causes the end-user to expect something that the software is not intended to deliver. It can be as simple as the use of inappropriate/confusing icons, or misleading program names that the user will see. It can be as complicated as a blatantly inaccurate user manual written by a technical writer who recently died of acute dyslexia. If you choose to name your latest e-mail application "cd_player," you have an obvious documentation defect.

Documentation defects are usually easy to detect, and often just as easy to correct. After you have corrected the documentation problems, you may still be left with a training problem. If you were tenacious enough to create detailed documentation for your project, and you were fortunate enough to get your users to read that documentation, your users have been trained with defective material. It may take a lot of effort to get those users to read the corrected literature, and you will probably have to keep answering questions until they do.

Training bugs can be caused by defects in a formal classroom-training program, defects in documentation, or misinterpretation of either by the end-user. In addition, a user may have developed an incorrect expectation from prior experiences with legacy or other similar software. As stated above, documentation defects are easy to correct. Formal training defects are usually easy to correct as well. User misinterpretation, if it occurs on a large scale, usually indicates a documentation or training defect—even when the entire development staff is convinced otherwise.

User Perception Defects

Software defect reports or enhancement requests will often be subjective in nature. If the user is complaining that the XYZ gadget is too <small, big, bright, dark, blurry, clear, etc.>, and many other users think it's fine as is, it would be a bad idea to change the software to meet this user's expectation, because it is nearly certain that it's her *expectation* that's defective. You can usually discourage such reports by giving the user a large stack of carefully designed (and impossible to complete) "Software Specification Committee, Request for Formal Hearing to Discuss Potential Change" forms to fill out.

If a large number of users are making similar complaints, it probably indicates a design defect. These are easy to correct, but a developer will need to exercise caution when addressing complaints based on purely subjective detail.

Software Defects

A software defect can be defined as any software behavior that deviates from the design. The software may be dumping core (Linux and friends) or causing "Dr. Watson" dialogs to pop up, or the software may be adding two plus two and calculating a sum of three. Sometimes, software defects are easy to correct. Other times, a developer can spend weeks trying to track a specific problem down.

Bugs that aren't detected during the initial testing or beta release phases of the development cycle are usually more difficult to correct—both in terms of debugging/correction, and the imminent redeployment of the software that usually results.

If you haven't already, please read the online Qt documentation for debugging techniques. Qt provides some useful mechanisms to assist in problem solving.

Since every developer has her own idea of the "best" way to debug a software defect, I'll offer mine to those who have little experience. If one is inappropriate or fails to detect the problem, try another. It may take a long time, but every problem can be solved.

Defect Event Capture

Capture the details of what takes place as, or just before, the defect occurs. This is an obvious first step in the debugging process. You can temporarily add hard-coded print statements, use the qDebug() macro, or add ASSERT() macro statements. It helps a great deal to have a complete understanding of what is taking place within your code when the problem(s) occur. It is my experience that up to ninety-five percent of all software defects can be analyzed and corrected in a matter of minutes using this method.

The following example code represents a possible event logging class that can help you to spot a defect easily and (important for many) remotely. By adding calls to Log::lprint() within your code, you can easily view exactly what worked and what didn't in a postmortem. The class provides millisecond-accuracy timestamps (within the limits of the OS), limited log file size, and log sequence numbers (to help coordinate a support effort over the phone).

```
Log.h

#ifndef _LOG_H
#define _LOG_H

#include <stdio.h>
#include <stdlib.h>
#include <stdarg.h>
#include <qobject.h>
#include <qstring.h>
#include <qfile.h>
```

```
// Simplifies specifying the filename and line number
#define FLI      __FILE__, __LINE__

class Log : public QObject
{
    Q_OBJECT
public:
    enum Sizes { HalfMeg = 524288, OneMeg = 1048576 };

    Log( const QString &file=0, int size=HalfMeg,
        bool stdredir=false );
    virtual ~Log();

    // Usage is identical to printf(3C)
    virtual void  print( const char *fmt, ... );
    // Typically, you'll pass the macro FLI to this method
    // followed by standard printf(3C) arguments
    virtual void  lprint( const char *file, int line,
        const char *fmt, ... );
    // This method will print data to the log without the
    // timestamp and log sequence ID.
    virtual void  raw( const char *fmt, ... );

    // Tests whether the file is open
    bool          isOpen() { return(opensuccess); }
    // Tests whether sequence IDs are enabled
    bool          sequence();

public slots:
    // Flush the buffer stream to the log
    void          flush();
    // Flushes then closes the stream
    void          close();
    // ASCII/hexidecimal data buffer dump
    void          buf_dump( void *buf, int bytes );
    // Enable/disable sequence IDs
    void          setSequence( bool );

protected slots:
    // Called by the ctor
    virtual void  create( const QString &file,
            int size, bool stdredire );

private:
    bool          doseq;
    bool          redir;
    bool          opensuccess;
    QString       fname;
    int           limit;
    QFile        *ofp;
    unsigned long seq;
};
```

```
#endif


Log.cpp

#include <Log.h>
#include <qdatetime.h>
#include <qfile.h>
#ifdef WIN32
#include <io.h>
#endif
#include <ctype.h>

// Ctor: filename, max size, redirect stdout/stderr
Log::Log( const QString &file, int size, bool stdredir )
{
    doseq = true;
    redir = stdredir;
    limit = size;
    opensuccess = false;
    seq = 0L;
    if(strcmp(file, "stderr")) {
        create( file, size, stdredir );
    } else {
        ofp = new QFile();
        ofp->open( IO_WriteOnly, stderr );
        opensuccess = true;
    }
}

// Create file method, rotate log files
void
Log::create( const QString &file, int size, bool stdredir )
{
    if(file != 0) {
        fname = file;
        ofp = new QFile( file );
    } else {
        ofp = new QFile();
        ofp->open( IO_WriteOnly, stderr );
        if(stdredir == true) {
            opensuccess = true;
#ifndef WIN32
            dup2(ofp->handle(), 1);
#else
            _dup2(ofp->handle(), 1);
#endif
        }
        return;
    }

    if(ofp->size() >= limit) {
```

```
            QString nn;
            nn.sprintf("%s.old", file);
#ifndef WIN32
                link(file, nn);
                unlink(file);
#else
                rename( file, nn );
#endif
            if(ofp->open( IO_WriteOnly|IO_Truncate ) == false) {
                opensuccess = false;
                delete ofp;
                ofp = new QFile();
                ofp->open( IO_WriteOnly, stderr );
            } else {
                opensuccess = true;
            }
            if(stdredir == true) {
#ifdef WIN32
                _dup2(ofp->handle(), 1);
                _dup2(ofp->handle(), 2);
#else
                dup2(ofp->handle(), 1);
                dup2(ofp->handle(), 2);
#endif
            }
    } else {
            if(ofp->open( IO_WriteOnly|IO_Append ) == false) {
                opensuccess = false;
                delete ofp;
                ofp = new QFile();
                ofp->open( IO_WriteOnly, stderr );
            } else {
                opensuccess = true;
            }
            if(stdredir == true) {
#ifdef WIN32
                _dup2(ofp->handle(), 1);
                _dup2(ofp->handle(), 2);
#else
                dup2(ofp->handle(), 1);
                dup2(ofp->handle(), 2);
#endif
            }
    }
}

Log::~Log()
{
    ofp->flush();
    ofp->close();
}

void
```

```
Log::raw(const char *fmt, ...)
{
    char p[4096];
    va_list ap;

    if(ofp == 0) return;

    va_start(ap, fmt);
#ifdef _HPUX_SOURCE
    vsprintf(p, fmt, ap);
#endif
#ifdef WIN32
    vsprintf(p, fmt, ap);
#endif
#ifdef LINUX
    vsnprintf(p, 4095, fmt, ap);
    va_end(ap);
#endif

    ofp->writeBlock(p, strlen(p));

    if(ofp->size() >= limit && ofp->handle() != fileno(stderr)) {
        ofp->flush();
        ofp->close();
        create(fname, limit, redir);
    }
}

void
Log::print(const char *fmt, ...)
{
    char p[4096];
    QString buf;
    va_list ap;

    if(ofp == 0) return;
    memset(p, 0, 4096);

    va_start(ap, fmt);
#ifdef _HPUX_SOURCE
    vsprintf(p, fmt, ap);
#endif
#ifdef WIN32
    vsprintf(p, fmt, ap);
#endif
#ifdef LINUX
    vsnprintf(p, 4095, fmt, ap);
    va_end(ap);
#endif

    QDateTime t = QDateTime::currentDateTime();
    if(doseq == true) {
```

```
                        buf.sprintf("%06ld %02d:%02d:%02d.%03ld %02d/%02d: %s",
                                    seq++,
                                    t.time().hour(),
                                    t.time().minute(),
                                    t.time().second(),
                                    t.time().msec(),
                                    t.date().month(),
                                    t.date().day(), p );
        } else {
                buf.sprintf("%02d:%02d:%02d.%03ld %02d/%02d: %s",
                                    t.time().hour(),
                                    t.time().minute(),
                                    t.time().second(),
                                    t.time().msec(),
                                    t.date().month(),
                                    t.date().day(), p );
        }
        ofp->writeBlock(buf, strlen(buf));
        if(ofp != 0 && ofp->size() >= limit &&
                ofp->handle() != fileno(stderr)) {
                ofp->flush();
                ofp->close();
                strcpy(p, fname);
                create((const char *)p, limit, redir);
        }
}

void
Log::lprint(const char *file, int line, const char *fmt, ...)
{
    char p[4096];
    QString buf;
    va_list ap;

    if(ofp == NULL) return;
    memset(p, 0, 4096);

    va_start(ap, fmt);
#ifdef _HPUX_SOURCE
    vsprintf(p, fmt, ap);
#endif
#ifdef WIN32
    vsprintf(p, fmt, ap);
#endif
#ifdef LINUX
    vsnprintf(p, 4095, fmt, ap);
    va_end(ap);
#endif

    QDateTime t = QDateTime::currentDateTime();
    if(doseq == true) {
        buf.sprintf("%06ld %02d:%02d:%02d.%03ld "
```

```
                         "%02d/%02d: (%s:%d) %s",
                              seq++,
                              t.time().hour(),
                              t.time().minute(),
                              t.time().second(),
                              t.time().msec(),
                              t.date().month(),
                              t.date().day(), file, line, p );
        } else {
              buf.sprintf("%02d:%02d:%02d.%03ld "
                         "%02d/%02d: (%s:%d) %s",
                              t.time().hour(),
                              t.time().minute(),
                              t.time().second(),
                              t.time().msec(),
                              t.date().month(),
                              t.date().day(), file, line, p );
        }
        ofp->writeBlock(buf, strlen(buf));
        ofp->flush();
        if(ofp != 0 && ofp->size() >= limit &&
              ofp->handle() != fileno(stderr)) {
              ofp->close();
              strcpy(p, fname);
              create((const char *)p, limit, redir);
        }
}

void
Log::buf_dump(void *data, int len)
{
        size_t a, b;
        unsigned char c, *dat;

        dat = (unsigned char *)data;
        if(!len || len < 0) return;

        raw("  Hexadecimal                               ASCII\n");
        raw("  ------------------------------------------"
              "--------\n");
        raw("  ");
        for(a=0;a<len;a++) {
              c = (unsigned char)dat[a];
              if(a && !(a%8)) raw(" ");
              if(a && !(a%16)) {
                      raw("  [");
                      for(b=a-16;b<a;b++) {
                              c = (unsigned char)dat[b];
                              if(!isspace(dat[b]) &&
                                      isprint(dat[b])) {
                                              raw("%c", c);
                              } else raw("-");
                      } else raw("-");
```

```
                }
                raw("]\n  %02x", c);
            } else {
                raw("%02x", c);
            }
        }
        for(b=a;(b%16);b++) raw("   ");
        raw("   [");
        for(b-=16;b<a;b++) {
            c = (unsigned char)dat[b];
            if(isprint(dat[b])) raw("%c", c);
            else raw("-");
        }
        for(;(b%16);b++) raw(" ");
        raw("]\n");
        raw("   ---------------------------------------------"
            "--------\n");
}

void
Log::flush()
{
    ofp->flush();
}

bool
Log::sequence()
{
    return( doseq );
}

void
Log::setSequence( bool val )
{
    doseq = val;
}

void
Log::close()
{
    ofp->flush();
    ofp->close();
}

#include <Log.moc>
```

This is not a pretty or graceful class, but it does work. Using the Log class is simple.
Create an instance in a superclass of your application in a manner similar to:

```
...
    // Create a global log instance
```

```
log = new Log( ".myapp.log", Log::OneMeg, true );
...

// Scattered about your code...
log->lprint( FLI, "IP: %s\n", (const char *)sock->ip() );

// Dump the structure to the log
log->buf_dump( &db_buffer, sizeof(db_buffer) );
...
```

This will generate lines similar to:

```
...
000127 14:29:27.240 04/16: (Project/ci_con.cpp:254) IP: 11.27.32.3
  Hexadecimal                          ASCII
  --------------------------------------------------
  0000000000000000 0000000000000000   [————]
  0000000000000000 0000000000000000   [————]
  0000000000000000 0000000000000000   [————]
  000000                              [--    ]
  --------------------------------------------------
...
```

The first value in the first line is a sequence ID that increments for each non-raw log entry. The next value is the HH:MM:SS:ms timestamp for the log entry. The next value is the MM/DD (month/day) stamp. Next is the source file name and the line number, followed by the argument output string. The remaining lines are the output of the dump of the db_buffer contents.

Core Dump Analysis (Linux/UNIX only)

If you're lucky, your application has a defect that attempts to violate program memory segmentation constraints. This almost always results in a *core dump,* which will provide virtually all the information you're likely to need to isolate the cause. When such violations occur, the operating system will likely send your application a *signal* that triggers default (or custom) behavior. The default behavior is to dump the contents of the application's memory space, including a stack trace, and perhaps even some information from the OS' system tables (such as the process, user, and file tables) that pertain to this application's runtime environment. Unless you are very knowledgeable, you will not want to override the default handling of these signals. The most common causes of a core dump are:

- Your application explicitly calls the abort(2) system call.
- SIGSEGV—This causes the stderr message "memory fault—core dumped" to be displayed. This is the most common cause of a core dump. Your application has attempted to access or modify a memory address that is not within the software's assigned address space. This is usually the result of uninitialized or NULL pointers, but may very well be caused by the overrun of a fixed length array. A stack trace

will usually show you *where* it detected a problem, but won't necessarily give you any information about *why* it occurred.

- SIGIOT—The stderr message, "illegal instruction—core dumped" will be displayed. Your application has corrupted its own "text" segment—the memory segment assigned to the executing code of this application has been overwritten with instructions that are illegal or that make no sense. This error is almost always caused by an array overrun condition. These defects are often difficult to analyze and correct.

- SIGBUS—A stderr message "bus error—core dumped" is displayed. A method within your application has exhausted its available stack segment. This is almost always caused by runaway recursion—a method has called itself too many times—and each time, the method's arguments (or just the return address) will be pushed onto the stack. Eventually, the software will exceed its quota, or available resources will be exhausted. These defects are usually easy to locate because there should be very few methods in your application that call themselves.

Dr. Watson (Windows only)

NT-based operating systems (this includes Windows 2000) and Windows 98 systems with the *Resource Toolkit* installed have a software fault logging agent called Dr. Watson (presumably named for the fictional character in Sir Arthur Conan Doyle's Sherlock Holmes stories). It will gather and log information pertaining to software faults and the state of the computer at the time the fault occurred. Dr. Watson can generate scripts that a debugger (or other application) can parse to retrieve the details it has logged. Dr. Watson can also take a "snapshot" of the current state of the system as long as Windows is not actually "hung"—a condition where all application and system software is completely unresponsive—a condition that many Windows users surprisingly accept as normal. Go figure.

Dr. Watson does not start in the default (as installed) startup configuration, and usually has to be started manually or by adding a shortcut to the "Startup" folder. To start Dr. Watson manually, select the Start menu, click on "Run" and type in "drwatson" and hit the Enter key (or click OK). Starting Dr. Watson from the "System Information" tool will give you the opportunity to configure the locations for the various files it will create, and various other parameters such as the number of previous instructions executed prior to the fault.

Using A Debugger

It's beyond the scope of this (or any) book to teach the reader how to use every debugger, so I'll stick to very generalized terms and procedures. Your debugger should have plenty of documentation that explains how to perform these procedures.

If you can easily reproduce a software defect, and the defect causes abnormal termination of the software, you can save yourself some time by recompiling the software with the compiler's debugging option(s) enabled. Next, start your debugger and load/-execute the software. When you reproduce the defect, a stack trace should clearly indicate where the defect is *detected* within the source code. The point where the error actually occurs will require inspection of the code. You may need to set breakpoints and step through the code's execution, but that is seldom necessary and usually time-consuming.

Intermittent defects require a great deal more work and require a very clear problem description. You will have to analyze every line in the code that can possibly result in the reported behavior. You may find other defects that haven't been reported during this process, so don't consider the time completely wasted.

RAPID APPLICATION DEVELOPMENT

Face it: Creating large, complicated dialog screens is a tedious chore, no matter what platform you're developing for or what toolkit you're using to get the job done. Qt is no exception. While a future Qt product may include a "what you see is what you get" (WYSIWYG) dialog editor and code generator, the current releases don't. All the same, there are several useable RAD utilities available from developers that have been kind enough to make their work available to the public. The following pages describe their current feature sets and all are available via links from the Troll Web site at www.trolltech.com.

While Troll does not currently provide a WYSIWYG builder, it is likely that they'll include one in some future release. You shouldn't let that discourage you from creating your own or modifying one of the editors mentioned below to suit your needs. The following are just a few of the IDEs and WYSIWYG editors available for Qt.

Qt Architect

This is my favorite, just because it's the one I began working with first and because it does most of the things I needed such a tool to do (and there is a binary for Windows). Your mileage may vary. As of this writing, Qt Architect supports most of the functionality of Qt version 2.0.2, so no native support is available for the QCanvas or QDial widgets—although you can add native support using Qt Architect's Widget Modules feature. The Qt Architect authors are very good at updating the software and seem dedicated to making a comprehensive product. It's reasonable to assume that in the time it takes to read this far in this book, the authors will have a version ready for Qt 2.1 functionality.

Qt Architect supports both layout and hard-coded geometry for widgets that are added to a dialog. Multiple dialogs can be edited simultaneously and grouped together in project-fashion. Each dialog is created as a separate set of files for the dialog parameters and source code. The dialog project files are saved as XML. (See Fig. 7.1.)

QtEZ

QtEZ is more of a complete IDE than Qt Architect, but is reliant on KDE development tools and libraries, making a port to the Windows platform difficult.

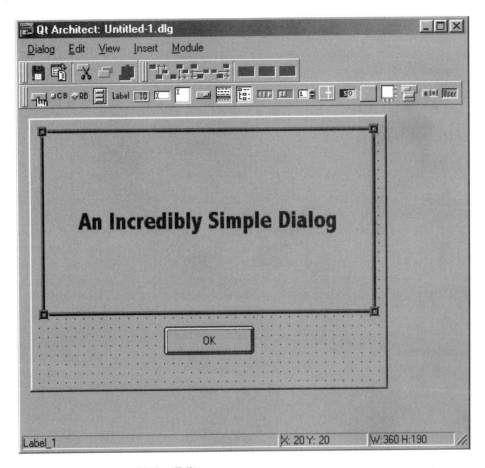

Figure 7.1   Qt Architect's Dialog Editor.

KDevelope

If you do most of your work in a UNIX environment (as I do), you will want to take a look at what the KDevelope environment offers. This IDE promises to become the standard IDE for Linux platforms. It supports development for KDE, Qt, C++, or C applications, provides "wizards" for framework generation, and the usual array of C++ development tools such as class browsers, language savvy editors, and the like.

Windows developers are not likely to see a binary for Windows platforms.

Ebuilder

Ebuilder is another WYSIWYG GUI editor; its best feature is undoubtedly its hierarchical widget view of the project being edited. Projects are application-oriented instead of the dialog-oriented approach of Qt Architect, making it more like the ground-up editors that many Motif programmers will remember.

Another nice feature of Ebuilder is the Member Function View that makes it easy to add member functions to a widget you're designing. You can also add additional include files for external code. You will see how important that is when you begin adding your own code to that generated by Ebuilder.

No Ebuilder binary was available for Windows at this writing.

SUMMARY

There are a great many other considerations related to application development, but they aren't affected by a choice to use the Qt toolkit and were therefore left out of this discussion. If you subscribe to the qt-interest mailing list, you will hear a lot of discussion on these unrelated topics. Those discussions are usually discouraged by the vigilant Trolls who tend to keep discussions on-topic.

For discussions on source code management, software licensing practices, and all the many other topics, there are dedicated newsgroups that discuss nothing else.

CHAPTER

8

Windows 2000 Topics

I have heard Windows developers claim that Qt isn't capable of interfacing with other Windows applications. This chapter, as does much of the material that precedes it, should help to dispel that myth. Throughout this book, I have intermixed Windows and Linux development terms because, to put it simply and correctly, Qt doesn't care what platform you use. Everything in this book, except when noted otherwise, applies to both platforms. That does not mean that Windows and Linux are the same. Microsoft Windows has features that don't translate well to features on UNIX platforms (and vice-versa). This chapter is devoted exclusively to Windows issues and provides examples of Qt programming for Windows-dependent functionality.

It *can* be a little difficult to perform some of the more extreme platform-dependent tasks—such as adding a systray icon for your application—but it can be done. The following examples make use of some extremely Windows-dependent functionality that many developers are likely to encounter.

DDE SERVER CLASS

Turning your Windows Qt application into a DDE server is as easy as it is nonportable. The following example class provides a very simple DDE Execute server.

```
DDE Execute Server—dde.h

#ifndef __DDE_H_
#define __DDE_H_
#include <qwidget.h>
#include <qlist.h>
#include <qstring.h>
#include <windows.h>
#include <ddeml.h>
#include <tchar.h>


// DdeTopics store a function/handle pair
// DdeExecutes search a list of these for a topic and
// execute the function which returns true for ACK or
// false for others.
class DdeTopic
{
public:
    DdeTopic( bool (*func)( const char * ), HSZ name )
            { hConv = NULL, fun = func, topica = name; }
    HSZ    topic() { return( topica ); }
    void   setConversation( HCONV h ) { hConv = h; }
    HCONV  conversation() { return( hConv ); }
    bool (*function())( const char * ) { return( fun ); }

private:
    bool (*fun)(const char *);
    HSZ topica;
    HCONV hConv;
};


class DdeServer : public QObject
{
    Q_OBJECT
public:
    DdeServer( QString &svc_name );
    virtual ~DdeServer();
    void        insertTopic( bool (*func)( const char * ),
                    const char *name );

signals:
    void        execute( void * );

private:
    DWORD       idInst;
    HINSTANCE   hinst;
    HSZ         svc;
};


#endif // __DDE_H_



DDE Execute Server—dde.cpp
```

```
#include <Dde.h>

static QList<DdeTopic> topics;

static HDDEDATA CALLBACK
Callback( UINT wType, UINT wFmt, HCONV hConv, HSZ hsz1,
    HSZ hsz2, HDDEDATA hDDEData, DWORD dwData1,
    DWORD dwData2 )
{
    DdeTopic *p;
    DWORD len;
    bool (*fun)(const char *);
    const char *s;

  switch (wType)
  {
    case XTYP_REGISTER:
    case XTYP_UNREGISTER:
      return( (HDDEDATA)false );

    case XTYP_ADVDATA:
      return( (HDDEDATA)DDE_FACK );

    case XTYP_XACT_COMPLETE:
      return( (HDDEDATA)false );

    case XTYP_DISCONNECT:
      return( (HDDEDATA)false );

    case XTYP_EXECUTE:
      s = (const char *)DdeAccessData( hDDEData,
        &len );
        for(p=topics.first();p!=0;p=topics.next()) {
        if(p->topic() == hsz1) {
          fun = p->function();
          if( fun( s ) == true )
            return( (HDDEDATA)DDE_FACK );
          else
            return((HDDEDATA)DDE_FNOTPROCESSED);
        }
      }
      return( (HDDEDATA)DDE_FNOTPROCESSED );

    case XTYP_CONNECT:
      for(p=topics.first();p!=0;p=topics.next()) {
        if(p->topic() == hsz1) {
          p->setConversation( hConv );
          return( (HDDEDATA)true );
        }
      }
      return( (HDDEDATA)false );

    default:
```

```
          return( (HDDEDATA)false );
    }
}

DdeServer::DdeServer( QString &svc_name )
{
    idInst = 0;

    DdeInitialize( &idInst, Callback,
         APPCLASS_STANDARD|CBF_SKIP_ALLNOTIFICATIONS, 0 );

    svc = DdeCreateStringHandle( idInst,
           (const char *)svc_name, CP_WINANSI );

    if(!DdeNameService( idInst, svc, 0,
         DNS_REGISTER|DNS_FILTERON )) {
         // Ctor failed...
    }
}

DdeServer::~DdeServer()
{
    DdeUninitialize( idInst );
}

void
DdeServer::insertTopic( bool (*func)(const char *),
    const char *name )
{
    HSZ n = DdeCreateStringHandle( idInst, name,
         CP_WINANSI );
    topics.append( new DdeTopic( func, n ) );
}

#include <Dde.moc>
```

To use this class in an application, all you need to do is define the functions to be called for a specific topic and instantiate a DdeServer object for the application. Here's a useless sample:

```
#include <qmessagebox.h>
#include <Dde.h>

static bool
myfunc( const char *p )
{
    QMessageBox::information( 0, "DDE Execute", p );
    return( true );
}
...
    dde = new DdeServer( QString("DDESample") );
    dde->insertTopic( myfunc, "TestTopic" );
...
```

This sample will pop up a message box whenever another Windows application performs a DDE Execute to application "DDESample," topic "TestTopic," displaying the client's execute string in the process.

MULTIMEDIA SUPPORT

The following example provides very simple audio support for different types of media. Each of the slots assumes you already determined what type of media is being used (MIDI, WAV, etc.). The class transparently supports the Microsoft SAPI 3.0 TTS (Text To Speech) API calls if the target platform has the SAPI runtime installed. The SAPI SDK is required to build this support into the class, however. You can obtain the SDK from the MSDN Web site—http://www.msdn.microsoft.com.

It should be a simple exercise to add MIME typing support to this class to eliminate the need to know what media type is involved.

```
Audio.h
#ifndef _AUDIO_H
#define _AUDIO_H

#ifndef WIN32
#error
#endif

#include <qwidget.h>
// Avoids the warning caused by lack of #pragma once
#ifdef STRICT
#undef STRICT
#endif

#include <windows.h>
#include <Midi.h>

class Audio : public QObject
{
    Q_OBJECT
public:
    Audio();
    ~Audio();

    enum        { Idle=0, Speech, Midi, Wav };

    int         pitch();
    int         speed();
    int         voice();
    bool        isSpeaking();
    bool        canSpeak() { return(cantalk); }

public slots:
```

```
    void            speak( const char * );
    void            midiPlay( const char * );
    void            wavPlay( const char * );
    void            setPitch( int );
    void            setSpeed( int );
    void            setVoice( int );
    void            properties( QWidget *parent );
    void            pause();
    void            resume();
    void            stop();
    void            repeat();

private:
    int             state;
    LilMidi         *midi;
    WCHAR           spkbuffer[2048];
    char            file[1024];
    bool            cantalk;
};

#endif // _AUDIO_H



Midi.h

#ifndef __MIDI_H__
#define __MIDI_H__

#ifndef WIN32
#error // Only supported on Win32
#endif

#include <qobject.h>
#include <qstring.h>

class LilMidi : public QObject
{
    Q_OBJECT
public:
    LilMidi();
    virtual         ~LilMidi();

    enum            { Stopped=0, Playing, Paused };

    int             tempo();
    int             status();
    int             divisionType();
    bool            open( const QString & );
    bool            seek( unsigned long msec );
    unsigned long pos();

public slots:
```

```
    void        setTempo( int );
    void        close();
    void        play();
    void        stop();
    void        pause();
    void        fastFwd( int sec );
    void        rewind( int sec );

private:
    int         state;
    WORD        device;
    bool        isopen;
};

#endif //__MIDI_H__



Audio.cpp

#include <Audio.h>
#include <string.h>
#include <stdio.h>

// Zap this if you don't want to use the SAPI stuff
#define TTS

#ifdef TTS

#include <mmsystem.h>
#include <initguid.h>
#include <objbase.h>
#include <objerror.h>
#include <ole2ver.h>
#include <spchwrap.h>
#include <qmessagebox.h>

static CTTSMode    *speech;
#endif // TTS

#define GOOFY_MS_GLITCH
#ifdef GOOFY_MS_GLITCH
int errno;
#endif

Audio::Audio()
{
#ifdef TTS
    HRESULT hRes;
    // Initialize Speech
    TTSMODEINFOW mode;
    memset(&mode, 0, sizeof(TTSMODEINFOW));
    speech = NULL;
    memset(file, 0, 1024);
```

```
    memset(spkbuffer, 0, 2048*sizeof(WCHAR));
    state = Idle;
    SetMessageQueue(96);
    CoInitialize(NULL);
    speech = new CTTSMode();
    wcscpy(mode.szSpeaker, L"Mary");
    if((hRes = speech->Init( &mode, NULL )) == NOERROR) {
        cantalk = true;
        QString s = QString( (QChar *)mode.szSpeaker,
            TTSI_NAMELEN );
    } else cantalk = false;
#endif // TTS
    midi = new LilMidi();
}


Audio::~Audio()
{
#ifdef TTS
    if(cantalk == true || speech != NULL) {
        delete speech;
    }
    CoUninitialize();
#endif
    delete midi;
}


int
Audio::pitch()
{
#ifdef TTS
    if(cantalk == false || speech == NULL) return(-1);
#endif
    return( 0 );
}


int
Audio::speed()
{
#ifdef TTS
    if(cantalk == false || speech == NULL) return(-1);
    return( speech->SpeedGet() );
#endif
    return(0);
}


// Pops a dialog with the properties dialog (if supported
// by TTS engine)
void
Audio::properties( QWidget *p )
{
#ifdef TTS
    if(cantalk == false || speech == NULL) return;
    speech->GeneralDlg( p->winId(), L"TTS Properties" );
#endif
```

```
}

int
Audio::voice()
{
#ifdef TTS
    if(cantalk == false || speech == NULL) return(-1);
#endif
    return(0);
}

void
Audio::speak( const char *p )
{
#ifdef TTS
    if(cantalk == false || speech == NULL) return;
    state = Speech;
    memset(spkbuffer, 0, 2048*sizeof(WCHAR));
    QString mqs = QString(p);
    wcsncpy( spkbuffer,
            (WCHAR *)(mqs.unicode()), 1023);
    spkbuffer[strlen(p)] = 0;
    speech->Speak( (PCWSTR)spkbuffer, true, NULL );
#endif
}

void
Audio::midiPlay( const char *p )
{
    state = Midi;

    memset(file, 0, 1024);
    strncpy(file, p, 1023);

    midi->close();
    midi->open( p );
    midi->play();
}

void
Audio::wavPlay( const char *p )
{
    state = Wav;
    memset(file, 0, 1024);
    strncpy(file, p, 1023);
    PlaySound( file, NULL, SND_ASYNC|SND_FILENAME );
}

void
Audio::setPitch( int v )
{
}

void
```

```
Audio::setSpeed( int v )
{
#ifdef TTS
    speech->SpeedSet(v);
#endif
}

void
Audio::setVoice( int v )
{
}

void
Audio::pause()
{
    switch(state) {
    case Speech:
#ifdef TTS
    speech->AudioPause();
#endif
        break;
    case Wav:
        PlaySound( NULL, NULL, SND_PURGE );
        break;
    case Midi:
        midi->pause();
        break;
    default:
        break;
    }
}

void
Audio::resume()
{
    switch(state) {
    case Speech:
#ifdef TTS
        speech->AudioResume();
#endif
        break;
    case Wav:
        PlaySound( file, NULL,
            SND_ASYNC|SND_FILENAME );
        break;
    case Midi:
        midi->play();
        break;
    default:
        break;
    }
}
```

```
void
Audio::stop()
{
    switch(state) {
    case Speech:
#ifdef TTS
            speech->AudioReset();
#endif
            break;
    case Wav:
            PlaySound( NULL, NULL, SND_PURGE );
            break;
    case Midi:
            midi->stop();
            break;
    default:
            break;
    }
}

void
Audio::repeat()
{
    switch(state) {
    case Speech:
#ifdef TTS
            speech->Speak( spkbuffer, true, NULL );
#endif
            break;
    case Wav:
            PlaySound( file, NULL,
                    SND_ASYNC|SND_FILENAME );
            break;
    case Midi:
            midi->seek( 0L );
            midi->play();
            break;
    default:
            break;
    }
}

#include <Audio.moc>


Midi.cpp

#include <afxwin.h>
#include <mmsystem.h>
// Avoids the warning caused by lack of #pragma once
#ifdef STRICT
#undef STRICT
```

```
#endif
#include <Midi.h>
#include <qfile.h>

// LilMidi ctor
LilMidi::LilMidi()
{
    state = Stopped;
    device = 0;
    isopen = false;
}

// Default dtor
LilMidi::~LilMidi()
{
    close();
}

// bool open( const QString &file_name )
// Open the midi file, set stream position to 0
bool
LilMidi::open( const QString &filename )
{
    QFile f( filename );

    // If we aren't stopped, stop and close.
    if ( isopen == true ) {
        if( state != Stopped ) stop();
        close();
    }

    device = 0;

    // See if the file exists
    if( f.exists() == false ) {
        return( false );
    }

    // Get the device
    MCI_OPEN_PARMS parms;
    parms.lpstrDeviceType = (LPCSTR)MCI_DEVTYPE_SEQUENCER;
    parms.lpstrElementName= (LPCSTR)(const char *)filename;
    parms.wDeviceID = 0;

    if( mciSendCommand( NULL,
        MCI_OPEN,
        MCI_WAIT | MCI_OPEN_TYPE |
        MCI_OPEN_TYPE_ID | MCI_OPEN_ELEMENT,
        (DWORD)(LPVOID)&parms ) ) {
        return( false );
    }
    device = parms.wDeviceID;
    isopen = true;
```

```
        // Set the time format to milliseconds
        MCI_SET_PARMS sparms;
        sparms.dwTimeFormat = MCI_FORMAT_MILLISECONDS;
        if ( mciSendCommand( device,
              MCI_SET,
              MCI_SET_TIME_FORMAT,
              (DWORD)(LPVOID)&sparms ) ) {
              close ();
              return( false );
        }
        mciSendCommand( device, MCI_SEEK, MCI_SEEK_TO_START,
              NULL );
        return( true );
}

// void close()
// Stop and close the mci stream
void
LilMidi::close()
{
    if( isopen == true ) {
          // Stop playing and close
          mciSendCommand( device, MCI_STOP, NULL, NULL );
          state = Stopped;

          mciSendCommand( device, MCI_CLOSE, NULL, NULL );

          device = 0;
          isopen = false;
    }
}

// void play()
// begin play from current stream position
void
LilMidi::play()
{
    if( isopen == true ) {
          MCI_STATUS_PARMS sparms;
          MCI_PLAY_PARMS parms;

          // Start playing from current position
          // if paused
          if( state == Paused ) {
                sparms.dwItem = MCI_STATUS_POSITION;
                if( mciSendCommand(
                      device,
                      MCI_STATUS,
                      MCI_WAIT | MCI_STATUS_ITEM,
                      (DWORD)(LPVOID)&sparms )) {
                      return;
                }
          } else {
```

```
                            sparms.dwReturn = 0;
                }
            parms.dwCallback = NULL;
            parms.dwFrom = sparms.dwReturn;
            if( mciSendCommand(
                    device,
                    MCI_PLAY,
                    MCI_FROM,
                    (DWORD)(LPVOID)&parms) ) {
                    return;
                }
            state = Playing;
        }
}

// void stop()
// Stop and reposition stream to 0
void
LilMidi::stop()
{
    if( isopen == true ) {
            if(state == Playing ) {
                    mciSendCommand( device, MCI_STOP,
                            NULL, NULL );
            }
            mciSendCommand( device, MCI_SEEK,
                    MCI_SEEK_TO_START, NULL );
            state = Stopped;
        }
}

// void pause()
void
LilMidi::pause()
{
    if( isopen == true && state == Playing ){
            MCI_PLAY_PARMS parms;
            if( mciSendCommand( device, MCI_PAUSE, 0,
                    (DWORD)(LPVOID)&parms ) )
                    return;
            state = Paused;
        }
}

// unsigned long pos()
// Returns current stream position
unsigned long
LilMidi::pos()
{
    if( isopen == true ) {
            MCI_STATUS_PARMS parms;
            parms.dwItem = MCI_STATUS_POSITION;
            if( mciSendCommand(
```

```
                        device,
                        MCI_STATUS,
                        MCI_WAIT | MCI_STATUS_ITEM,
                        (DWORD)(LPVOID)&parms) ) {
                        return( 0L );
                }
                return( parms.dwReturn );
        }
        return( 0L );
}

// int status()
// update and return current state
// LilMidi::(Stopped, Playing, or Paused)
int
LilMidi::status()
{
    if( isopen == true ) {
            MCI_STATUS_PARMS parms;
            parms.dwItem = MCI_STATUS_MODE;
            if( mciSendCommand(
                    device,
                    MCI_STATUS,
                    MCI_WAIT | MCI_STATUS_ITEM,
                    (DWORD)(LPVOID)&parms) ) {
                    return( Stopped );
            }

            switch( parms.dwReturn ) {
            case MCI_MODE_PLAY:
                    state = Playing;
                    break;
            case MCI_MODE_PAUSE:
                    state = Paused;
                    break;
            default:
                    state = Stopped;
                    break;
            }
    } else {
            state = Stopped;
    }

    return( state );
}

// bool seek( unsigned long milliseconds )
// seek to the stream position
bool
LilMidi::seek( unsigned long msec )
{
    if( isopen == true ) {
            MCI_SEEK_PARMS parms;
```

```
                    parms.dwTo = msec;
                    switch( status() ) {
                    case Playing:
                            if( mciSendCommand( device,
                                    MCI_PAUSE, 0, NULL ) )
                                    return( false );
                            if( mciSendCommand( device,
                                    MCI_SEEK,
                                    MCI_TO | MCI_WAIT,
                                    (DWORD)(LPVOID)&parms) ) {
                                    return( false );
                            }
                            state = Paused;
                            play();
                            break;
                    default:
                            if( mciSendCommand( device,
                                    MCI_SEEK,
                                    MCI_TO | MCI_WAIT,
                                    (DWORD)(LPVOID)&parms) ) {
                                    return( false );
                            }
                            break;
                    }
            }
        return( true );
}


// void fastFwd( int seconds )
// advance the stream position
void
LilMidi::fastFwd( int sec )
{
    if( isopen == true ) {
            unsigned long p = pos();
            p += (unsigned long)( sec * 1000 );
            seek( p );
    }
}


// void rewind( int seconds )
// rewind the stream
void
LilMidi::rewind( int sec )
{
    if( isopen == true ) {
            unsigned long p = pos();
            if( p < (unsigned long)( sec * 1000 ) )
                    p = 0;
            else
                    p -= (unsigned long)( sec * 1000 );
            seek( p );
```

```
        }
}

// int divisionType()
// Returns 0 on error or MCI_SEQ_DIV_???? value
int
LilMidi::divisionType()
{
    if( isopen == true ) {
        MCI_STATUS_PARMS parms;
        parms.dwItem = MCI_SEQ_STATUS_DIVTYPE;
        if( mciSendCommand( device,
            MCI_STATUS,
            MCI_WAIT | MCI_STATUS_ITEM,
            (DWORD)(LPVOID)&parms) ) {
            return( 0 );
        }
        return( (int)parms.dwReturn );
    }
    return( 0 );
}

// int tempo()
// -1 on error, else tempo value
int
LilMidi::tempo()
{
    if( isopen == true ) {
        MCI_STATUS_PARMS parms;
        parms.dwItem = MCI_SEQ_STATUS_TEMPO;
        if( mciSendCommand( device,
            MCI_STATUS,
            MCI_WAIT | MCI_STATUS_ITEM,
            (DWORD)(LPVOID)&parms) ) {
            return( -1 );
        }
        return( (int)parms.dwReturn );
    }
    return( -1 );
}

// void setTempo( int tempo )
void
LilMidi::setTempo( int tempo )
{
    if( isopen == true ) {
        MCI_SEQ_SET_PARMS parms;
        parms.dwTempo = tempo;
        mciSendCommand( device,
            MCI_SET,
            MCI_WAIT | MCI_SEQ_SET_TEMPO,
            (DWORD)(LPVOID)&parms );
    }
```

```
}

#include <Midi.moc>
```

Using this class is extremely easy. The following sample demonstrates instantiation and use:

```
#include <Audio.h>

...

    Audio *aud = new Audio();

    aud->wavPlay( "sounds\\hello.wav" );
    aud->speak( "This is a test." );
...
```

Of course, Audio::speak won't do anything if the target system hasn't installed a TTS engine (likely on Win98 or NT4 systems) but should work fine on Windows 2000 and won't cause problems on systems that *don't* have a TTS engine installed.

It should be a simple matter to add MIDI support or adapt the Audio class to use a different TTS engine than the SPCHAPI from Microsoft.

SUMMARY

While I still consider Linux to be my OS of choice (as a development platform), Windows 2000 offers a lot of features, making it increasingly difficult to choose a favorite. Most of the examples that ship with the Qt distribution are targeted primarily at a Linux audience. I base that statement on the fact that some of the examples won't build (and aren't relevant) on a Windows platform. I expect to see some examples in future Qt releases that are only relevant on Windows. We'll see.

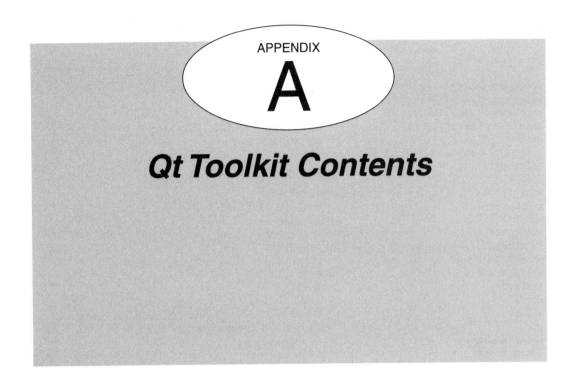

Qt Toolkit Contents

The following table provides a detailed accounting of the method-level functionality of the Qt toolkit, as provided in the 2.1 release. The table is an alphabetical listing of methods, cross-referenced with the class or classes in which the methods are found. Refer to current documentation for access specifications as periodic refinements by the vendor tend to change the access permissions from one release to another.

Alphabetical Listing Of Qt Class Methods

The following table provides a comprehensive listing of Qt class methods, signals, slots, and the classes that expose them.

Slot, signal, or method	Class(es) that expose it
AsciiToUnicode()	QJpUnicodeConv
Jisx0201KanaToUnicode()	QJpUnicodeConv
Jisx0201LatinToUnicode()	QJpUnicodeConv
Jisx0201ToUnicode()	QJpUnicodeConv
Jisx0208ToUnicode()	QJpUnicodeConv
Jisx0212ToUnicode()	QJpUnicodeConv

(continued)

SjisToUnicode()   QJpUnicodeConv

UnicodeToAscii()   QJpUnicodeConv
UnicodeToJisx0201()   QJpUnicodeConv
UnicodeToJisx0201Kana()   QJpUnicodeConv
UnicodeToJisx0201Latin()   QJpUnicodeConv
UnicodeToJisx0208()   QJpUnicodeConv
UnicodeToJisx0212()   QJpUnicodeConv
UnicodeToSjis()   QJpUnicodeConv

abort()   QPrinter
aborted()   QPrinter
about()   QMessageBox
aboutQt()   QMessageBox
aboutToQuit()   QApplication
aboutToShow()   QWidgetStack QTabDialog QPopupMenu
absFilePath()   QFileInfo QDir
absPath()   QDir
accel()   QButton QMenuData
accept()   QDropEvent QWheelEvent QCloseEvent QKeyEvent
                                             QDialog QDragMoveEvent
acceptAction()   QDropEvent
acceptDrop()   QIconViewItem
acceptDrops()   QWidget
accum()   QGLFormat
action()   QDropEvent
activate()   QListViewItem QCheckListItem QLayout QSignal
activate_filters()   QObject
activate_signal()   QObject
activate_signal_bool()   QObject
activate_signal_string()   QObject
activate_signal_strref()   QObject
activated()   QAccel QComboBox QMenuBar QPopupMenu QSocketNo-
                                             tifier
activatedPos()   QListViewItem
activatedRedirect()   QPopupMenu
active()   QPalette
activeModalWidget()   QApplication
activePopupWidget()   QApplication
activeWindow()   QWorkspace QApplication
actual()   QNPlugin
add()   QWhatsThis QLayout QGridLayout QToolTip
addChild()   QScrollView
addChildLayout()   QLayout
addColSpacing()   QGridLayout
addColumn()   QListView
addDays()   QDateTime QDate
addFilePath()   QMimeSourceFactory
addFilter()   QFileDialog
addItem()   QBoxLayout QGridLayout QLayout
addLabel()   QHeader

(continued)

addLayout()	QGridLayout QBoxLayout
addLeftWidget()	QFileDialog
addLine()	QRangeControl
addMSecs()	QTime
addMultiCell()	QGridLayout
addMultiCellWidget()	QGridLayout
addOperation()	QNetworkProtocol
addPage()	QWizard QRangeControl
addPath()	QUrl
addRightWidget()	QFileDialog
addRowSpacing()	QGridLayout
addSecs()	QTime QDateTime
addSeparator()	QToolBar
addSpace()	QGroupBox
addSpacing()	QBoxLayout
addStep()	QSlider
addStretch()	QBoxLayout
addStrut()	QBoxLayout
addTab()	QTabWidget QTabDialog QTabBar
addToolBar()	QMainWindow
addToolButton()	QFileDialog
addWidget()	QStatusBar QGridLayout QWidgetStack QBoxLayout
addWidgets()	QFileDialog
adjustItems()	QIconView
adjustPos()	QSplitter
adjustSize()	QWidget QSimpleRichText QMessageBox
alignment()	QMultiLineEdit QLayoutItem QGroupBox
	QStyleSheetItem QLineEdit QLabel
alignmentRect()	QLayout
allColumnsShowFocus()	QListView
allGray()	QImage
alloc()	QColor
allowedInContext()	QStyleSheetItem
allowsErrorInteraction()	QSessionManager
allowsInteraction()	QSessionManager
allWidgets()	QApplication
alpha()	QGLFormat
anchor()	QSimpleRichText
anchorAt()	QSimpleRichText
animateClick()	QButton
answerRect()	QDragMoveEvent
append()	QGList QMultiLineEdit QList QTextView QString
	QCString QValueList QIconDrag
applyButtonPressed()	QTabDialog
appropriate()	QWizard
arg()	QNPInstance QNetworkOperation QString
argc()	QApplication QNPInstance
argn()	QNPInstance
argv()	QNPInstance QApplication
arrangeItemsInGrid()	QIconView
arrangement()	QIconView
asBitmap()	QVariant

(continued)

asBool()	QVariant
asBrush()	QVariant
ascent()	QFontMetrics
ascii()	QString QKeyEvent
asColor()	QVariant
asColorGroup()	QVariant
asCString()	QVariant
asCursor()	QVariant
asDouble()	QVariant
asFont()	QVariant
asIconSet()	QVariant
asImage()	QVariant
asInt()	QVariant
asList()	QVariant
asPalette()	QVariant
asPixmap()	QVariant
asPoint()	QVariant
asPointArray()	QVariant
asRect()	QVariant
asRegion()	QVariant
asSize()	QVariant
asString()	QVariant
asStringList()	QVariant
assign()	QArray QByteArray QGArray
asUInt()	QVariant
at()	QGList QList QValueList QGVector QBuffer QFile QBitArray QByteArray QGArray QVector QIODevice QArray QString
atBeginning()	QMultiLineEdit
atEnd()	QIODevice QDataStream QMultiLineEdit QFile QTextStream
atFirst()	QGCacheIterator QIntCacheIterator QAsciiCacheIterator QGListIterator QListIterator QStrListIterator QCacheIterator
atLast()	QGCacheIterator QAsciiCacheIterator QListIterator QCacheIterator QStrListIterator QGListIterator QIntCacheIterator
autoAdd()	QLayout
autoArrange()	QIconView
autoBufferSwap()	QGLWidget
autoClose()	QProgressDialog
autoCompletion()	QComboBox
autoDefault()	QPushButton
autoDelete()	QCollection QStack QQueue QNetworkProtocol
autoMask()	QWidget
autoRaise()	QToolButton
autoRepeat()	QButton
autoReset()	QProgressDialog
autoResize()	QButton QComboBox QLabel
autoUpdate()	QMultiLineEdit QTableView
back()	QWizard
backButton()	QWizard

(continued)

background()	QColorGroup
backgroundColor()	QWidget QPainter QMovie
backgroundColorChange()	QWidget
backgroundMode()	QWidget QPainter
backgroundOrigin()	QWidget
backgroundPixmap()	QWidget
backgroundPixmapChange()	QWidget
backspace()	QLineEdit QMultiLineEdit
backward()	QTextBrowser
backwardAvailable()	QTextBrowser
badSuperclassWarning()	QObject
base()	QColorGroup
baseName()	QFileInfo
baseSize()	QWidget
basicDirection()	QString
beep()	QApplication
begin()	QByteArray QPainter QArray QValueList QMap
bevelButtonRect()	QStyle
bitmap()	QCursor
bitOrder()	QImage
bits()	QImage
block()	QSignal
blockSignals()	QObject
blue()	QColor
bold()	QFont QFontInfo QFontDatabase
bottom()	QRect QDoubleValidator QIntValidator
bottomLeft()	QRect
bottomMargin()	QScrollView
bottomRight()	QRect
bound()	QRangeControl
boundedTo()	QSize
boundingRect()	QPointArray QRegion QFontMetrics QPainter
brightText()	QColorGroup
brush()	QPalette QPainter QColorGroup
brushOrigin()	QPainter
bsearch()	QByteArray QGVector QArray QGArray QVector
buddy()	QLabel
buffer()	QBuffer
button()	QColorGroup QMouseEvent
buttonClicked()	QButtonGroup
buttonDefaultIndicatorWidth()	QStyle
buttonPressed()	QButtonGroup
buttonRect()	QStyle QPlatinumStyle
buttonReleased()	QButtonGroup
buttonSymbols()	QSpinBox
buttonText()	QColorGroup QMessageBox
buttonToggled()	QButtonGroup
byteOrder()	QDataStream
bytesPerLine()	QImage
cacheLimit()	QPixmapCache
cacheStatistics()	QFont
caching()	QFileInfo

(continued)

calcRect()	QIconViewItem
calcTmpText()	QIconViewItem
canCast()	QVariant
cancel()	QProgressDialog QSessionManager
cancelButton()	QWizard
cancelButtonPressed()	QTabDialog
cancelled()	QProgressDialog
canDecode()	QUriDrag QColorDrag QImageDrag QIconDrag QTextDrag
canEncode()	QTextCodec
canonicalPath()	QDir
capStyle()	QPen
caption()	QWidget
cascade()	QWorkspace
caseSensitive()	QRegExp
category()	QChar
cd()	QDir
cdUp()	QUrlOperator QUrl QDir
cell()	QChar
cellAt()	QHeader
cellGeometry()	QGridLayout
cellHeight()	QTableView
cellPos()	QHeader
cellSize()	QHeader
cellUpdateRect()	QTableView
cellWidth()	QTableView
center()	QRect QScrollView
centerCurrentItem()	QListBox
centerIndicator()	QProgressBar
centralWidget()	QMainWindow
cfirst()	QGList
changed()	QImageConsumer
changeInterval()	QTimer
changeItem()	QMenuData QListBox QComboBox
changeSize()	QSpacerItem
changeTab()	QTabWidget QTabDialog
charSet()	QFontInfo QFont
charSetForLocale()	QFont
charSets()	QFontDatabase
charSetSample()	QFontDatabase
checkConnectArgs()	QObject
checkConnection()	QNetworkProtocol
checkOverflow()	QLCDNumber
checkValid()	QUrlOperator
child()	QObject QChildEvent
childCount()	QListViewItem QListView
childEvent()	QMainWindow QSplitter QGroupBox QWidgetStack QObject QWorkspace
childIsVisible()	QScrollView
children()	QObject
childrenRect()	QWidget
childrenRegion()	QWidget

(continued)

childX()	QScrollView
childY()	QScrollView
chooseContext()	QGLContext
classInfo()	QMetaObject
className()	QObject QMetaObject
clast()	QGList
cleanBuffers()	QPointArray
cleanDirPath()	QDir
cleanText()	QSpinBox
cleanup()	QFont QPainter QColor QCursor
clear()	QToolBar QToolTip QMultiLineEdit QIntCache
	QVariant QCollection QStack QValueList
	QListView QAccel QLineEdit QList QCache QList-
	Box QIconView QGVector QIntDict QAsciiCache QS-
	tatusBar QGCache QTranslator QVector QGDict
	QMap QLabel QPtrDict QAsciiDict QClipboard
	QMenuData QComboBox QPixmapCache QDict QQueue
	QGList
clearBit()	QBitArray
clearEdit()	QComboBox
clearEntries()	QUrlOperator
clearFlags()	QMetaProperty
clearFocus()	QWidget
clearInputString()	QListBox
clearMask()	QWidget
clearOperationQueue()	QNetworkProtocol
clearSelection()	QIconView QListBox QListView
clearTableFlags()	QTableView
clearValidator()	QLineEdit QComboBox
clearWFlags()	QWidget
clearWState()	QWidget
clicked()	QHeader QListBox QIconView QButtonGroup
	QListView QButton
clipboard()	QApplication
clipper()	QScrollView
clipRegion()	QPainter
close()	QBuffer QIODevice QWidget QFile
closeAllWindows()	QApplication
closeEvent()	QProgressDialog QPopupMenu QWidget QDialog
closingDown()	QApplication
cmd()	QPaintDevice QPicture QPrinter
codecForContent()	QTextCodec
codecForIndex()	QTextCodec
codecForLocale()	QTextCodec
codecForMib()	QTextCodec
codecForName()	QTextCodec
colIsVisible()	QTableView
collapsed()	QListView
color()	QBrush QColorGroup QPen QImage QPalette
	QStyleSheetItem
colorGroup()	QWidget
colorIndex()	QGLContext

(continued)

`colorMode()`	QPrinter
`colorSpec()`	QApplication
`colorTable()`	QImage
`colStretch()`	QGridLayout
`columnAlignment()`	QListView
`columnMode()`	QListBox
`columns()`	QPopupMenu QListView QGroupBox
`columnText()`	QListView
`columnWidth()`	QListView
`columnWidthMode()`	QListView
`colXPos()`	QTableView
`comboButtonFocusRect()`	QWindowsStyle QStyle QPlatinumStyle QMotifStyle QCommonStyle
`comboButtonRect()`	QStyle QCommonStyle QPlatinumStyle QWindowsStyle QMotifStyle
`commitData()`	QApplication
`compare()`	QIconViewItem QString
`compareItems()`	QGList QSortedList QGVector
`compile()`	QRegExp
`complete()`	QNPStream
`compose()`	QString
`connect()`	QSignal QAsyncIO QObject
`connectionStateChanged()`	QUrlOperator QNetworkProtocol
`connectItem()`	QMenuData QAccel
`connectNotify()`	QClipboard QObject
`connectResize()`	QMovie
`connectStatus()`	QMovie
`connectUpdate()`	QMovie
`constPolish()`	QWidget
`constref()`	QString
`contains()`	QGArray QList QRegion QTranslator QGVector QMap QCString QVector QArray QGList QValueList QIconViewItem QRect QByteArray QString
`containsRef()`	QGList QList QGVector QVector
`contentsDragEnterEvent()`	QIconView QScrollView
`contentsDragLeaveEvent()`	QIconView QScrollView
`contentsDragMoveEvent()`	QIconView QScrollView
`contentsDropEvent()`	QScrollView QIconView
`contentsHeight()`	QScrollView
`contentsMouseDoubleClickEvent()`	QIconView QListView QScrollView
`contentsMouseMoveEvent()`	QScrollView QIconView QListView
`contentsMousePressEvent()`	QListView QScrollView QIconView
`contentsMouseReleaseEvent()`	QListView QScrollView QIconView
`contentsMoving()`	QScrollView
`contentsRect()`	QFrame
`contentsToViewport()`	QScrollView
`contentsWheelEvent()`	QScrollView
`contentsWidth()`	QScrollView
`contentsX()`	QScrollView
`contentsY()`	QScrollView
`context()`	QGLWidget QTextView QSimpleRichText
`contexts()`	QStyleSheetItem

(continued)

`convertBitOrder()`	QImage
`convertDepth()`	QImage
`convertDepthWithPalette()`	QImage
`convertFromImage()`	QPixmap
`convertFromPlainText()`	QStyleSheet
`convertSeparators()`	QDir
`convertToAbs()`	QFileInfo QDir
`convertToImage()`	QPixmap
`coords()`	QRect
`copy()`	QCString QLineEdit QByteArray QImage QString QArray QPointArray QPalette QUrlOperator QMultiLineEdit QTextView QBitArray
`copyText()`	QMultiLineEdit
`cornerWidget()`	QScrollView
`count()`	QGDict QCache QStrListIterator QQueue QPtrDict QPtrDictIterator QStack QArray QKeyEvent QValueList QGList QMap QComboBox QIntDictIterator QGVector QAsciiCache QDictIterator QGCacheIterator QCacheIterator QListIterator QCollection QFocusData QDict QIntCacheIterator QAsciiDict QIntCache QDir QIconView QByteArray QListBox QButtonGroup QAsciiCacheIterator QIntDict QGCache QHeader QAccel QMenuData QVector QList QAsciiDictIterator
`create()`	QImage QGLContext QNPlugin QWidget
`createAlphaMask()`	QImage
`createdDirectory()`	QUrlOperator QNetworkProtocol
`createHeuristicMask()`	QPixmap QImage
`creator()`	QPrinter
`critical()`	QMessageBox
`current()`	QDictIterator QStack QLayoutIterator QPtrDictIterator QIntDictIterator QListBoxItem QIntCacheIterator QListIterator QGLayoutIterator QDir QCacheIterator QList QQueue QListViewItemIterator QStrListIterator QAsciiDictIterator QAsciiCacheIterator
`currentAllocContext()`	QColor
`currentChanged()`	QIconView QListBox QListView
`currentContext()`	QGLContext
`currentDate()`	QDate
`currentDateTime()`	QDateTime
`currentDirPath()`	QDir
`currentItem()`	QIconView QListBox QListView QComboBox QAsciiCacheIterator QIntCacheIterator QDictIterator QPtrDictIterator QIntDictIterator QCacheIterator QAsciiDictIterator
`currentKey()`	QGList QList
`currentNode()`	QGList QList
`currentPage()`	QTabWidget QTabDialog QWizard
`currentTab()`	QTabBar
`currentText()`	QComboBox QListBox
`currentTime()`	QTime
`currentValueText()`	QSpinBox

(continued)

cursor()	QWidget
cursorDown()	QMultiLineEdit
cursorFlashTime()	QApplication
cursorLeft()	QLineEdit QMultiLineEdit
cursorPoint()	QMultiLineEdit
cursorPosition()	QLineEdit QMultiLineEdit
cursorRight()	QLineEdit QMultiLineEdit
cursorUp()	QMultiLineEdit
cursorWordBackward()	QMultiLineEdit QLineEdit
cursorWordForward()	QLineEdit QMultiLineEdit
customColor()	QColorDialog
customCount()	QColorDialog
customEvent()	QWidget
customWhatsThis()	QPopupMenu QWidget QMenuBar
cut()	QMultiLineEdit QLineEdit
dark()	QColor QColorGroup
data()	QArray QByteArray QMimeSourceFactory QVector QPicture QMapIterator QGVector QUrlOperator QNetworkProtocol QIconDragItem QMapConstIterator QGArray QCustomEvent QDropEvent QClipboard
dataChanged()	QClipboard
dataTransferProgress()	QUrlOperator QNetworkProtocol
date()	QDateTime
day()	QDate
dayName()	QDate
dayOfWeek()	QDate
dayOfYear()	QDate
daysInMonth()	QDate
daysInYear()	QDate
daysTo()	QDate QDateTime
decimals()	QDoubleValidator
deciPointSize()	QFont
decode()	QTextDrag QImageDrag QUriDrag QImageFormat QImageDecoder QUrl QColorDrag
decodeLocalFiles()	QUriDrag
decodeName()	QFile
decoderFor()	QImageFormatType
decodeToUnicodeUris()	QUriDrag
decomposition()	QChar
decompositionTag()	QChar
defaultButtonPressed()	QTabDialog
defaultCodec()	QApplication
defaultDepth()	QPixmap
defaultFactory()	QMimeSourceFactory
defaultFamily()	QFont
defaultFont()	QFont
defaultFormat()	QGLFormat
defaultFrameWidth()	QCDEStyle QCommonStyle QStyle
defaultOptimization()	QPixmap
defaultOverlayFormat()	QGLFormat
defaultSheet()	QStyleSheet
defaultTabStop()	QMultiLineEdit

(continued)

defineIOHandler()	QImageIO
definesFontItalic()	QStyleSheetItem
definesFontUnderline()	QStyleSheetItem
del()	QLineEdit QMultiLineEdit
delay()	QToolTipGroup
deleteAllCodecs()	QTextCodec
deleteAllItems()	QLayout
deleteCurrent()	QLayoutIterator
deleteData()	QBitArray QGArray
deleteItem()	QCollection
deleteNetworkProtocol()	QUrlOperator
delta()	QWheelEvent
depth()	QPaintDeviceMetrics QListViewItem QImage
	QPixmap QGLFormat
dequeue()	QQueue
descent()	QFontMetrics
description()	QImageIO
deselect()	QLineEdit QMultiLineEdit
designable()	QMetaProperty
desktop()	QApplication
desktopSettingsAware()	QApplication
destroy()	QWidget
destroyAllocContext()	QColor
destroyed()	QObject
detach()	QGArray QValueList QImage QMap QByteArray
	QPixmap QIconSet QArray QBitArray
	QTextStream QDataStream QPainter QGLContext
device()	QGLContext
deviceIsPixmap()	QPaintDevice
devType()	QChar
digitValue()	QFileDialog QFileInfo
dir()	QChar QBoxLayout
direction()	QGLFormat
directRendering()	QRangeControl
directSetValue()	QFileDialog
dirEntered()	QDir
dirName()	QUrl QFileInfo QFileDialog
dirPath()	QFont
dirty()	QPalette
disabled()	QSessionManager
discardCommand()	QObject QSignal
disconnect()	QAccel QMenuData
disconnectItem()	QObject
disconnectNotify()	QMovie
disconnectResize()	QMovie
disconnectStatus()	QMovie
disconnectUpdate()	QLCDNumber
display()	QStyleSheetItem
displayMode()	QLineEdit
displayText()	QListView QIconView
doAutoScroll()	QPrinter
docName()	QTextView
documentTitle()	

(continued)

`doLayout()`	QListBox
`done()`	QDialog
`doneCurrent()`	QGLContext
`dotsPerMeterX()`	QImage
`dotsPerMeterY()`	QImage
`doubleBuffer()`	QGLFormat QGLWidget
`doubleClicked()`	QIconView QListView QListBox
`doubleClickInterval()`	QApplication
`downButton()`	QSpinBox
`drag()`	QDragObject
`dragAutoScroll()`	QScrollView
`dragCopy()`	QDragObject
`dragEnabled()`	QIconViewItem
`dragEntered()`	QIconViewItem
`dragEnterEvent()`	QLineEdit QWidget QMultiLineEdit
`draggingSlider()`	QScrollBar
`dragLeaveEvent()`	QMultiLineEdit QWidget
`dragLeft()`	QIconViewItem
`dragMove()`	QDragObject
`dragMoveEvent()`	QMultiLineEdit QWidget
`dragObject()`	QIconView
`draw()`	QSimpleRichText
`drawArc()`	QPainter
`drawArrow()`	QWindowsStyle QStyle QMotifStyle QCDEStyle
`drawBackground()`	QIconView
`drawBevelButton()`	QStyle QMotifStyle QWindowsStyle QPlatinumStyle
`drawButton()`	QToolButton QButton QCheckBox QWindowsStyle QRadioButton QMotifStyle QPlatinumStyle QStyle QPushButton
`drawButtonLabel()`	QPushButton QCheckBox QRadioButton QToolButton QButton
`drawButtonMask()`	QStyle
`drawCheckMark()`	QStyle QPlatinumStyle QMotifStyle QWindowsStyle
`drawChord()`	QPainter
`drawComboButton()`	QPlatinumStyle QMotifStyle QStyle QCommonStyle QWindowsStyle
`drawComboButtonMask()`	QCommonStyle QStyle
`drawContents()`	QFrame QProgressBar QLCDNumber QScrollView QIconView QLabel QMenuBar QPopupMenu
`drawContentsMask()`	QLabel QProgressBar QFrame
`drawContentsOffset()`	QListView QScrollView QTextView
`drawEllipse()`	QPainter
`drawExclusiveIndicator()`	QStyle QWindowsStyle QPlatinumStyle QCDEStyle QMotifStyle
`drawExclusiveIndicatorMask()`	QMotifStyle QWindowsStyle QStyle
`drawFocusRect()`	QMotifStyle QStyle QWindowsStyle
`drawFrame()`	QFrame
`drawFrameMask()`	QFrame
`drawImage()`	QPainter
`drawIndicator()`	QStyle QPlatinumStyle QWindowsStyle QMotifStyle QCDEStyle
`drawIndicatorMask()`	QStyle QPlatinumStyle

(continued)

`drawItem()`	QPopupMenu QStyle
`drawLine()`	QPainter
`drawLineSegments()`	QPainter
`drawPanel()`	QWindowsStyle QStyle
`drawPicture()`	QPainter
`drawPie()`	QPainter
`drawPixmap()`	QPainter
`drawPoint()`	QPainter
`drawPoints()`	QPainter
`drawPolygon()`	QPainter
`drawPolyline()`	QPainter
`drawPopupMenuItem()`	QStyle QPlatinumStyle QMotifStyle QWindowsStyle
`drawPopupPanel()`	QStyle QWindowsStyle QPlatinumStyle
`drawPushButton()`	QPlatinumStyle QWindowsStyle QMotifStyle QStyle
`drawPushButtonLabel()`	QCommonStyle QStyle QPlatinumStyle
`drawQuadBezier()`	QPainter
`drawRect()`	QPainter QStyle
`drawRectStrong()`	QStyle
`drawRiffles()`	QPlatinumStyle
`drawRoundRect()`	QPainter
`drawRubber()`	QIconView
`drawScrollBarBackground()`	QPlatinumStyle
`drawScrollBarControls()`	QWindowsStyle QStyle QPlatinumStyle QMotifStyle
`drawSeparator()`	QStyle
`drawSlider()`	QMotifStyle QPlatinumStyle QStyle QWindowsStyle
`drawSliderGroove()`	QWindowsStyle QMotifStyle QPlatinumStyle QStyle
`drawSliderGrooveMask()`	QCommonStyle QStyle
`drawSliderMask()`	QStyle QWindowsStyle QPlatinumStyle QCommon-Style
`drawSplitter()`	QWindowsStyle QSplitter QStyle QMotifStyle
`drawTab()`	QStyle QCommonStyle QWindowsStyle QMotifStyle
`drawTabMask()`	QMotifStyle QCommonStyle QStyle QWindowsStyle
`drawText()`	QWidget QPainter
`drawTicks()`	QSlider
`drawTiledPixmap()`	QPainter
`drawToolBarHandle()`	QStyle
`drawToolButton()`	QStyle
`drawWinFocusRect()`	QPainter
`drawWinGroove()`	QSlider
`drawWinShades()`	QWindowsStyle
`drives()`	QDir
`dropEnabled()`	QIconViewItem
`dropEvent()`	QMultiLineEdit QWidget QLineEdit
`dropped()`	QIconView QIconViewItem
`dumpObjectInfo()`	QObject
`dumpObjectTree()`	QObject
`duplicate()`	QByteArray QArray QGArray
`duplicatesEnabled()`	QComboBox
`dx()`	QWMatrix
`dy()`	QWMatrix
`echoMode()`	QLineEdit QMultiLineEdit
`edited()`	QMultiLineEdit QLineEdit

(continued)

`editor()`	QSpinBox
`elapsed()`	QTime
`emitRenamed()`	QIconView
`emitSelectionChanged()`	QIconView
`enableClipper()`	QScrollView
`enabled()`	QToolTipGroup QToolTip
`enabledChange()`	QListView QButton QWidget
`enableRewind()`	QIODeviceSource QDataSource
`encode()`	QUrl
`encodedData()`	QStoredDrag QDropEvent QIconDrag QTextDrag QImageDrag QMimeSource
`encodedEntryList()`	QDir
`encodedPathAndQuery()`	QUrl
`encodeName()`	QFile
`encodingName()`	QFont
`end()`	QMultiLineEdit QImageConsumer QByteArray QMap QPainter QNPStream QValueList QArray QLineEdit
`endMovingToolBar()`	QMainWindow
`enforceSortOrder()`	QListViewItem
`enqueue()`	QQueue
`ensureCurrentVisible()`	QListBox
`ensureItemVisible()`	QIconView QListView
`ensureVisible()`	QScrollView
`enter_loop()`	QApplication
`enterAllocContext()`	QColor
`enterEvent()`	QToolButton QIconView QWidget
`enterInstance()`	QNPWidget
`enterWhatsThisMode()`	QWhatsThis
`entryInfoList()`	QDir
`entryList()`	QDir
`enumKeys()`	QMetaProperty
`eof()`	QDataStream QTextStream QDataSink
`eor()`	QRegion
`equal()`	QUrlInfo
`erase()`	QWidget
`erased()`	QPaintEvent
`eraseRect()`	QPainter
`error()`	QStyleSheet
`errorCode()`	QNetworkOperation
`event()`	QClipboard QWidget QMainWindow QTimer QToolBar QSocketNotifier QSplitter QObject
`eventFilter()`	QWorkspace QMenuBar QFileDialog QLayout QScrollView QMainWindow QComboBox QFontDialog QListView QIconView QAccel QWizard QTabWidget QObject QSpinBox QToolBar
`exactMatch()`	QFont QFontInfo
`exclusiveIndicatorSize()`	QWindowsStyle QMotifStyle QPlatinumStyle QStyle
`exec()`	QPopupMenu QApplication QDialog
`exists()`	QFileInfo QDir QFile
`exit()`	QApplication
`exit_loop()`	QApplication

(continued)

expand()	QGridLayout
expanded()	QListView
expandedTo()	QSize
expanding()	QLayoutItem QSpacerItem QLayout QBoxLayout
	QGridLayout QSizePolicy QWidgetItem
extension()	QFileInfo
extraData()	QWidget
extraPopupMenuItemWidth()	QPlatinumStyle QWindowsStyle QMotifStyle QStyle
families()	QFontDatabase
family()	QFont QFontInfo
familyListBox()	QFontDialog
fileHighlighted()	QFileDialog
fileName()	QFileInfo QUrl QImageIO
filePath()	QDir QMimeSourceFactory QFileInfo
fileSelected()	QFileDialog
fill()	QGArray QBitArray QCString QString QByteArray
	QArray QGVector QTextStream QImage QVector
	QPixmap
fillRect()	QPainter
filter()	QDir
find()	QGList QVector QWidget QAsciiDict QGArray
	QAsciiCache QIntCache QButtonGroup QCache QInt-
	Dict QCString QMap QList QPixmapCache QVal-
	ueList QArray QTranslator QGVector QPtrDict
	QDict QByteArray QString
find_other()	QGCache
find_string()	QGCache
findCol()	QTableView
findFirstVisibleItem()	QIconView
findIndex()	QValueList
findItem()	QIconView QMenuData QListBox
findKey()	QAccel
findLastVisibleItem()	QIconView
findNext()	QList
findNextRef()	QList
findPopup()	QMenuData
findRef()	QList QGList QVector QGVector
findRev()	QCString QString
findRow()	QTableView
findWidget()	QGridLayout QBoxLayout
finishButton()	QWizard
finished()	QNetworkProtocol QUrlOperator QMovie
first()	QList QValueList QGList
firstChild()	QListViewItem QListView
firstItem()	QIconView QListBox
fixedPitch()	QFont QFontInfo
fixup()	QValidator
flags()	QTextStream QIODevice
flush()	QFile QIODevice QBuffer QPainter
flushX()	QApplication
focusData()	QWidget

(continued)

focusInEvent()	QListBox QTabBar QGroupBox QLineEdit QRadioButton QSlider QMultiLineEdit QComboBox QButton QWidget QIconView QPushButton QTextView QMenuBar QPopupMenu QListView
focusNextPrevChild()	QScrollView QPopupMenu QButton QWidget
focusOutEvent()	QListView QIconView QSlider QTextView QLineEdit QMultiLineEdit QTabBar QWidget QListBox QPopupMenu QMenuBar QButton QPushButton
focusPolicy()	QWidget
focusProxy()	QWidget
focusWidget()	QFocusData QApplication QWidget
font()	QWidget QToolTip QPainter QApplication QFontDatabase
fontChange()	QMenuBar QLabel QWidget QGroupBox
fontFamily()	QStyleSheetItem
fontHighlighted()	QFontDialog
fontInf()	QPaintDevice
fontInfo()	QWidget QPainter
fontItalic()	QStyleSheetItem
fontMet()	QPaintDevice
fontMetrics()	QPainter QApplication QWidget
fontPropagation()	QWidget
fontSelected()	QFontDialog
fontSize()	QStyleSheetItem
fontUnderline()	QStyleSheetItem
fontWeight()	QStyleSheetItem
foreground()	QColorGroup
foregroundColor()	QWidget
format()	QImageDrag QMimeSource QStoredDrag QGLWidget QGLContext QTextDrag QDropEvent QIconDrag QImageIO QImageDecoder
formatName()	QImageFormatType QImageDecoder
forward()	QTextBrowser
forwardAvailable()	QTextBrowser
frame()	QLineEdit
frameChanged()	QFrame QWidgetStack QGrid QHBox QScrollView
frameDone()	QImageConsumer
frameGeometry()	QWidget
frameNumber()	QMovie
framePixmap()	QMovie
frameRect()	QFrame
frameShadow()	QFrame
frameShape()	QFrame
frameSize()	QWidget
frameStyle()	QFrame
frameWidth()	QFrame
free()	QNetworkOperation
fromLast()	QValueList
fromLatin1()	QString
fromLocal8Bit()	QString
fromPage()	QPrinter

(continued)

fromStrList()	QStringList
fromUnicode()	QTextCodec QJisCodec QEucKrCodec QTextEncoder QEucJpCodec QGbkCodec
fromUtf8()	QString
fullPage()	QPrinter
fullSpan()	QCustomMenuItem
geometry()	QLayout QSpacerItem QWidget QLayoutItem QWidgetItem
get()	QGListIterator QGCacheIterator QUrlOperator QGList QGDictIterator
getButtonShift()	QWindowsStyle QStyle QPlatinumStyle QCommonStyle
getch()	QFile QIODevice QBuffer
getColor()	QColorDialog
getCursorPosition()	QMultiLineEdit
getData()	QLNode
getDouble()	QInputDialog
getExistingDirectory()	QFileDialog
getFirst()	QList
getFont()	QFontDialog
getHsv()	QColor
getInteger()	QInputDialog
getItem()	QInputDialog
getJavaClass()	QNPlugin
getJavaEnv()	QNPlugin
getJavaPeer()	QNPInstance
getKeyAscii()	QGDictIterator QGCacheIterator
getKeyInt()	QGCacheIterator QGDictIterator
getKeyPtr()	QGDictIterator
getKeyString()	QGDictIterator QGCacheIterator
getLast()	QList
getLocation()	QMainWindow
getMarkedRegion()	QMultiLineEdit
getMIMEDescription()	QNPlugin
getNetworkProtocol()	QNetworkProtocol QUrlOperator
getOpenFileName()	QFileDialog
getOpenFileNames()	QFileDialog
getPluginDescriptionString()	QNPlugin
getPluginNameString()	QNPlugin
getRange()	QSplitter
getRgba()	QColorDialog
getSaveFileName()	QFileDialog
getString()	QMultiLineEdit
getText()	QInputDialog
getURL()	QNPInstance
getURLNotify()	QNPInstance
getValidRect()	QMovie
getVersionInfo()	QNPlugin
getWFlags()	QWidget
getWState()	QWidget
glDraw()	QGLWidget
glInit()	QGLWidget

(continued)

`globalPos()`	QWheelEvent QMouseEvent
`globalX()`	QWheelEvent QMouseEvent
`globalY()`	QMouseEvent QWheelEvent
`gotFocus()`	QFocusEvent
`grabKeyboard()`	QWidget
`grabMouse()`	QWidget
`grabWidget()`	QPixmap
`grabWindow()`	QPixmap
`greaterThan()`	QUrlInfo
`green()`	QColor
`greg2jul()`	QDate
`grep()`	QStringList
`gridX()`	QIconView
`gridY()`	QIconView
`group()`	QUrlInfo QToolTip QFileInfo QButton
`groupId()`	QFileInfo
`guiStyle()`	QStyle
`guiThreadAwake()`	QApplication
`handle()`	QFile
`hasAlphaBuffer()`	QImage
`hasApplyButton()`	QTabDialog
`hasCancelButton()`	QTabDialog
`hasClipping()`	QPainter
`hasDefaultButton()`	QTabDialog
`hasFocus()`	QWidget
`hasGlobalMouseTracking()`	QApplication
`hasHeightForWidth()`	QBoxLayout QLayoutItem QWidgetItem QGridLayout QSizePolicy
`hasHelpButton()`	QTabDialog
`hashKeyAscii()`	QGDict
`hashKeyString()`	QGDict
`hasHost()`	QUrl
`hasMarkedText()`	QMultiLineEdit QLineEdit
`hasMouseTracking()`	QWidget
`hasOkButton()`	QTabDialog
`hasOnlyLocalFileSystem()`	QNetworkProtocol
`hasOpenGL()`	QGLFormat
`hasOpenGLOverlays()`	QGLFormat
`hasOverlay()`	QGLFormat
`hasPassword()`	QUrl
`hasPath()`	QUrl
`hasRef()`	QUrl
`hasSelectedText()`	QTextView
`hasUser()`	QUrl
`hasViewXForm()`	QPainter
`hasWorldXForm()`	QPainter
`head()`	QQueue
`header()`	QListView
`height()`	QWidget QPaintDeviceMetrics QFontMetrics QList-BoxPixmap QRect QListViewItem QPixmap QIcon-ViewItem QListBoxItem QImage QSize QSimpleRich-Text QListBoxText

(continued)

heightForWidth()	QWidget QGridLayout QBoxLayout QTextView QLabel QWidgetItem QMenuBar QLayoutItem
heightMM()	QPaintDeviceMetrics
help()	QWizard
helpButton()	QWizard
helpButtonPressed()	QTabDialog
helpClicked()	QWizard
heuristicContentMatch()	QTextCodec QGbkCodec QJisCodec QEucKrCodec QEucJpCodec
heuristicNameMatch()	QEucJpCodec QGbkCodec QEucKrCodec QJisCodec QTextCodec
hide()	QWidget QMenuBar QDialog QToolBar QPopupMenu QToolTip
hideEvent()	QWidget
highlight()	QColorGroup
highlighted()	QMenuBar QTextBrowser QPopupMenu QListBox QComboBox
highlightedRedirect()	QPopupMenu
highlightedText()	QColorGroup
hideOrShow()	QStatusBar
highPriority()	QObject
hitButton()	QRadioButton QButton
home()	QDir QMultiLineEdit QFocusData QLineEdit QTextBrowser
hMargin()	QMultiLineEdit
homeDirPath()	QDir
horData()	QSizePolicy
horizontalScrollBar()	QScrollView QTableView
host()	QUrl
hotSpot()	QCursor
hour()	QTime
hScrollBarMode()	QScrollView
hsv()	QColor
icon()	QWidget QMessageBox
iconPixmap()	QMessageBox
iconProvider()	QFileDialog
iconSet()	QToolButton QMenuData QPushButton QHeader
iconText()	QWidget
iconView()	QIconViewItem
id()	QWidgetStack QButtonGroup
idAfter()	QSplitter
idAt()	QPopupMenu QMenuData
ignore()	QKeyEvent QDragMoveEvent QDropEvent QCloseEvent QWheelEvent
ignoreWhatsThis()	QAccel
image()	QImageDecoder QImageIO QClipboard
imageFormat()	QImageIO QImage QPixmap
inactive()	QPalette
indent()	QLabel
index()	QListBox QIconViewItem QIconView
indexChange()	QHeader
indexOf()	QMenuData

(continued)

indicatorFollowsStyle()	QProgressBar
indicatorSize()	QWindowsStyle QStyle QMotifStyle QPlatinumStyle
info()	QUrlOperator
inFont()	QFontMetrics
information()	QMessageBox
inherits()	QObject QMetaObject
initialize()	QPainter QColor QFont QCursor
initialized()	QGLContext
initializeGL()	QGLWidget
initializeOverlayGL()	QGLWidget
initMetaObject()	QObject
inputFormatList()	QImage
inputFormats()	QImageIO QImage QImageDecoder
insert()	QLineEdit QPtrDict QString QVector QCache QC-String QList QAsciiCache QStyleSheet QIntDict QAsciiDict QTranslator QValueList QMultiLineEdit QPixmapCache QMap QButtonGroup QIntCache QGVector QDict
insert_other()	QGCache
insert_string()	QGCache
insertAt()	QGList QMultiLineEdit
insertChar()	QMultiLineEdit
insertChild()	QObject
inserted()	QChildEvent
insertExpand()	QGVector
insertionPolicy()	QComboBox
insertInGrid()	QIconView
insertItem()	QAccel QComboBox QMenuData QListView QIconView QListViewItem QBoxLayout QListBox
insertLayout()	QBoxLayout
insertLine()	QMultiLineEdit
insertSeparator()	QMenuData
insertSpacing()	QBoxLayout
insertStretch()	QBoxLayout
insertStringList()	QListBox QComboBox
insertStrList()	QListBox QComboBox
insertSubstitution()	QFont
insertTab()	QTabDialog QTabWidget QTabBar
insertTearOffHandle()	QPopupMenu
insertWidget()	QBoxLayout
inSort()	QList QGList
installEventFilter()	QObject
installTranslator()	QApplication
instance()	QNPWidget QNPStream
interpretText()	QSpinBox
intersect()	QRegion QRect
intersects()	QRect QIconViewItem
inText()	QSimpleRichText
invalidate()	QBoxLayout QLayoutItem QLayout QGridLayout
invalidateHeight()	QListViewItem
intValue()	QLCDNumber
invert()	QWMatrix

(continued)

invertPixels()	QImage
invertSelection()	QIconView QListBox QListView
inWhatsThisMode()	QWhatsThis
ioDevice()	QImageIO
isA()	QObject
isAccepted()	QDropEvent QCloseEvent QKeyEvent QWheelEvent
isActionAccepted()	QDropEvent
isActive()	QTimer QPainter
isActiveWindow()	QXtWidget QWidget
isAnchor()	QStyleSheetItem
isAsynchronous()	QIODevice
isAutoRepeat()	QKeyEvent
isBitmapScalable()	QFontDatabase
isBlocked()	QSignal
isBuffered()	QIODevice
isCheckable()	QPopupMenu
isChecked()	QRadioButton QCheckBox
isClickEnabled()	QHeader
isCombinedAccess()	QIODevice
isConnected()	QConnection
isContentsPreviewEnabled()	QFileDialog
isCopyOf()	QFont QPalette
isDefault()	QPushButton
isDefaultUp()	QMenuBar
isDesktop()	QWidget
isDigit()	QChar
isDir()	QFileInfo QUrlInfo QUrlOperator
isDirectAccess()	QIODevice
isDirty()	QColor
isDockEnabled()	QMainWindow
isDockMenuEnabled()	QMainWindow
isDown()	QButton
isEmpty()	QIntCacheIterator QStack QCache QAsciiDictIterator QSpacerItem QArray QList QIntCache QPtrDictIterator QMap QValueList QRect QAsciiCacheIterator QString QPtrDict QRegExp QWidgetItem QQueue QLayout QStrListIterator QAsciiDict QSize QRegion QCString QAsciiCache QIntDictIterator QDictIterator QListIterator QVector QLayoutItem QCacheIterator QDict QByteArray QIntDict
isEnabled()	QWidget QSocketNotifier QAccel
isEnabledTo()	QWidget
isEnabledToTLW()	QWidget
isEndOfParagraph()	QMultiLineEdit
isEnumType()	QMetaProperty
isEqual()	QGArray
isExclusive()	QButtonGroup
isExclusiveToggle()	QButton
isExecutable()	QUrlInfo QFileInfo
isExpandable()	QListViewItem
isExtDev()	QPaintDevice

(continued)

`isFile()`	QUrlInfo QFileInfo
`isFocusEnabled()`	QWidget
`isGenerated()`	QIconSet
`isGrayscale()`	QImage
`isHorizontalStretchable()`	QToolBar
`isInactive()`	QIODevice
`isInfoPreviewEnabled()`	QFileDialog
`isItemChecked()`	QMenuData
`isItemEnabled()`	QAccel QMenuData
`isLetter()`	QChar
`isLetterOrNumber()`	QChar
`isLocalFile()`	QUrl
`isMark()`	QChar
`isMenuButton()`	QPushButton
`isMinimized()`	QWidget
`isModal()`	QWidget
`isMovingEnabled()`	QHeader
`isMultiSelection()`	QListBox QListView
`isNull()`	QGuardedPtr QSize QPixmap QPicture QArray QTime QChar QByteArray QMovie QRegion QVector QDateTime QIconSet QRect QImage QString QPoint QDate QCString
`isNumber()`	QChar
`isOn()`	QButton QCheckListItem
`isOpen()`	QListViewItem QListView QIODevice
`isOverwriteMode()`	QMultiLineEdit
`isPhase2()`	QSessionManager
`isPopup()`	QWidget
`isPrint()`	QChar
`isPrintableData()`	QDataStream
`isPunct()`	QChar
`isQBitmap()`	QPixmap
`isRadioButtonExclusive()`	QButtonGroup
`isRaw()`	QIODevice
`isReadable()`	QIODevice QFileInfo QUrlInfo QDir
`isReadOnly()`	QMultiLineEdit QLineEdit
`isReadWrite()`	QIODevice
`isRelative()`	QDir QFileInfo
`isRelativePath()`	QDir
`isRelativeUrl()`	QUrl
`isResizeEnabled()`	QHeader
`isRoot()`	QDir
`isScalable()`	QFontDatabase
`isSelectable()`	QListViewItem QIconViewItem QListBoxItem
`isSelected()`	QIconViewItem QListBox QListViewItem QListView
`isSeparator()`	QCustomMenuItem
`isSequentialAccess()`	QIODevice
`isSessionRestored()`	QApplication
`isSetType()`	QMetaProperty
`isSharing()`	QGLContext QGLWidget
`isSizeGripEnabled()`	QStatusBar
`isSmoothlyScalable()`	QFontDatabase

(continued)

isSpace()	QChar
isSymLink()	QFileInfo QUrlInfo
isSynchronous()	QIODevice
isTabEnabled()	QTabWidget QTabDialog QTabBar
isToggleButton()	QButton
isTopLevel()	QLayout QWidget
isTranslated()	QIODevice
isUndoEnabled()	QMultiLineEdit
isUpdatesEnabled()	QWidget
isValid()	QUrl QGLWidget QSize QMetaProperty QColor QRect QDate QGLContext QVariant QDateTime QTime QRegExp
isVerticalStretchable()	QToolBar
isVisible()	QWidget
isVisibleTo()	QWidget
isVisibleToTLW()	QWidget
isWidgetType()	QObject
isWritable()	QIODevice QFileInfo QUrlInfo
italic()	QFontDatabase QFontInfo QFont
item()	QStyleSheet QListBox
itemAbove()	QListViewItem
itemAt()	QListView QListBox
itemBelow()	QListViewItem
itemChanged()	QNetworkProtocol QUrlOperator
itemHeight()	QPopupMenu QListBox
itemMargin()	QListView
itemParameter()	QMenuData
itemPos()	QListView QListViewItem
itemRect()	QListView QStyle QListBox
itemRenamed()	QIconView
itemsMovable()	QIconView
itemTextBackground()	QIconView
itemTextPos()	QIconView
itemVisible()	QListBox
iterator()	QLayoutItem QBoxLayout QGridLayout QLayout
join()	QStringList
joining()	QChar
joinStyle()	QPen
jul2greg()	QDate
jumpTable()	QImage
key()	QKeyEvent QMapIterator QIconViewItem QFont QMapConstIterator QListViewItem QAccel
keyboardFocusTab()	QTabBar
keyboardGrabber()	QWidget
keyPressEvent()	QListBox QComboBox QDialog QListView QMessageBox QPopupMenu QLineEdit QIconView QMultiLineEdit QMenuBar QTabBar QTextBrowser QScrollBar QButton QTextView QFileDialog QSlider QWidget
keyReleaseEvent()	QButton QWidget
keysToValue()	QMetaProperty
keyToString()	QAccel
keyToValue()	QMetaProperty

(continued)

`killLine()`	QMultiLineEdit
`killTimer()`	QObject
`killTimers()`	QObject
`label()`	QToolBar QHeader
`labelText()`	QProgressDialog
`last()`	QGList QValueList QList
`lastColVisible()`	QTableView
`lastItem()`	QIconView
`lastModified()`	QUrlInfo QFileInfo QNPStream
`lastRead()`	QFileInfo QUrlInfo
`lastResortFamily()`	QFont
`lastResortFont()`	QFont
`lastRowVisible()`	QTableView
`lastWindowClosed()`	QApplication
`latin1()`	QChar QString
`layout()`	QWidget QLayout QLayoutItem
`layOutButtonRow()`	QWizard
`layoutTabs()`	QTabBar
`layOutTitleRow()`	QWizard
`lazyAlloc()`	QColor
`leading()`	QFontMetrics
`leapYear()`	QDate
`leaveAllocContext()`	QColor
`leaveEvent()`	QWidget QMultiLineEdit QLineEdit QMenuBar QToolButton QSpinBox
`leaveInstance()`	QNPWidget
`leaveWhatsThisMode()`	QWhatsThis
`left()`	QString QRect QCString
`leftBearing()`	QFontMetrics
`leftCell()`	QTableView
`leftJustify()`	QString QCString
`leftMargin()`	QScrollView
`length()`	QCString QMultiLineEdit QString
`lessThan()`	QUrlInfo
`light()`	QColor QColorGroup
`lineEdit()`	QComboBox
`lineLength()`	QMultiLineEdit
`lineSpacing()`	QFontMetrics
`lineStep()`	QScrollBar QRangeControl QSpinBox QSlider
`lineTo()`	QPainter
`lineUpToolBars()`	QMainWindow
`lineWidth()`	QFontMetrics QFrame
`linkColor()`	QTextView
`linkUnderline()`	QTextView
`listBegin()`	QVariant
`listBox()`	QListBoxItem QComboBox
`listChildren()`	QUrlOperator
`listEnd()`	QVariant
`listStyle()`	QStyleSheetItem
`listView()`	QListViewItem
`load()`	QPixmap QImage QTranslator QVariant QPicture
`loadCharmap()`	QTextCodec

(continued)

loadCharmapFile()	QTextCodec
loadFromData()	QImage QPixmap
local8Bit()	QString
locale()	QTextCodec
locale_init()	QFont
localFileToUri()	QUriDrag
logicalDpiX()	QPaintDeviceMetrics
logicalDpiY()	QPaintDeviceMetrics
logicalFontSize()	QStyleSheetItem
logicalFontSizeStep()	QStyleSheetItem
look_ascii()	QGDict
look_int()	QGDict
look_ptr()	QGDict
look_string()	QGDict
loopLevel()	QApplication
lostFocus()	QFocusEvent
lower()	QWidget QCString QString QChar
m11()	QWMatrix
m12()	QWMatrix
m21()	QWMatrix
m22()	QWMatrix
mainWidget()	QLayout QApplication
mainWindow()	QToolBar
makeAbsolute()	QMimeSourceFactory
makeArc()	QPointArray
makeCurrent()	QGLContext QGLWidget
makeDecoder()	QGbkCodec QEucJpCodec QTextCodec QJisCodec QEucKrCodec
makeEllipse()	QPointArray
makeEncoder()	QTextCodec
makeOverlayCurrent()	QGLWidget
makeRowLayout()	QIconView
manhattanLength()	QPoint
map()	QWMatrix QSignalMapper
mapFromGlobal()	QWidget
mapFromParent()	QWidget
mapped()	QSignalMapper
mapTextToValue()	QSpinBox
mapToActual()	QHeader
mapToGlobal()	QWidget
mapToIndex()	QHeader
mapToLogical()	QHeader
mapToParent()	QWidget
mapToSection()	QHeader
mapValueToText()	QSpinBox
margin()	QStyleSheetItem QTabWidget QLayout QFrame
margins()	QPrinter
markedText()	QMultiLineEdit QLineEdit
mask()	QPixmap QCursor
match()	QRegExp QDir
matchAllDirs()	QDir
matchstr()	QRegExp

(continued)

`maxColOffset()`	QTableView
`maxColors()`	QColor
`maxCost()`	QCache QAsciiCache QIntCache QGCache
`maxCount()`	QComboBox
`maximumHeight()`	QWidget
`maximumSize()`	QLayoutItem QGridLayout QWidgetItem QWidget QLayout QBoxLayout QSpacerItem
`maximumSliderDragDistance()`	QCommonStyle QStyle QPlatinumStyle QWindowsStyle
`maximumWidth()`	QWidget
`maxItemTextLength()`	QIconView
`maxItemWidth()`	QListBox QIconView
`maxLength()`	QMultiLineEdit QLineEdit
`maxLineLength()`	QMultiLineEdit
`maxLines()`	QMultiLineEdit
`maxLineWidth()`	QMultiLineEdit
`maxPage()`	QPrinter
`maxRowOffset()`	QTableView
`maxValue()`	QSlider QScrollBar QSpinBox QRangeControl
`maxViewX()`	QTableView
`maxViewY()`	QTableView
`maxWidth()`	QFontMetrics
`maxXOffset()`	QTableView
`maxYOffset()`	QTableView
`maybeReady()`	QDataSource QDataSink
`maybeTip()`	QToolTip
`mayGrowHorizontally()`	QSizePolicy
`mayGrowVertically()`	QSizePolicy
`mayShrinkHorizontally()`	QSizePolicy
`mayShrinkVertically()`	QSizePolicy
`member()`	QConnection
`memberName()`	QConnection
`menuBar()`	QLayout QMainWindow
`menuButtonIndicatorWidth()`	QStyle
`menuContentsChanged()`	QMenuData QMenuBar
`menuDelPopup()`	QMenuData
`menuInsPopup()`	QMenuData
`menuStateChanged()`	QMenuData QMenuBar
`message()`	QStatusBar
`metaObject()`	QObject
`metric()`	QPicture QPrinter QPaintDevice QPixmap QWidget
`mibEnum()`	QEucKrCodec QEucJpCodec QGbkCodec QTextCodec QJisCodec
`microFocusHint()`	QWidget
`mid()`	QCString QString QColorGroup
`midlight()`	QColorGroup
`midLineWidth()`	QFrame
`mightBeRichText()`	QStyleSheet
`mimeSourceFactory()`	QTextView
`minimumDuration()`	QProgressDialog
`minimumHeight()`	QWidget

(continued)

`minimumSize()`	QGridLayout QWidgetItem QLayoutItem QLayout QBoxLayout QSpacerItem QToolBar QMenuBar QWidget
`minimumSizeHint()`	QWidget QMultiLineEdit QWidgetStack QLabel QSplitter QTabWidget QLineEdit QProgressBar QListView QMainWindow QSlider QIconView QListBox QToolBar QMenuBar QScrollView
`minimumWidth()`	QWidget
`minLeftBearing()`	QFontMetrics
`minPage()`	QPrinter
`minRightBearing()`	QFontMetrics
`minute()`	QTime
`minValue()`	QSlider QScrollBar QRangeControl QSpinBox
`minViewX()`	QTableView
`minViewY()`	QTableView
`mirror()`	QImage
`mirrored()`	QChar
`mirroredChar()`	QChar
`mixedColor()`	QPlatinumStyle
`mkdir()`	QUrlOperator QDir
`mode()`	QIODevice QLCDNumber QFileDialog
`month()`	QDate
`monthName()`	QDate
`mouseButtonClicked()`	QListView QListBox QIconView
`mouseButtonPressed()`	QListBox QIconView QListView
`mouseDoubleClickEvent()`	QComboBox QListBox QMultiLineEdit QWidget QLineEdit
`mouseGrabber()`	QWidget
`mouseMoveEvent()`	QWidget QLineEdit QMenuBar QSizeGrip QButton QComboBox QListBox QSlider QMultiLineEdit QPopupMenu QScrollBar QHeader
`mousePressEvent()`	QHeader QListBox QWidget QLineEdit QMultiLineEdit QSizeGrip QTabBar QSlider QComboBox QMenuBar QScrollBar QButton QPopupMenu
`mouseReleaseEvent()`	QSlider QButton QWidget QMenuBar QLineEdit QScrollBar QHeader QPopupMenu QTabBar QMultiLineEdit QListBox QComboBox
`move()`	QWidget QDialog QSemiModal QPushButton QIconViewItem
`moveBottomLeft()`	QRect
`moveBottomRight()`	QRect
`moveBy()`	QIconViewItem QRect
`moveCell()`	QHeader
`moveCenter()`	QRect
`moveChild()`	QScrollView
`moved()`	QHeader QIconView
`moveEvent()`	QXtWidget QWidget QToolButton
`moveFocus()`	QButtonGroup
`moveSection()`	QHeader
`moveSplitter()`	QSplitter
`moveTo()`	QPainter
`moveToFirst()`	QSplitter

(continued)

moveToLast()	QSplitter
moveTopLeft()	QRect
moveTopRight()	QRect
movie()	QLabel
msec()	QTime
msecsTo()	QTime
name()	QEucKrCodec QFile QTextCodec QObject QEucJp-Codec QUrlInfo QJisCodec QMetaProperty QSignal QStyleSheetItem QGbkCodec QColor
nameFilter()	QUrlOperator QDir
nameToType()	QVariant
networkOrdered()	QChar
new_classinfo()	QMetaObject
new_metadata()	QMetaObject
new_metaenum()	QMetaObject
new_metaenum_item()	QMetaObject
new_metaobject()	QMetaObject
new_metaproperty()	QMetaObject
newChild()	QNetworkProtocol
newChildren()	QUrlOperator QNetworkProtocol
newConverter()	QJpUnicodeConv
newInstance()	QNPlugin
newItem()	QCollection
newLine()	QMultiLineEdit
newPage()	QPrinter
newStream()	QNPInstance
newStreamCreated()	QNPInstance
newWindow()	QNPInstance
next()	QGList QListBoxItem QGLayoutIterator QList QFocusData QWizard
nextButton()	QWizard
nextItem()	QIconViewItem
nextLine()	QScrollBar
nextPage()	QScrollBar
nextSibling()	QListViewItem
normal()	QPalette
normalize()	QRect
notify()	QApplication
notifyURL()	QNPInstance
nrefs()	QArray QByteArray QGArray
numArgs()	QConnection
number()	QString
numberOfColumns()	QStyleSheetItem
numBitPlanes()	QColor
numBytes()	QImage
numClassInfo()	QMetaObject
numColors()	QImage QPaintDeviceMetrics
numCols()	QGridLayout QTableView
numColumns()	QListBox
numCopies()	QPrinter
numDigits()	QLCDNumber

(continued)

numItemsVisible()	QListBox
numLines()	QMultiLineEdit
numRows()	QListBox QGridLayout QTableView
numSignals()	QMetaObject
numSlots()	QMetaObject
object()	QConnection
objectTrees()	QObject
offIconSet()	QToolButton
offset()	QHeader QImage
okay()	QNPStream
oldPos()	QMoveEvent
oldSize()	QResizeEvent
onIconSet()	QToolButton
onItem()	QIconView QListBox QListView
onViewport()	QListBox QListView QIconView
opaqueMoving()	QMainWindow
opaqueResize()	QSplitter
open()	QFile QBuffer QIODevice
operation()	QNetworkOperation
operationGet()	QNetworkProtocol QLocalFs
operationInProgress()	QNetworkProtocol
operationListChildren()	QLocalFs QNetworkProtocol
operationMkDir()	QLocalFs QNetworkProtocol
operationPut()	QNetworkProtocol QLocalFs
operationRemove()	QNetworkProtocol QLocalFs
operationRename()	QNetworkProtocol QLocalFs
operator!()	QString
operator!=()	QWMatrix QPen QVariant QRegExp QGuardedPtr QDate QDateTime QByteArray QColorGroup QTime QMapConstIterator QRegion QDir QValueList QImage QArray QPalette QColor QValueListConstIterator QBrush QMapIterator QValueListIterator QFont
operator&()	QRegion QRect
operator&=()	QBitArray QRect QRegion
operator()()	QListIterator QAsciiDictIterator QAsciiCacheIterator QGCacheIterator QCacheIterator QGDictIterator QIntCacheIterator QGListIterator QPtrDictIterator QIntDictIterator QDictIterator
operator*()	QStrListIterator QGuardedPtr QMapIterator QMapConstIterator QValueListConstIterator QListIterator QValueListIterator
operator*=()	QWMatrix QSize QPoint
operator+()	QValueList QRegion
operator++()	QValueListIterator QGDictIterator QDictIterator QAsciiDictIterator QAsciiCacheIterator QIntCacheIterator QPtrDictIterator QIntDictIterator QGListIterator QStrListIterator QGCacheIterator QCacheIterator QLayoutIterator QValueListConstIterator QListViewItemIterator QListIterator

(continued)

operator+=()	QPoint QListIterator QString QListViewItemIterator QDictIterator QValueList QGDictIterator QPtrDictIterator QCacheIterator QCString QGCacheIterator QIntDictIterator QGListIterator QStrListIterator QAsciiCacheIterator QRegion QIntCacheIterator QAsciiDictIterator QSize
operator-()	QRegion
operator—()	QValueListIterator QCacheIterator QGCacheIterator QValueListConstIterator QGListIterator QListIterator QIntCacheIterator QStrListIterator QListViewItemIterator QAsciiCacheIterator
operator-=()	QAsciiCacheIterator QListIterator QCacheIterator QIntCacheIterator QListViewItemIterator QSize QRegion QGCacheIterator QGListIterator QStrListIterator QPoint
operator->()	QGuardedPtr
operator/=()	QSize QPoint
operator<()	QDate QDateTime QTime
operator<<()	QDataStream QTextStream QValueList
operator<=()	QTime QDateTime QDate
operator=()	QGDictIterator QGCache QPointArray QGList QPtrDict QQueue QAsciiDict QGDict QIconSet QIntCacheIterator QBitVal QVariant QBitArray QCursor QMovie QGVector QDict QBitmap QGuardedPtr QUrlOperator QAsciiCacheIterator QIntCache QPicture QStrList QFontMetrics QGCacheIterator QByteArray QVector QBrush QPen QCache QRegion QLayoutIterator QCacheIterator QGListIterator QList QPalette QUrl QDir QValueList QMap QCString QStack QPixmap QRegExp QFont QFileInfo QSortedList QIntDict QColor QUrlInfo QGArray QListViewItemIterator QListIterator QArray QImage QString QStrListIterator QFontInfo QAsciiCache
operator==()	QColorGroup QDir QValueListIterator QFont QTime QImage QGuardedPtr QList QBrush QWMatrix QValueList QRegion QByteArray QValueListConstIterator QDate QUrl QGList QPen QMapIterator QDateTime QArray QColor QMapConstIterator QVariant QUrlInfo QRegExp QPalette
operator>()	QDateTime QTime QDate
operator>=()	QDateTime QDate QTime
operator>>()	QTextStream QDataStream
operator[]()	QAsciiDict QString QDir QValueList QAsciiCache QBitArray QIntCache QCache QPtrDict QIntDict QByteArray QArray QDict QMap QVector
operator^()	QRegion
operator^=()	QBitArray QRegion
operator|()	QRect QRegion
operator|=()	QRegion QBitArray QRect
operator~()	QBitArray
optimization()	QPixmap

(continued)

`orientation()`	QGroupBox QScrollBar QPrinter QSplitter QSlider QToolBar QHeader
`orientationChanged()`	QToolBar
`outputFileName()`	QPrinter
`outputFormatList()`	QImage
`outputFormats()`	QImage QImageIO
`outputToFile()`	QPrinter
`overflow()`	QLCDNumber
`overlayContext()`	QGLWidget
`overlayTransparentColor()`	QGLContext
`overrideCursor()`	QApplication
`owner()`	QUrlInfo QFileInfo
`ownerId()`	QFileInfo
`packImage()`	QPNGImagePacker
`page()`	QWizard
`pageCount()`	QWizard
`pageDown()`	QMultiLineEdit
`pageOrder()`	QPrinter
`pageSize()`	QPrinter
`pageStep()`	QSlider QRangeControl QScrollBar
`pageUp()`	QMultiLineEdit
`paint()`	QListBoxItem QListBoxText QListBoxPixmap QTab-Bar QCustomMenuItem
`paintBranches()`	QCheckListItem QListViewItem
`paintCell()`	QListBox QMultiLineEdit QTableView QListViewItem QCheckListItem
`paintEmptyArea()`	QListView
`paintEvent()`	QSlider QWidget QMainWindow QLineEdit QFrame QScrollBar QButton QTableView QComboBox QSize-Grip QPopupMenu QStatusBar QGLWidget QTabDialog QToolBar QHeader QTabBar QGroupBox
`paintFocus()`	QCheckListItem QIconViewItem QListViewItem
`paintGL()`	QGLWidget
`paintingActive()`	QPaintDevice
`paintItem()`	QIconViewItem
`paintLabel()`	QTabBar
`paintOverlayGL()`	QGLWidget
`paintSection()`	QHeader
`paintSectionLabel()`	QHeader
`paintSlider()`	QSlider
`palette()`	QWidget QApplication QToolTip
`paletteChange()`	QTextView QWidget
`palettePropagation()`	QWidget
`paper()`	QTextView
`paperColorGroup()`	QTextView
`parameter()`	QSignal
`parameters()`	QImageIO
`parent()`	QObject QListViewItem
`parentWidget()`	QToolTip QWidget
`parse()`	QUrlOperator QUrl
`password()`	QUrl
`paste()`	QMultiLineEdit QLineEdit

(continued)

path()	QUrl QDir
pattern()	QRegExp
pause()	QMovie
paused()	QMovie
pen()	QPainter
permission()	QFileInfo
permissions()	QUrlInfo
pixel()	QImage QColor
pixelIndex()	QImage
pixelSize()	QFont
pixmap()	QListBoxPixmap QButton QListViewItem QBrush QListBoxItem QFileIconProvider QDragObject QLabel QMenuData QListBox QClipboard QComboBox QIconViewItem QIconSet
pixmapHotSpot()	QDragObject
pixmapRect()	QIconViewItem
pixmapSizeChanged()	QMainWindow
plane()	QGLFormat
play()	QPicture
point()	QPointArray
pointSize()	QFont QFontInfo
pointSizeFloat()	QFont
pointSizes()	QFontDatabase
polish()	QApplication QMotifStyle QWidget QStyle
polishPopupMenu()	QWindowsStyle QStyle QPlatinumStyle QMotifStyle
pop()	QValueStack QStack
popup()	QToolButton QComboBox QPushButton QPopupMenu
popupDelay()	QToolButton
popupMenuItemHeight()	QWindowsStyle QMotifStyle QPlatinumStyle QStyle
popupSubmenuIndicatorWidth()	QStyle QCommonStyle
port()	QUrl
pos()	QCursor QWidget QMoveEvent QDropEvent QMouseEvent QIconViewItem QPainter QWheelEvent
positionFromValue()	QRangeControl
postEvent()	QApplication
postURL()	QNPInstance
precision()	QTextStream
prefix()	QSpinBox
prepend()	QValueList QString QList QCString
pressed()	QButtonGroup QButton QListView QIconView QHeader QListBox
prev()	QList QListBoxItem QGList QFocusData
previewMode()	QFileDialog
previewUrl()	QFilePreview
prevItem()	QIconViewItem
prevLine()	QScrollBar
prevPage()	QScrollBar
prevValue()	QRangeControl
print()	QNPInstance
printerName()	QPrinter
printerSelectionOption()	QPrinter
printFullPage()	QNPInstance

(continued)

printProgram()	QPrinter
processEvents()	QApplication
processOneEvent()	QApplication
processOperation()	QNetworkProtocol
progress()	QProgressBar QProgressDialog
property()	QMetaObject QObject
propertyNames()	QMetaObject
protocol()	QUrl
protocolDetail()	QNetworkOperation
provides()	QMimeSource QDropEvent
push()	QValueStack QStack
pushButtonContentsRect()	QStyle
put()	QUrlOperator
putch()	QFile QBuffer QIODevice
putPoints()	QPointArray
qglClearColor()	QGLWidget
qglColor()	QGLWidget
quadBezier()	QPointArray
query()	QUrl
queryList()	QObject
quit()	QApplication
raise()	QWidget
raiseWidget()	QWidgetStack
rangeChange()	QRangeControl QSlider QScrollBar QSpinBox
rasterOp()	QPainter
rawArg()	QNetworkOperation
rawMode()	QFontInfo QFont
rawName()	QFont
rBottom()	QRect
read()	QImageIO QGDict QGVector QGList QTextStream
readAll()	QIODevice
readBlock()	QBuffer QIODevice QFile
readBytes()	QDataStream
readLine()	QFile QIODevice QBuffer QTextStream
readLink()	QFileInfo
readRawBytes()	QDataStream QTextStream
ready()	QAsyncIO
readyToReceive()	QDataSink
readyToSend()	QIODeviceSource QDataSource
reason()	QFocusEvent
receive()	QDataSink
receivers()	QObject
rect()	QPixmap QPaintEvent QImage QWidget QRect QIcon-ViewItem
rects()	QRegion
red()	QColor
redirect()	QPainter
redo()	QMultiLineEdit
redoAvailable()	QMultiLineEdit
ref()	QString QUrl
reformat()	QStatusBar
refresh()	QSplitter QFileInfo

(continued)

region()	QPaintEvent
registerDecoderFactory()	QImageDecoder
registerNetworkProtocol()	QNetworkProtocol
reject()	QDialog
release()	QSessionManager
released()	QHeader QButton QButtonGroup
releaseKeyboard()	QWidget
releaseMouse()	QWidget
relinkNode()	QGList
remove()	QVector QValueList QStack QQueue QIntCache QWhatsThis QString QCache QDict QGVector QPtr-Dict QAsciiCache QFile QDir QIntDict QTranslator QGList QList QAsciiDict QToolTip QButton-Group QMap QCString QUrlOperator
remove_ascii()	QGDict
remove_int()	QGDict
remove_other()	QGCache
remove_ptr()	QGDict
remove_string()	QGCache QGDict
removeAt()	QGList
removeChild()	QObject QScrollView
removeColumn()	QListView
removed()	QUrlOperator QChildEvent QNetworkProtocol
removeEventFilter()	QObject
removeFirst()	QGList QList
removeItem()	QListViewItem QMenuData QComboBox QListView QAccel QListBox
removeItemAt()	QMenuData
removeLabel()	QHeader
removeLast()	QList QGList
removeLine()	QMultiLineEdit
removeMappings()	QSignalMapper
removeNode()	QGList QList
removePage()	QTabWidget QWizard QTabDialog
removePostedEvents()	QApplication
removeRef()	QList QGList
removeRenameBox()	QIconViewItem
removeSubstitution()	QFont
removeTab()	QTabBar
removeTip()	QToolTipGroup
removeToolBar()	QMainWindow
removeTranslator()	QApplication
removeWidget()	QStatusBar QWidgetStack
rename()	QIconViewItem QDir QUrlOperator
renameEnabled()	QIconViewItem
renderPixmap()	QGLWidget
repaint()	QIconViewItem QWidget QTableView QListViewItem
repaintArea()	QLineEdit
repaintContents()	QScrollView
repaintItem()	QListView QIconView
repairEventFilter()	QAccel
reparent()	QWidget

(continued)

replace()	QAsciiDict QCString QIntDict QMap QDict QString QPtrDict
requestPhase2()	QSessionManager
requestRead()	QNPStream
rereadDir()	QFileDialog
reset()	QProgressBar QImage QProgressDialog QIODevice QTextStream QIconSet QWMatrix QUrlOperator QUrl QGLContext
resetRawData()	QGArray QArray QByteArray
resetReason()	QFocusEvent
resetStatus()	QIODevice
resetXForm()	QPainter
resize()	QDict QArray QGDict QGVector QWidget QPushButton QDialog QAsciiDict QGArray QVector QPtrDict QScrollView QByteArray QIntDict QCString QSemiModal QBitArray QPixmap
resizeContents()	QScrollView
resizeEvent()	QWorkspace QTextView QProgressDialog QSlider QMessageBox QScrollView QIconView QComboBox QGroupBox QListView QLineEdit QWidgetStack QTabDialog QMainWindow QSplitter QTabWidget QMultiLineEdit QXtWidget QTableView QListBox QFileDialog QFrame QScrollBar QRadioButton QToolBar QMenuBar QWidget QPushButton QGLWidget QSpinBox QTabBar QCheckBox
resizeGL()	QGLWidget
resizeMode()	QIconView QLayout
resizeOverlayGL()	QGLWidget
resizePolicy()	QScrollView
resizeSection()	QHeader
resolveProperty()	QMetaObject
resortDir()	QFileDialog
restart()	QTime QMovie
restartCommand()	QSessionManager
restartHint()	QSessionManager
restore()	QPainter
restoreOverrideCursor()	QApplication
restoreWorldMatrix()	QPainter
result()	QDialog
returnPressed()	QMultiLineEdit QListView QListBox QLineEdit QIconView
rewind()	QIODeviceSource QDataSource
rewindable()	QIODeviceSource QDataSource
rgb()	QColor
rgba()	QGLFormat
rheight()	QSize
richText()	QTextView
right()	QString QCString QRect
rightBearing()	QFontMetrics
rightButtonClicked()	QIconView QListBox QListView
rightButtonPressed()	QListView QListBox QIconView
rightJustification()	QMainWindow

(continued)

`rightJustify()`	QString QCString
`rightMargin()`	QScrollView
`rLeft()`	QRect
`rmdir()`	QDir
`root()`	QDir
`rootDirPath()`	QDir
`rootIsDecorated()`	QListView
`rotate()`	QWMatrix QPainter
`row()`	QChar
`rowIsVisible()`	QTableView
`rowMode()`	QListBox
`rowStretch()`	QGridLayout
`rowYPos()`	QTableView
`rRight()`	QRect
`rTop()`	QRect
`running()`	QMovie
`rwidth()`	QSize
`rx()`	QPoint
`ry()`	QPoint
`save()`	QImage QPainter QPicture QTranslator QPixmap QVariant
`saveState()`	QApplication
`saveWorldMatrix()`	QPainter
`scale()`	QPainter QWMatrix
`scaleFont()`	QStyleSheet
`scanLine()`	QImage
`scriptCombo()`	QFontDialog
`scroll()`	QWidget QTableView
`scrollBarExtent()`	QStyle
`scrollBarMetrics()`	QMotifStyle QPlatinumStyle QWindowsStyle QStyle
`scrollBarPointOver()`	QStyle
`scrollBy()`	QScrollView
`scrollToAnchor()`	QTextBrowser
`second()`	QTime
`secsTo()`	QTime QDateTime
`sectionAt()`	QHeader
`sectionClicked()`	QHeader
`sectionPos()`	QHeader
`sectionSize()`	QHeader
`seekable()`	QNPStream
`segmentStyle()`	QLCDNumber
`selectAll()`	QMultiLineEdit QFileDialog QTextView QIconView QListBox QListView QLineEdit
`selected()`	QListBoxItem QTabDialog QTabBar QTabWidget QListBox QButtonGroup
`selectedFile()`	QFileDialog
`selectedFiles()`	QFileDialog
`selectedFilter()`	QFileDialog
`selectedItem()`	QListView
`selectedText()`	QTextView
`selectionChanged()`	QListView QIconView QListBox
`selectionMode()`	QListBox QIconView QListView

(continued)

`selectTab()`	QTabBar
`selfMask()`	QPixmap
`selfNesting()`	QStyleSheetItem
`sender()`	QObject
`sendEvent()`	QApplication
`sendPostedEvents()`	QApplication
`sendTo()`	QDataSource QIODeviceSource
`separator()`	QDir QMenuBar
`serialNumber()`	QPalette QPixmap
`sessionId()`	QSessionManager QApplication
`setAccel()`	QButton QMenuData
`setAcceptDrops()`	QWidget
`setAccum()`	QGLFormat
`setAction()`	QDropEvent
`setActive()`	QPalette
`setActiveItem()`	QPopupMenu
`setActiveWindow()`	QXtWidget QWidget
`setAlignment()`	QGroupBox QLineEdit QLayoutItem QLabel QStyleSheetItem QMultiLineEdit
`setAllColumnsShowFocus()`	QListView
`setAlpha()`	QGLFormat
`setAlphaBuffer()`	QImage
`setAnchor()`	QStyleSheetItem
`setApplyButton()`	QTabDialog
`setAppropriate()`	QWizard
`setArg()`	QNetworkOperation
`setArrangement()`	QIconView
`setAutoAdd()`	QLayout
`setAutoArrange()`	QIconView
`setAutoBufferSwap()`	QGLWidget
`setAutoClose()`	QProgressDialog
`setAutoCompletion()`	QComboBox
`setAutoDefault()`	QPushButton
`setAutoDelete()`	QCollection QStack QNetworkProtocol QQueue
`setAutoMask()`	QWidget QLabel
`setAutoRaise()`	QToolButton
`setAutoRepeat()`	QButton
`setAutoReset()`	QProgressDialog
`setAutoResize()`	QLabel QButton QComboBox
`setAutoUpdate()`	QMultiLineEdit QTableView
`setBackEnabled()`	QWizard
`setBackgroundColor()`	QMovie QWidget QTableView QPainter QComboBox
`setBackgroundMode()`	QPainter QWidget
`setBackgroundOrigin()`	QWidget
`setBackgroundPixmap()`	QWidget
`setBar()`	QProgressDialog
`setBaseSize()`	QWidget
`setBinMode()`	QLCDNumber
`setBit()`	QBitArray
`setBold()`	QFont
`setBottom()`	QRect QIntValidator QDoubleValidator
`setBottomItem()`	QListBox

(continued)

setBrush()	QPalette QPainter QColorGroup
setBrushOrigin()	QPainter
setBuddy()	QLabel
setBuffer()	QBuffer
setButton()	QButtonGroup
setButtonDefaultIndicatorWidth()	QStyle
setButtonSymbols()	QSpinBox
setButtonText()	QMessageBox
setByteOrder()	QDataStream
setCacheLimit()	QPixmapCache
setCaching()	QFileInfo
setCancelButton()	QTabDialog QProgressDialog
setCancelButtonText()	QProgressDialog
setCapStyle()	QPen
setCaption()	QWidget
setCaseSensitive()	QRegExp
setCellHeight()	QTableView
setCellSize()	QHeader
setCellWidth()	QTableView
setCenterIndicator()	QProgressBar
setCentralWidget()	QMainWindow
setCharSet()	QFont
setCheckable()	QPopupMenu
setChecked()	QCheckBox QRadioButton
setChildGeometries()	QWidgetStack
setClickEnabled()	QHeader
setClipping()	QPainter
setClipRect()	QPainter
setClipRegion()	QPainter
setCodec()	QTextStream
setColor()	QPalette QStyleSheetItem QColorGroup QBrush QImage QPen QColorDrag
setColorMode()	QPrinter
setColorSpec()	QApplication
setColStretch()	QGridLayout
setColumnAlignment()	QListView
setColumnLayout()	QGroupBox
setColumnMode()	QListBox
setColumns()	QGroupBox
setColumnText()	QListView
setColumnWidth()	QListView
setColumnWidthMode()	QListView
setComplete()	QNPStream
setContentsPos()	QScrollView QIconView QListView
setContentsPreview()	QFileDialog
setContentsPreviewEnabled()	QFileDialog
setContexts()	QStyleSheetItem
setCoords()	QRect
setCornerWidget()	QScrollView
setCreator()	QPrinter
setCRect()	QWidget
setCurrent()	QDir

(continued)

setCurrentItem()	QIconView QListView QListBox QComboBox
setCurrentTab()	QTabBar
setCursor()	QWidget
setCursorFlashTime()	QApplication
setCursorPosition()	QMultiLineEdit QLineEdit
setCustomColor()	QColorDialog
setCustomHighlighting()	QListBoxItem
setData()	QCustomEvent QIconDragItem QMimeSourceFactory
	QClipboard QPicture
setDate()	QDateTime
setDecimals()	QDoubleValidator
setDecMode()	QLCDNumber
setDecodingFunction()	QFile
setDefault()	QPushButton
setDefaultButton()	QTabDialog
setDefaultCodec()	QApplication
setDefaultFactory()	QMimeSourceFactory
setDefaultFont()	QFont
setDefaultFormat()	QGLFormat
setDefaultOptimization()	QPixmap
setDefaultOverlayFormat()	QGLFormat
setDefaultSheet()	QStyleSheet
setDefaultTabStop()	QMultiLineEdit
setDefaultUp()	QMenuBar
setDelay()	QToolTipGroup
setDepth()	QGLFormat
setDescription()	QImageIO
setDesktopSettingsAware()	QApplication
setDevice()	QTextStream QDataStream
setDir()	QUrlInfo QFileDialog
setDirection()	QBoxLayout
setDirectRendering()	QGLFormat
setDisabled()	QPalette
setDiscardCommand()	QSessionManager
setDisplayMode()	QStyleSheetItem
setDockEnabled()	QMainWindow
setDockMenuEnabled()	QMainWindow
setDocName()	QPrinter
setDotsPerMeterX()	QImage
setDotsPerMeterY()	QImage
setDoubleBuffer()	QGLFormat
setDoubleClickInterval()	QApplication
setDown()	QButton
setDragAutoScroll()	QScrollView
setDragEnabled()	QIconViewItem
setDropEnabled()	QIconViewItem
setDuplicatesEnabled()	QComboBox
setEchoMode()	QLineEdit QMultiLineEdit
setEdited()	QLineEdit QMultiLineEdit
setEditText()	QComboBox
setEnabled()	QWidget QSpinBox QSocketNotifier QLineEdit QAccel QComboBox QToolTip QScrollView QToolTipGroup

(continued)

setEncodedData()	QStoredDrag
setEncodedPathAndQuery()	QUrl
setEncoding()	QTextStream
setEncodingFunction()	QFile
setErrorCode()	QNetworkOperation
setExclusive()	QButtonGroup
setExpand()	QCString QString QGArray
setExpandable()	QListViewItem
setExtensionType()	QMimeSourceFactory
setf()	QTextStream
setFamily()	QFont
setFile()	QUrlInfo QFileInfo
setFileName()	QImageIO QUrl
setFilenames()	QUriDrag
setFilePath()	QMimeSourceFactory
setFilter()	QFileDialog QDir
setFilters()	QFileDialog
setFinish()	QWizard
setFinishEnabled()	QWizard
setFixedHeight()	QWidget
setFixedPitch()	QFont
setFixedSize()	QWidget
setFixedVisibleLines()	QMultiLineEdit
setFixedWidth()	QWidget
setFlags()	QIODevice QMetaProperty
setFocus()	QWidget
setFocusPolicy()	QWidget
setFocusProxy()	QWidget
setFont()	QPopupMenu QWizard QComboBox QIconView QToolTip QListView QLineEdit QPainter QListBox QCustom-MenuItem QMultiLineEdit QWidget QApplication QTabDialog
setFontFamily()	QStyleSheetItem
setFontItalic()	QStyleSheetItem
setFontPropagation()	QWidget
setFontSize()	QStyleSheetItem
setFontUnderline()	QStyleSheetItem
setFontWeight()	QStyleSheetItem
setFormat()	QGLContext QImageIO
setFrame()	QLineEdit
setFramePeriod()	QImageConsumer
setFrameRect()	QFrame QWidgetStack
setFrameShadow()	QFrame
setFrameShape()	QFrame
setFrameStyle()	QFrame
setFRect()	QWidget
setFromTo()	QPrinter
setFullPage()	QPrinter
setGeometry()	QWidget QSemiModal QWidgetItem QBoxLayout QPushButton QLayout QLayoutItem QDialog QSpacerItem QGridLayout
setGlobalMouseTracking()	QApplication

(continued)

setGridX()	QIconView
setGridY()	QIconView
setGroup()	QUrlInfo
setHBarGeometry()	QScrollView
setHeight()	QSize QRect QListViewItem
setHeightForWidth()	QSizePolicy
setHelpButton()	QTabDialog
setHelpEnabled()	QWizard
setHexMode()	QLCDNumber
setHMargin()	QMultiLineEdit
setHMS()	QTime
setHorData()	QSizePolicy
setHorizontalStretchable()	QToolBar
setHost()	QUrl
setHScrollBarMode()	QScrollView
setHsv()	QColor
setIcon()	QMessageBox QWidget
setIconPixmap()	QMessageBox
setIconProvider()	QFileDialog
setIconSet()	QPushButton QToolButton
setIconText()	QWidget
setId()	QMenuData
setIgnoreWhatsThis()	QAccel
setImage()	QClipboard QImageDrag QMimeSourceFactory QImageIO
setInactive()	QPalette
setIndent()	QLabel
setIndicator()	QProgressBar
setIndicatorFollowsStyle()	QProgressBar
setInfoPreview()	QFileDialog
setInfoPreviewEnabled()	QFileDialog
setInitialized()	QGLContext
setInsertionPolicy()	QComboBox
setIODevice()	QImageIO
setIsMenuButton()	QPushButton
setItalic()	QFont
setItemChecked()	QMenuData
setItemEnabled()	QMenuData QAccel
setItemMargin()	QListView
setItemParameter()	QMenuData
setItemRect()	QIconViewItem
setItemsMovable()	QIconView
setItemTextBackground()	QIconView
setItemTextPos()	QIconView
setJoinStyle()	QPen
setKey()	QIconViewItem
setKeyCompression()	QWidget
setLabel()	QToolBar QProgressDialog QHeader
setLabelText()	QProgressDialog
setLastModified()	QUrlInfo
setLatin1()	QString
setLazyAlloc()	QColor

(continued)

setLeft()	QRect
setLeftCell()	QTableView
setLineStep()	QSlider QScrollBar QSpinBox
setLineWidth()	QFrame
setLinkColor()	QTextView
setLinkUnderline()	QTextView
setListBox()	QComboBox
setListStyle()	QStyleSheetItem
setLogicalFontSize()	QStyleSheetItem
setLogicalFontSizeStep()	QStyleSheetItem
setLooping()	QImageConsumer
setMainWidget()	QApplication
setMapping()	QSignalMapper
setMargin()	QLayout QStyleSheetItem QFrame QTabWidget
setMargins()	QScrollView
setMask()	QWidget QPixmap
setMatchAllDirs()	QDir
setMatrix()	QWMatrix
setMaxCost()	QCache QAsciiCache QIntCache QGCache
setMaxCount()	QComboBox
setMaximumHeight()	QWidget
setMaximumSize()	QWidget
setMaximumWidth()	QWidget
setMaxItemTextLength()	QIconView
setMaxItemWidth()	QIconView
setMaxLength()	QMultiLineEdit QLineEdit
setMaxLineLength()	QMultiLineEdit
setMaxLines()	QMultiLineEdit
setMaxValue()	QSlider QSpinBox QScrollBar
setMenuBar()	QLayout
setMicroFocusHint()	QWidget
setMidLineWidth()	QFrame
setMimeSourceFactory()	QTextView
setMinimumDuration()	QProgressDialog
setMinimumHeight()	QWidget
setMinimumSize()	QWidget
setMinimumWidth()	QWidget
setMinMax()	QPrinter
setMinValue()	QSlider QScrollBar QSpinBox
setMode()	QIODevice QLCDNumber QFileDialog
setMouseTracking()	QWidget
setMovie()	QLabel
setMovingEnabled()	QHeader
setMultiSelection()	QListBox QListView
setName()	QFile QSignal QUrlInfo QObject QWidget
setNamedColor()	QColor
setNameFilter()	QDir QUrlOperator
setNextEnabled()	QWizard
setNoChange()	QCheckBox
setNormal()	QPalette
setNum()	QLabel QString QCString
setNumberOfColumns()	QStyleSheetItem

(continued)

setNumColors()	QImage
setNumCols()	QTableView
setNumCopies()	QPrinter
setNumDigits()	QLCDNumber
setNumRows()	QTableView
setOctMode()	QLCDNumber
setOffIconSet()	QToolButton
setOffset()	QImage QTableView QHeader
setOkay()	QNPStream
setOkButton()	QTabDialog
setOn()	QPushButton QButton QToolButton QCheckListItem
setOnIconSet()	QToolButton
setOpaqueMoving()	QMainWindow
setOpaqueResize()	QSplitter
setOpen()	QListView QListViewItem
setOptimization()	QPixmap
setOption()	QGLFormat
setOrientation()	QToolBar QScrollBar QGroupBox QHeader QPrinter QSlider QSplitter
setOrigin()	QGridLayout
setOutputFileName()	QPrinter
setOutputToFile()	QPrinter
setOverlay()	QGLFormat
setOverrideCursor()	QApplication
setOverwriteMode()	QMultiLineEdit
setOwner()	QUrlInfo
setPageOrder()	QPrinter
setPageSize()	QPrinter
setPageStep()	QScrollBar QSlider
setPalette()	QScrollBar QListView QComboBox QSlider QLineEdit QWidget QToolTip QApplication QTableView QIconView
setPalettePropagation()	QWidget
setPaper()	QTextView
setPaperColorGroup()	QTextView
setParameter()	QSignal
setParameters()	QImageIO
setPassword()	QUrl
setPath()	QDir QUrlOperator QUrl
setPen()	QPainter
setPermissions()	QUrlInfo
setPixel()	QImage
setPixelAlignment()	QPNGImagePacker
setPixelSize()	QFont
setPixelSizeFloat()	QFont
setPixmap()	QIconSet QClipboard QMimeSourceFactory QLabel QIconViewItem QButton QBrush QDragObject QListViewItem
setPixmapRect()	QIconViewItem
setPlane()	QGLFormat
setPoint()	QDropEvent QPointArray
setPoints()	QPointArray

(continued)

setPointSize()	QFont
setPointSizeFloat()	QFont
setPopup()	QPushButton QToolButton
setPopupDelay()	QToolButton
setPort()	QUrl
setPos()	QCursor
setPrefix()	QSpinBox
setPreviewMode()	QFileDialog
setPrintableData()	QDataStream
setPrinterName()	QPrinter
setPrinterSelectionOption()	QPrinter
setPrintProgram()	QPrinter
setProgress()	QProgressBar QProgressDialog
setProperty()	QSessionManager QObject
setProtocol()	QUrl
setProtocolDetail()	QNetworkOperation
setQuery()	QUrl
setRadioButtonExclusive()	QButtonGroup
setRange()	QRangeControl QDoubleValidator QIntValidator
setRasterOp()	QPainter
setRawArg()	QNetworkOperation
setRawData()	QGArray QByteArray QArray
setRawMode()	QFont
setRawName()	QFont
setReadable()	QUrlInfo
setReadOnly()	QLineEdit QMultiLineEdit
setReason()	QFocusEvent
setRect()	QRect
setRef()	QUrl
setRenameEnabled()	QIconViewItem
setResizeEnabled()	QHeader
setResizeMode()	QSplitter QLayout QIconView
setResizePolicy()	QScrollView
setRestartCommand()	QSessionManager
setRestartHint()	QSessionManager
setResult()	QDialog
setRgb()	QColor
setRgba()	QGLFormat
setRight()	QRect
setRightJustification()	QMainWindow
setRootIsDecorated()	QListView
setRowMode()	QListBox
setRowStretch()	QGridLayout
setRubberband()	QSplitter
setScrollBarExtent()	QStyle
setSegmentStyle()	QLCDNumber
setSelectable()	QIconViewItem QListBoxItem QListViewItem
setSelected()	QIconViewItem QIconView QListViewItem QListBox QListView
setSelection()	QLineEdit QFileDialog QMultiLineEdit
setSelectionMode()	QListView QIconView QListBox
setSelfNesting()	QStyleSheetItem

(continued)

`setSeparator()`	QMenuBar
`setShape()`	QTabBar QCursor
`setSharedBlock()`	QGArray
`setShowHiddenFiles()`	QFileDialog
`setShowSortIndicator()`	QListView
`setShowToolTips()`	QIconView
`setSize()`	QImageConsumer QUrlInfo QRect
`setSizeGripEnabled()`	QStatusBar
`setSizeIncrement()`	QWidget
`setSizeLimit()`	QComboBox
`setSizes()`	QSplitter
`setSmallDecimalPoint()`	QLCDNumber
`setSortIndicator()`	QHeader
`setSorting()`	QListView QDir QIconView
`setSource()`	QTextBrowser
`setSpacing()`	QLayout QGrid QIconView QHBox
`setSpecialValueText()`	QSpinBox
`setSpeed()`	QMovie
`setStartDragDistance()`	QApplication
`setStartDragTime()`	QApplication
`setState()`	QButton QNetworkOperation QIODevice
`setStatus()`	QIODevice QImageIO
`setStencil()`	QGLFormat
`setSteps()`	QRangeControl
`setStereo()`	QGLFormat
`setStr()`	QCString
`setStretchableWidget()`	QToolBar
`setStretchFactor()`	QBoxLayout QHBox
`setStrikeOut()`	QFont
`setStyle()`	QApplication QWidget QBrush QPen
`setStyleHint()`	QFont
`setStyleSheet()`	QTextView
`setSubtype()`	QTextDrag
`setSuffix()`	QSpinBox
`setSupportsMargin()`	QLayout
`setSymLink()`	QUrlInfo
`setTabArray()`	QPainter
`setTabBar()`	QTabWidget QTabDialog
`setTabEnabled()`	QTabWidget QTabBar QTabDialog
`setTableFlags()`	QTableView
`setTabOrder()`	QWidget
`setTabPosition()`	QTabWidget
`setTabStops()`	QPainter
`setTarget()`	QDragObject
`setText()`	QMimeSourceFactory QTextBrowser QImage QLineEdit QClipboard QIconViewItem QListBoxItem QMessageBox QListViewItem QMultiLineEdit QButton QTextDrag QTextView QLabel
`setTextFormat()`	QMessageBox QLabel QTextView
`setTextLabel()`	QToolButton
`setTextRect()`	QIconViewItem
`setTickInterval()`	QSlider

(continued)

setTickmarks()	QSlider
setTime()	QDateTime
setTime_t()	QDateTime
setTitle()	QGroupBox
setToggleButton()	QPushButton QToolButton QButton
setToggleType()	QButton
setToolBarsMovable()	QMainWindow
setTop()	QRect QIntValidator QDoubleValidator
setTopCell()	QTableView
setTopItem()	QListBox
setTopLeftCell()	QTableView
setTotalSteps()	QProgressBar QProgressDialog
setTracking()	QHeader QScrollBar QSlider
setTreeStepSize()	QListView
setTristate()	QCheckBox
setType()	QIODevice
setUnderline()	QFont
setUndoDepth()	QMultiLineEdit
setUndoEnabled()	QMultiLineEdit
setUnicode()	QString
setUnicodeCodes()	QString
setUnicodeUris()	QUriDrag
setup()	QCheckListItem QPrinter QListViewItem
setupPainter()	QTableView
setUpdatesEnabled()	QWidget
setUpLayout()	QMainWindow
setUris()	QUriDrag
setUrl()	QFileDialog QNetworkProtocol
setUseHighlightColors()	QMotifStyle
setUser()	QUrl
setUsesBigPixmap()	QToolButton
setUsesBigPixmaps()	QMainWindow
setUsesTextLabel()	QMainWindow QToolButton
setValidator()	QMultiLineEdit QComboBox QLineEdit QSpinBox
setValue()	QSlider QRangeControl QScrollBar QSpinBox
setVariableHeight()	QListBox
setVariableWidth()	QListBox
setVBarGeometry()	QScrollView
setVerData()	QSizePolicy
setVersion()	QDataStream
setVerticalStretchable()	QToolBar
setViewMode()	QFileDialog
setViewport()	QPainter
setViewXForm()	QPainter
setVScrollBarMode()	QScrollView
setWeight()	QFont
setWFlags()	QWidget
setWhatsThis()	QMenuData QAccel
setWheelScrollLines()	QApplication
setWhiteSpaceMode()	QStyleSheetItem
setWidth()	QRect QSimpleRichText QPen QSize
setWildcard()	QRegExp

(continued)

setWinStyleHighlightColor()	QApplication
setWindow()	QPainter QNPWidget
setWindowCreated()	QGLContext
setWordWrap()	QMultiLineEdit
setWordWrapIconText()	QIconView
setWorldMatrix()	QPainter
setWorldXForm()	QPainter
setWrapColumnOrWidth()	QMultiLineEdit
setWrapping()	QSpinBox
setWrapPolicy()	QMultiLineEdit
setWritable()	QUrlInfo
setWState()	QWidget
setX()	QRect QPoint
setXOffset()	QTableView
setY()	QPoint QRect
setYMD()	QDate
setYOffset()	QTableView
shadow()	QColorGroup
shape()	QTabBar QCursor
sharedBlock()	QGArray
shear()	QPainter QWMatrix
shortcutKey()	QAccel
shortPoints()	QPointArray
show()	QMainWindow QTabBar QDialog QScrollView QWidget QProgressBar QPopupMenu QTableView QListView QSemiModal QMenuBar QWidgetStack QWizard QTab-Dialog QToolBar
showChild()	QScrollView
showEvent()	QListView QWidget QIconView QProgressDialog QListBox QWorkspace QTextView QTextBrowser QTabWidget
showFullScreen()	QWidget
showHiddenFiles()	QFileDialog
showMaximized()	QWidget
showMinimized()	QWidget
showNormal()	QWidget
showPage()	QWizard QTabWidget QTabDialog
showSortIndicator()	QListView
showTip()	QToolTipGroup
showToolTips()	QIconView
signal()	QMetaObject
signalNames()	QMetaObject
signalsBlocked()	QObject
simpleHeuristicNameMatch()	QTextCodec
simplifyWhiteSpace()	QCString QString
singleShot()	QTimer
size()	QFontMetrics QGVector QByteArray QPixmap QDict QAsciiDict QGCache QUrlInfo QArray QPtrDict QIconViewItem QImage QFile QWidget QAsciiCache QCache QIntCache QGArray QBuffer QResizeEvent QIODevice QBitArray QVector QFileInfo QRect QGDict QPicture QIntDict

(continued)

sizeChange()	QHeader
sizeChanged()	QFontDialog
sizeHint()	QScrollBar QTabBar QHBox QLCDNumber QGridLayout QWidgetItem QSpinBox QSlider QFrame QPushButton QProgressDialog QMultiLineEdit QLineEdit QList-Box QProgressBar QLabel QBoxLayout QWidget QSpacerItem QIconView QGrid QComboBox QLay-outItem QSizeGrip QMenuBar QRadioButton QTool-Button QPopupMenu QWidgetStack QCustomMenuItem QTabWidget QMainWindow QCheckBox QHeader QListView QScrollView QSplitter QWorkspace
sizeIncrement()	QWidget
sizeLimit()	QComboBox
sizeListBox()	QFontDialog
sizePolicy()	QHeader QToolButton QIconView QFrame QRadioBut-ton QWorkspace QLineEdit QSlider QLCDNumber QWidget QScrollView QPushButton QProgressBar QComboBox QMultiLineEdit QScrollBar QSizeGrip QSpinBox QSplitter QCheckBox QTabBar QLabel
sizes()	QSplitter
skipWhiteSpace()	QTextStream
sliderLength()	QMotifStyle QPlatinumStyle QWindowsStyle QStyle
sliderMoved()	QSlider QScrollBar
sliderPressed()	QScrollBar QSlider
sliderRect()	QScrollBar QSlider
sliderReleased()	QScrollBar QSlider
sliderStart()	QScrollBar
slot()	QMetaObject
slotNames()	QMetaObject
slotUpdate()	QIconView
smallDecimalPoint()	QLCDNumber
smoothScale()	QImage
smoothSizes()	QFontDatabase
socket()	QSocketNotifier
sort()	QGVector QIconView QListViewItem QByteArray QStringList QGArray QList QVector QArray QList-Box QGList QListView
sortChildItems()	QListViewItem
sortDirection()	QIconView
sorting()	QIconView QDir
source()	QDragObject QDropEvent QTextBrowser
spacerItem()	QSpacerItem QLayoutItem
spacing()	QIconView QLayout
specialValueText()	QSpinBox
speed()	QMovie
split()	QStringList
splitterWidth()	QWindowsStyle QStyle QMotifStyle
spontaneous()	QHideEvent QShowEvent
sprintf()	QString QCString
squeeze()	QTranslator
sRect()	QHeader
standardIcon()	QMessageBox

(continued)

standardSizes()	QFontDatabase
start()	QNetworkProtocol QTime QTimer QUrlOperator
	<div align="right">(continued)</div>
startDrag()	QIconView
startDragDistance()	QApplication
startDragTime()	QApplication
startedNextCopy()	QUrlOperator
startingUp()	QApplication
startMovingToolBar()	QMainWindow
startTimer()	QObject
state()	QMouseEvent QIODevice QNetworkOperation QButton QKeyEvent QWheelEvent
stateAfter()	QKeyEvent QMouseEvent
stateChange()	QCheckListItem
stateChanged()	QButton
staticMetaObject()	QObject
statistics()	QGDict QAsciiCache QIntCache QIntDict QDict QAsciiDict QCache QGCache QPtrDict
status()	QImageIO QIODevice QNPInstance
statusBar()	QMainWindow
stencil()	QGLFormat
step()	QMovie
stepChange()	QScrollBar QRangeControl
stepDown()	QSpinBox
steps()	QMovie
stepUp()	QSpinBox
stereo()	QGLFormat
stop()	QTimer QUrlOperator QNetworkProtocol
store()	QGArray
stored()	QMetaProperty
streamAsFile()	QNPInstance
streamDestroyed()	QNPInstance
strikeOut()	QFontInfo QFont
strikeOutPos()	QFontMetrics
string()	QConstString
stringListBegin()	QVariant
stringListEnd()	QVariant
stringShown()	QMultiLineEdit
stringToKey()	QAccel
stripWhiteSpace()	QString QCString
style()	QPen QBrush QApplication QWidget
styleChange()	QScrollBar QMainWindow QComboBox QMenuBar QPop- upMenu QTabDialog QIconView QListView QWidget QProgressDialog QTabWidget QSpinBox QSplitter QProgressBar QSlider
styleChanged()	QMessageBox
styleHint()	QFontInfo QFont
styleListBox()	QFontDialog
styles()	QFontDatabase
styleSheet()	QTextView QStyleSheetItem
styleString()	QFontDatabase
substitute()	QFont

(continued)

substitutions()	QFont
subtract()	QRegion
subtractLine()	QRangeControl
subtractPage()	QRangeControl

(continued)

subtractStep()	QSlider
suffix()	QSpinBox
superClass()	QMetaObject
superClasses()	QObject
superClassName()	QMetaObject
supportedOperations()	QLocalFs QNetworkProtocol
supportsMargin()	QLayout
swapBuffers()	QGLContext QGLWidget
swapRGB()	QImage
syncX()	QApplication
systemBitOrder()	QImage
systemByteOrder()	QImage
tab()	QTabBar
tabArray()	QPainter
tabBar()	QTabWidget QTabDialog
tabbarMetrics()	QCommonStyle QStyle QWindowsStyle QMotifStyle
tabLabel()	QTabDialog QTabWidget
tableFlags()	QTableView
tabList()	QTabBar
tabPosition()	QTabWidget
tabStops()	QPainter
tag()	QStyleSheet
take()	QVector QAsciiCache QIntCache QIntDict QAsciiDict QGList QDict QPtrDict QCache QList
take_ascii()	QGDict
take_int()	QGDict
take_other()	QGCache
take_ptr()	QGDict
take_string()	QGCache QGDict
takeAt()	QGList
takeCurrent()	QLayoutIterator QGLayoutIterator
takeFirst()	QGList
takeItem()	QIconView QListViewItem QListView QListBox
takeLast()	QGList
takeNode()	QList QGList
target()	QDragObject
testBit()	QBitArray
testFlags()	QMetaProperty
testOption()	QGLFormat
testTableFlags()	QTableView
testWFlags()	QWidget
testWState()	QWidget
text()	QButton QLineEdit QCheckListItem QMultiLineEdit QLabel QIconViewItem QListBox QImage QColorGroup QMenuData QKeyEvent QWhatsThis QTextView QComboBox QMessageBox QListBoxItem QListViewItem QClipboard QSpinBox

(continued)

`textChanged()`	QSpinBox QLineEdit QMultiLineEdit QTextBrowser QComboBox
`textFor()`	QWhatsThis
`textFormat()`	QLabel QTextView QMessageBox
`textKeys()`	QImage
`textLabel()`	QToolButton
`textLanguages()`	QImage
`textLine()`	QMultiLineEdit
`textList()`	QImage
`textRect()`	QIconViewItem
`textWidth()`	QMultiLineEdit
`thickness()`	QSlider
`tickInterval()`	QSlider
`tickmarks()`	QSlider
`tile()`	QWorkspace
`time()`	QDateTime
`timeout()`	QTimer
`timerEvent()`	QPopupMenu QObject QMultiLineEdit
`timerId()`	QTimerEvent
`tip()`	QToolTip
`title()`	QWizard QGroupBox
`toBitmap()`	QVariant
`toBool()`	QVariant
`toBrush()`	QVariant
`toColor()`	QVariant
`toColorGroup()`	QVariant
`toCString()`	QVariant
`toCursor()`	QVariant
`toDouble()`	QVariant QString QCString
`toFirst()`	QPtrDictIterator QGListIterator QAsciiDictIterator QIntCacheIterator QGCacheIterator QGDictIterator QDictIterator QCacheIterator QIntDictIterator QListIterator QAsciiCacheIterator QStrListIterator
`toFloat()`	QString QCString
`toFont()`	QVariant
`toggle()`	QPushButton QButton QToolButton
`toggleBit()`	QBitArray
`toggleCurrentItem()`	QListBox
`toggled()`	QButton
`toggleType()`	QButton
`toIconSet()`	QVariant
`toImage()`	QVariant
`toInt()`	QVariant QCString QString
`toLast()`	QIntCacheIterator QListIterator QAsciiCacheIterator QGListIterator QCacheIterator QGCacheIterator QStrListIterator
`toList()`	QVector QGVector QVariant
`toLong()`	QCString QString
`toolBarHandleExtend()`	QStyle
`toolBarPositionChanged()`	QMainWindow
`toolBars()`	QMainWindow

(continued)

toolBarsMovable()	QMainWindow
toolButtonRect()	QStyle
toolTipGroup()	QMainWindow
top()	QDoubleValidator QValueStack QStack QIntValidator QRect
toPage()	QPrinter
toPalette()	QVariant
topCell()	QTableView
topData()	QWidget
topItem()	QListBox
toPixmap()	QVariant
topLeft()	QRect
topLevelWidget()	QWidget
topLevelWidgets()	QApplication
topMargin()	QScrollView
toPoint()	QVariant
toPointArray()	QVariant
toRect()	QVariant
toRegion()	QVariant
topRight()	QRect
toShort()	QCString QString
toSize()	QVariant
toString()	QVariant QTime QDateTime QDate QUrl
toStringList()	QVariant
totalCost()	QCache QIntCache QGCache QAsciiCache
totalHeight()	QListViewItem QTableView
totalHeightForWidth()	QLayout
totalMaximumSize()	QLayout
totalMinimumSize()	QLayout
totalSizeHint()	QLayout
totalSteps()	QProgressDialog QProgressBar
totalWidth()	QTableView
toUInt()	QString QVariant QCString
toULong()	QCString QString
toUnicode()	QJisCodec QTextCodec QEucKrCodec QEucJpCodec QGbkCodec QTextDecoder
toUShort()	QCString QString
toVector()	QList QGList
tr()	QObject
tracking()	QSlider QScrollBar QHeader
translate()	QPointArray QRegion QApplication QPainter QWMatrix
transpose()	QSize
treeStepSize()	QListView
triggerUpdate()	QListView QListBox
trueMatrix()	QPixmap
truncate()	QString QCString QByteArray QArray
turnOffChild()	QCheckListItem
type()	QSocketNotifier QEvent QNPStream QMetaProperty QVariant QCheckListItem
typeName()	QVariant

(continued)

typeToName()	QVariant
underline()	QFont QFontInfo
underlinePos()	QFontMetrics
undo()	QMultiLineEdit
undoAvailable()	QMultiLineEdit
undoDepth()	QMultiLineEdit
ungetch()	QIODevice QFile QBuffer
unicode()	QChar QString
unicodeUriToUri()	QUriDrag
unite()	QRegion QRect
unpause()	QMovie
unPolish()	QStyle
unregisterDecoderFactory()	QImageDecoder
unsetCursor()	QWidget
unsetDevice()	QDataStream QTextStream
unsetf()	QTextStream
unsetFont()	QWidget
unsetPalette()	QWidget
unsetWindow()	QNPWidget
unsqueeze()	QTranslator
unuseJavaClass()	QNPlugin
upButton()	QSpinBox
update()	QWidget
updateCell()	QTableView
updateContents()	QListView QIconView QScrollView
updateDisplay()	QSpinBox
updateFamilies()	QFontDialog
updateGL()	QGLWidget
updateGeometry()	QWidget
updateItem()	QPopupMenu QMenuBar QListBox QMenuData
updateMask()	QPushButton QGroupBox QFrame QWidget QRadioButton QComboBox QTabWidget QCheckBox QTabBar QSlider
updateOverlayGL()	QGLWidget
updateScripts()	QFontDialog
updateScrollBars()	QScrollView
updateSizes()	QFontDialog
updateStyles()	QFontDialog
updateTableSize()	QTableView
upper()	QChar QString QCString
uriToLocalFile()	QUriDrag
uriToUnicodeUri()	QUriDrag
url()	QNetworkProtocol QNPStream QFileDialog
useHighlightColors()	QMotifStyle
user()	QUrl
userAgent()	QNPInstance
uses3D()	QToolButton
usesBigPixmap()	QToolButton
usesBigPixmaps()	QMainWindow
usesTextLabel()	QToolButton QMainWindow
usesTextLabelChanged()	QMainWindow
utf8()	QString

(continued)

valid()	QImage
validate()	QIntValidator QDoubleValidator QValidator
validateAndSet()	QLineEdit
validator()	QSpinBox QComboBox QMultiLineEdit QLineEdit
value()	QLCDNumber QScrollBar QSlider QSpinBox QRange-Control
valueChange()	QRangeControl QSlider QScrollBar QSpinBox
valueChanged()	QSlider QScrollBar QSpinBox
valueFromPosition()	QRangeControl
valueToKey()	QMetaProperty
valueToKeys()	QMetaProperty
variableHeight()	QListBox
variableWidth()	QListBox
verboseCharSetName()	QFontDatabase
verData()	QSizePolicy
version()	QDataStream
verticalScrollBar()	QTableView QScrollView
viewHeight()	QTableView
viewMode()	QFileDialog
viewport()	QScrollView QPainter
viewportDragEnterEvent()	QScrollView
viewportDragLeaveEvent()	QScrollView
viewportDragMoveEvent()	QScrollView
viewportDropEvent()	QScrollView
viewportMouseDoubleClickEvent()	QScrollView QListBox
viewportMouseMoveEvent()	QListBox QScrollView QTextView QTextBrowser
viewportMousePressEvent()	QTextBrowser QListBox QScrollView QTextView
viewportMouseReleaseEvent()	QListBox QTextView QTextBrowser QScrollView
viewportPaintEvent()	QScrollView QListBox
viewportResizeEvent()	QTextView QScrollView
viewportSize()	QScrollView
viewportToContents()	QScrollView
viewportWheelEvent()	QScrollView
viewRect()	QTableView
viewWidth()	QTableView
visibleHeight()	QScrollView
visibleRect()	QWidget
visibleWidget()	QWidgetStack
visibleWidth()	QScrollView
visual()	QString
vScrollBarMode()	QScrollView
wakeUpGuiThread()	QApplication
warning()	QMessageBox
wasCancelled()	QProgressDialog
weight()	QFont QFontInfo QFontDatabase
whatsThis()	QAccel QMenuData QMainWindow
whatsThisButton()	QWhatsThis
wheelEvent()	QScrollView QWidget QSlider QSpinBox QMultiLineEdit QScrollBar
wheelScrollLines()	QApplication
whiteSpaceMode()	QStyleSheetItem

(continued)

widget()	QWidgetItem QLayoutItem QNPInstance QWidget-Stack
widgetAt()	QApplication
width()	QRect QPen QCheckListItem QListViewItem QSimpleRichText QListBoxItem QTextStream QFontMetrics QImage QPaintDeviceMetrics QListBoxText QListBoxPixmap QPixmap QWidget QIconViewItem QSize
widthChanged()	QListViewItem
widthMM()	QPaintDeviceMetrics
widthUsed()	QSimpleRichText
wildcard()	QRegExp
winId()	QWidget
window()	QPainter
windowActivated()	QWorkspace
windowCreated()	QGLContext
windowList()	QWorkspace
winStyleHighlightColor()	QApplication
wmapper()	QWidget
wordWrap()	QMultiLineEdit
wordWrapIconText()	QIconView
worldMatrix()	QPainter
wrapColumnOrWidth()	QMultiLineEdit
wrapping()	QSpinBox
wrapPolicy()	QMultiLineEdit
write()	QGDict QGVector QGList QNPStream QImageIO QNPInstance
writeable()	QMetaProperty
writeBlock()	QBuffer QFile QIODevice
writeBytes()	QDataStream
writeRawBytes()	QTextStream QDataStream
writeReady()	QNPInstance
x()	QWidget QMouseEvent QWheelEvent QPoint QRect QIconViewItem
x11Event()	QXtWidget
xForm()	QPixmap QBitmap QPainter
xFormDev()	QPainter
xOffset()	QTableView
xtWidget()	QXtWidget
y()	QIconViewItem QWheelEvent QMouseEvent QWidget QRect QPoint
year()	QDate
yOffset()	QTableView

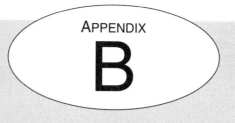

APPENDIX

B

How to Learn More

You have many options for learning more about the Qt toolkit. Due primarily to Qt's presence in the Open Source community, but also due to the fact that Qt is a truly fine product, there are more freely available examples of Qt application code than any other GUI toolkit. There are many Web sites—other than the site Trolltech maintains—that are geared toward distribution of useful Qt widgets and classes. The Trolls maintain an excellent mailing list, monitored by many Qt gurus whose knowledge of Qt dwarfs my own.

The following are reliable sources (there are many sources, but these are virtually always available) of additional information on the Qt toolkit:

Source	Description
qt-interest	The qt-interest mailing list is maintained by Trolltech. It is devoted to discussion of Qt development topics, how-to information exchange, and the discussion of ideas. Check for current instructions on how to join this list at the Trolltech Web site shown below.
www.trolltech.com	This is the main Trolltech site. You will find current releases of the Qt toolkit, as well as many user-contributed widgets and applications. This is also where you can find the current tmake utility.

www.kde.org	The home page for the "K" Desktop Environment, or KDE. This is the leading desktop environment for Linux systems and is based on Qt.
developer.kde.org	The home page for KDE developers.
ftp.sunsite.edu	An excellent source of KDE and Qt application examples for Linux.
ftp.cc.gatech.edu	Much of the sunsite FTP server is mirrored here.

There are a large number of Qt-based Open Source software projects in development that are independent of Trolltech and the KDE group. Most of these are available on one FTP site or another, and are excellent sources of real-world example code.

CONTENTS OF THE CD-ROM

As mentioned in Chapter 1, the CD-ROM that accompanies this book is in ISO9660 format with Joliet extensions; i.e., it should be mountable from Linux (or other UNIX-like systems) as long as you have an ISO9660 driver loaded that can talk to the CD-ROM drive.

On Linux systems, some of the folder and file names will be mangled if your driver doesn't support the Joliet file system extensions, but the files should read without problems. If you experience problems under a Linux environment, I recommend reading the ample HOWTO information that comes with every distribution.

On Windows platforms, you should have no problems reading the CD-ROM just as you would any CD-ROM. However, you will not be able to build the Qt Free Edition distribution that is on the CD-ROM on a Windows platform. To do so requires either a "Pro" license from Trolltech or an evaluation license. You will also need a compiler. I use Microsoft's Visual Studio 6.0 with Visual C++, but you may prefer to use the Borland compiler. It is my experience that there is very little to recommend one over the other, except I have grown more accustomed to the Microsoft environment.

The file, contents.txt, provides a detailed listing of the CD-ROM's contents. The CD-ROM is organized into subdirectories:

```
./Distribution
./Distribution/qt-2.1.0
```

These folders contain the Qt Free Edition in both compressed-tar format and the uncompressed and extracted format. These images are directly from the Qt distribution and are completely unconfigured. On supported platforms, all you should need to do is copy the entire directory tree to a hard disk, set the QTDIR environment variable to point to the top of the new directory tree, execute ./configure, and type `make`.

Platforms not directly supported by Qt will require a bit of tweaking.

```
./Distribution/tmake-1.4
```

This folder contains the source code for the tmake utility that translates platform-independent project description files into platform-dependent makefiles or Microsoft projects. Building tmake is just as easy as building Qt.

```
./Distribution/Redhat-6.1/static
./Distribution/Redhat-6.1/shared
```

These folders contain prebuilt copies of the Qt Free Edition source for RedHat Linux Version 6.1, with the egcs-1.1.2 compiler. This is (arguably) the most common Linux distribution, but it will still behave correctly on many other Linux distributions.

I provided both dedicated static-linkage and dedicated dynamic-linkage builds. Which method you choose to use depends greatly on your end-user environment.

```
./Book/Examples/chap2
./Book/Examples/chap3
./Book/Examples/chap4
./Book/Examples/chap5
./Book/Examples/chap7
./Book/Examples/chap8
```

As you may have guessed, these folders contain the examples from the book. Some of the examples have been altered to provide "demo" capabilities. If you wish to use them in an application, you will need to either rip out the main() function definitions or enclose them within a conditional compile.

```
./Binaries/Windows/examples
```

While a Pro license is required to build Qt for Windows platforms, it may help Windows users to see the examples that come with the Qt distribution execute in a Windows environment. For that reason, the executable forms of the Qt examples are provided in this folder.

```
./Extras
```

This folder contains some useful classes and HTML documentation that I've written over the years. You are encouraged to improve on these classes and to share those improvements—but remember to give credit where credit is due.

It is important to note that the SpinTime widget, a weekend kluge that works very well, contains chunks of code that are taken directly from the Qt QSpinBox widget, and are therefore the property of Trolltech and subject to their generous licensing. It is reproduced in SpinTime by their kind permission. I will eventually rewrite the widget to support QString, QDateTime, and internationalization of the display format—a task that would already be complete had I not been busy writing a book.

Index

A

AlignmentFlags type, 158
Alphabetical class list, 8
Alphabetical listing of Qt class methods, 211-65
Annotated class list, 8
API references section, 8
Application development, 163-92
   internalization, 166-72
   rapid application development (RAD), 190-92
Arrays, *See* Collections/arrays/linked-lists
ArrowType, 160
Athena Widget (Xaw) libraries, 15

B

-bg/-background *<color>*, 23
BGMode, 159
Border width, 84
"Breadboarding", 53-54
BrushStyle, 161
BSD with GNU g++ compiler, 11
-btn/-button *<color>*, 23
Buttons, 64-69
   QCheckBox, 64
   QPushButton, 64-66
   QRadioButton, 66-67
   QToolBar, 67-68
   QToolButton, 68-69
ButtonState, 158

C

Callback functions, 53
CD-ROM, xvii
   contents of, 267-68
   DDE server class, 193-97
   multimedia support, 197-210
-cmap, 23
Collections/arrays/linked-lists, 145-50
   QArray, 145
   QAsciiCache, 145
   QAsciiCacheIterator, 145
   QAsciiDict, 146
   QAsciiDictIterator, 146
   QBitArray, 146
   QByteArray, 146
   QCache, 146-47
   QCacheIterator, 147
   QCollection, 147
   QDict, 147
   QDictIterator, 148
   QIntCache, 148
   QIntCacheIterator, 148
   QIntDict, 148
   QIntDictIterator, 148
   QIntValidator, 148
   QList, 148-49
   QMap, 149
   QMapConstiterator, 149
   QMapIterator, 149
   QPtrDict, 149
   QPtrDictIterator, 149
   QQueue, 149

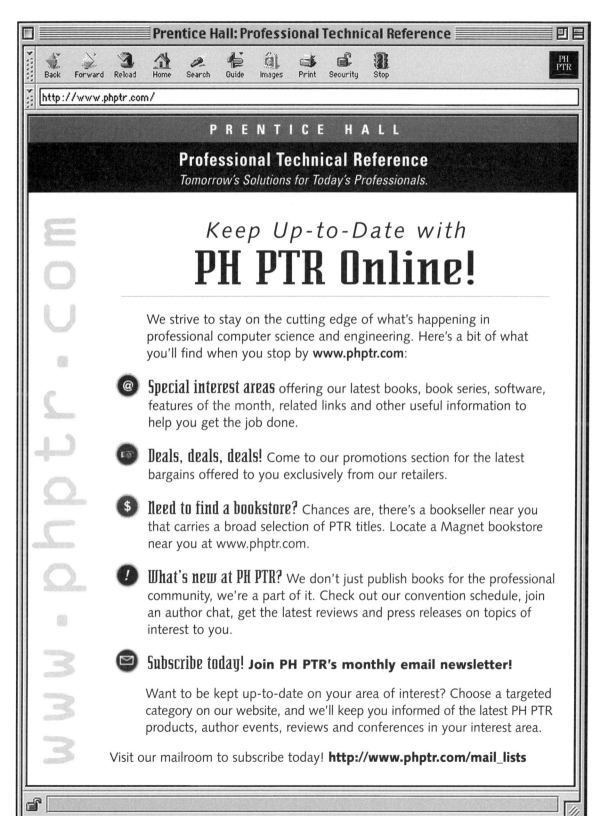

LICENSE AGREEMENT AND LIMITED WARRANTY

READ THE FOLLOWING TERMS AND CONDITIONS CAREFULLY BEFORE OPENING THIS SOFTWARE PACKAGE. THIS LEGAL DOCUMENT IS AN AGREEMENT BETWEEN YOU AND PRENTICE-HALL, INC. (THE "COMPANY"). BY OPENING THIS SEALED SOFTWARE PACKAGE, YOU ARE AGREEING TO BE BOUND BY THESE TERMS AND CONDITIONS. IF YOU DO NOT AGREE WITH THESE TERMS AND CONDITIONS, DO NOT OPEN THE SOFTWARE PACKAGE. PROMPTLY RETURN THE UNOPENED SOFTWARE PACKAGE AND ALL ACCOMPANYING ITEMS TO THE PLACE YOU OBTAINED THEM FOR A FULL REFUND OF ANY SUMS YOU HAVE PAID.

1.   **GRANT OF LICENSE:** In consideration of your payment of the license fee, which is part of the price you paid for this product, and your agreement to abide by the terms and conditions of this Agreement, the Company grants to you a nonexclusive right to use and display the copy of the enclosed software program (hereinafter the "software") on a single computer (i.e., with a single CPU) at a single location so long as you comply with the terms of this Agreement. The Company reserves all rights not expressly granted to you under this Agreement.

2.   **OWNERSHIP OF SOFTWARE:** You own only the magnetic or physical media (the enclosed software) on which the software is recorded or fixed, but the Company retains all the rights, title, and ownership to the software recorded on the original software copy(ies) and all subsequent copies of the software, regardless of the form or media on which the original or other copies may exist. This license is not a sale of the original software or any copy to you.

3.   **COPY RESTRICTIONS:** This software and the accompanying printed materials and user manual (the "Documentation") are the subject of copyright. You may not copy the Documentation or the software, except that you may make a single copy of the software for backup or archival purposes only. You may be held legally responsible for any copying or copyright infringement which is caused or encouraged by your failure to abide by the terms of this restriction.

4.   **USE RESTRICTIONS:** You may not network the software or otherwise use it on more than one computer or computer terminal at the same time. You may physically transfer the software from one computer to another provided that the software is used on only one computer at a time. You may not distribute copies of the software or Documentation to others. You may not reverse engineer, disassemble, decompile, modify, adapt, translate, or create derivative works based on the software or the Documentation without the prior written consent of the Company.

5.   **TRANSFER RESTRICTIONS:** The enclosed software is licensed only to you and may not be transferred to any one else without the prior written consent of the Company. Any unauthorized transfer of the software shall result in the immediate termination of this Agreement.

6.   **TERMINATION:** This license is effective until terminated. This license will terminate automatically without notice from the Company and become null and void if you fail to comply with any provisions or limitations of this license. Upon termination, you shall destroy the Documentation and all copies of the software. All provisions of this Agreement as to warranties, limitation of liability, remedies or damages, and our ownership rights shall survive termination.

7.   **MISCELLANEOUS:** This Agreement shall be construed in accordance with the laws of the United States of America and the State of New York and shall benefit the Company, its affiliates, and assignees.

8.   **LIMITED WARRANTY AND DISCLAIMER OF WARRANTY:** The Company warrants that the software, when properly used in accordance with the Documentation, will operate in substantial conformity with the description of the software set forth in the Documentation. The Company does not warrant that the software will meet your requirements or that the operation of the software will be uninterrupted or error-free. The Company warrants that the media on which the software is delivered shall be free from defects in materials and workmanship under normal use

for a period of thirty (30) days from the date of your purchase. Your only remedy and the Company's only obligation under these limited warranties is, at the Company's option, return of the warranted item for a refund of any amounts paid by you or replacement of the item. Any replacement of software or media under the warranties shall not extend the original warranty period. The limited warranty set forth above shall not apply to any software which the Company determines in good faith has been subject to misuse, neglect, improper installation, repair, alteration, or damage by you. EXCEPT FOR THE EXPRESSED WARRANTIES SET FORTH ABOVE, THE COMPANY DISCLAIMS ALL WARRANTIES, EXPRESS OR IMPLIED, INCLUDING WITHOUT LIMITATION, THE IMPLIED WARRANTIES OF MERCHANTABILITY AND FITNESS FOR A PARTICULAR PURPOSE. EXCEPT FOR THE EXPRESS WARRANTY SET FORTH ABOVE, THE COMPANY DOES NOT WARRANT, GUARANTEE, OR MAKE ANY REPRESENTATION REGARDING THE USE OR THE RESULTS OF THE USE OF THE SOFTWARE IN TERMS OF ITS CORRECTNESS, ACCURACY, RELIABILITY, CURRENTNESS, OR OTHERWISE.

IN NO EVENT, SHALL THE COMPANY OR ITS EMPLOYEES, AGENTS, SUPPLIERS, OR CONTRACTORS BE LIABLE FOR ANY INCIDENTAL, INDIRECT, SPECIAL, OR CONSEQUENTIAL DAMAGES ARISING OUT OF OR IN CONNECTION WITH THE LICENSE GRANTED UNDER THIS AGREEMENT, OR FOR LOSS OF USE, LOSS OF DATA, LOSS OF INCOME OR PROFIT, OR OTHER LOSSES, SUSTAINED AS A RESULT OF INJURY TO ANY PERSON, OR LOSS OF OR DAMAGE TO PROPERTY, OR CLAIMS OF THIRD PARTIES, EVEN IF THE COMPANY OR AN AUTHORIZED REPRESENTATIVE OF THE COMPANY HAS BEEN ADVISED OF THE POSSIBILITY OF SUCH DAMAGES. IN NO EVENT SHALL LIABILITY OF THE COMPANY FOR DAMAGES WITH RESPECT TO THE SOFTWARE EXCEED THE AMOUNTS ACTUALLY PAID BY YOU, IF ANY, FOR THE SOFTWARE.

SOME JURISDICTIONS DO NOT ALLOW THE LIMITATION OF IMPLIED WARRANTIES OR LIABILITY FOR INCIDENTAL, INDIRECT, SPECIAL, OR CONSEQUENTIAL DAMAGES, SO THE ABOVE LIMITATIONS MAY NOT ALWAYS APPLY. THE WARRANTIES IN THIS AGREEMENT GIVE YOU SPECIFIC LEGAL RIGHTS AND YOU MAY ALSO HAVE OTHER RIGHTS WHICH VARY IN ACCORDANCE WITH LOCAL LAW.

ACKNOWLEDGMENT

YOU ACKNOWLEDGE THAT YOU HAVE READ THIS AGREEMENT, UNDERSTAND IT, AND AGREE TO BE BOUND BY ITS TERMS AND CONDITIONS. YOU ALSO AGREE THAT THIS AGREEMENT IS THE COMPLETE AND EXCLUSIVE STATEMENT OF THE AGREEMENT BETWEEN YOU AND THE COMPANY AND SUPERSEDES ALL PROPOSALS OR PRIOR AGREEMENTS, ORAL, OR WRITTEN, AND ANY OTHER COMMUNICATIONS BETWEEN YOU AND THE COMPANY OR ANY REPRESENTATIVE OF THE COMPANY RELATING TO THE SUBJECT MATTER OF THIS AGREEMENT.

Should you have any questions concerning this Agreement or if you wish to contact the Company for any reason, please contact in writing at the address below.

Robin Short
Prentice Hall PTR
One Lake Street
Upper Saddle River, New Jersey 07458

ABOUT THE CD-ROM

The CD-ROM included with *Qt Programming for Linux and Windows 2000* contains the following—

- The complete source code for the Qt Free Edition (Version 2.1.1).
- Compiled binaries (static and dynamic linkage) for Red Hat Linux, Version 6.1.
- Source code for all the book examples.
- Additional examples, utilities, and useful routines.

The CD-ROM can be used on any system that supports ISO9660 CD-ROM filesystems, e.g., Linux, HP/UX, AIX, IRIX, Solaris, Microsoft Windows 95/98/2000/ME.

LICENSE AGREEMENT

Use of the software accompanying *Qt Programming for Linux and Windows 2000* is subject to the terms of the License Agreement and Limited Warranty, found on the previous two pages.

TECHNICAL SUPPORT

Prentice Hall does not offer technical support for any of the programs on the CD-ROM. However, if the CD-ROM is physically damaged, you may obtain a replacement copy by sending an email that describes the problem to: disc_exchange@prenhall.com.